UNE FEMME FRANÇAISE

CATHERINE
MALANDRINO

UNE FEMME
FRANÇAISE

*The seductive
style
of French
Women*

St. Martin's Press
New York

www.stmartins.com

The Library of Congress Cataloging-in-Publication Data is
available upon request.

ISBN 978-1-250-09765-1 (hardcover)
ISBN 978-1-250-09766-8 (ebook)

Our books may be purchased in bulk for promotional, educational, or business
use. Please contact your local bookseller or the Macmillan Corporate and
Premium Sales Department at 1-800-221-7945, extension 5442, or by email at
MacmillanSpecialMarkets@macmillan.com.

First Edition: November 2017

10 9 8 7 6 5 4 3 2 1

For my son, Oscar, my family,
and everybody in love with French style

CONTENTS

Acknowledgments

A big thank-you to:

Cait Hoyt and John Fierson, my agents at CAA; Elizabeth Beier, my editor; and Nicole Williams, Michael Storrings, and the team at St. Martin's Press for believing in me, my style, and my fantasy.

CFDA Diane von Furstenberg and Steven Kolb for their fabulous organization and support to designers.

FIAF and Marie Monique Steckel for enhancing French culture in the United States.

Pascale Richard for starting the process with me.

Valerie Frankel for accompanying me all the way through the book's writing. Veronique Gabai, Olga Krutoi, Valerie Pasquiou, Celia de la Varenne, Kristen Ingersoll, Selima Salaun, Michelle Gradin, Aline Matsika, Susan Seigel, Claudine Choquette, Kelly Rutherford, Akiko Kaneko, Delphine De Causans, and Julie De Noailles for their friendship, patience, and honest opinions.

My parents and sisters in France, Anne, Helene, Elisabeth, and their children Charlotte, Alexandre et Victoria, whom I love so much.

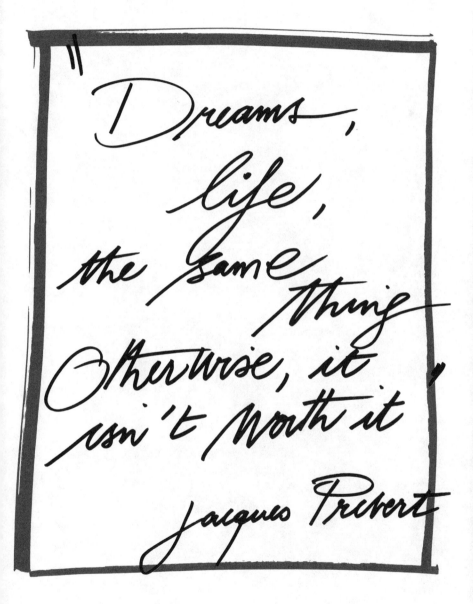

"Dreams,
life,
the same
thing

Otherwise, it
isn't worth it,"

Jacques Prévert

French women don't talk about "having it all," or checking things off a list. They aspire to have "it," a charm, a quality, an attitude toward seduction, style, and confidence that will make life and everything beautiful.

There is one woman who represented a blend of French culture with American idealism in her marriage to her husband, and in her own style and personality: Jacqueline Bouvier Kennedy.

From a young age, she was drawn to European culture. At Vassar, Jackie majored in French literature. During her undergraduate year in Paris, she studied art at the Sorbonne and become fluent in French, later translating French texts into English.

In the White House, Jackie hired French interior designer Stéphane Boudin to redecorate and chef René Verdon to cook state dinners of her favorite cuisine. (In later years, her taste for *carré d'agneau bouquetière* and *haricots verts almondine* had her lunching at New York society bistros La Côte Basque and La Grenouille.) When she and her husband John visited Paris in 1961, Jackie charmed Parisians and Charles de Gaulle with her style and intelligence. President Kennedy felt a bit overshadowed by his wife, and he jokingly referred to himself as "the man who accompanied Jackie Kennedy to Paris." During that visit and for two years after, she used all of her powers of persuasion to convince reluctant French officials to allow a grande dame of Paris—the *Mona Lisa*—to travel to Washington, D.C., for a historic visit at the National Gallery.

Not a legendary beauty, Jackie's chic Francophile style—the feminine hair, clean lines, and romantic rounded necklines—made her a fashion icon. French-born Oleg Cassini created most of her couture wardrobe of satin pink gowns, cashmere coats, and bright dresses, but she also wore Chanel (like the pink suit she had on the day JFK was assassinated), Givenchy, Dior, and Hermès. During the White House years, the "Jackie look" was the A-line skirt, three-quarter sleeves, kid gloves, pillbox hats, a three-strand pearl necklace, and gold and enamel bracelets by French jeweler Jean Schlumberger. But my favorite era was when she lived on Fifth Avenue and wore wide-leg trousers, white jeans, turtlenecks, trench coats, head scarves, and her ubiquitous black sunglasses, lending her a French air of mystery despite her very public life.

Over the years, she proved herself in every realm, as a diplomat, mother, lover (she allegedly had affairs with Warren Beatty, Paul Newman, and Frank Sinatra, among others), and in her career. Perfectly balancing American casualness and competence with a French style and flair, she set trends and captivated people all over the world. I grew up admiring this dignified survivor. She reinvented herself after John's death to have a second life with Aristotle Onassis, and a third life as an editor at Viking and Doubleday. Her journey was intense, with fascinating chapters. She's an example of an accomplished woman who grappled life with style.

Confidence, style, and charm aren't birthrights even for icons or movie stars. They have to be developed for women to reach their full potential and become successful. Through my experience of living in America for twenty years, I've built a bridge between Paris and New York. Today, **I want to share what I've learned about our differences and similarities.**

Girl from the wood

I grew up in Seyssinet-Pariset, a small town of twelve thousand people, located on the outskirts of Grenoble in southeastern France, one hour away from Lyon. My parents came to Grenoble when they were very young, when their parents, involved in the resistance, followed the dream of freedom by fighting dictators' ideas (Mussolini in Italy, Franco in Spain). After leaving the Mediterranean, my parents grew up, met, and married in France and raised their four daughters in the European way of life, happily at the foot of the French Alps.

I remember my childhood in colors. The blond hair of my Andalusian mother, the dark eyes of my Sicilian father, the pink cheeks of my sisters. Outside, it was a winter world with white peaks along a chain of mountains cutting into a clear blue sky right outside my window. The scheme changed in springtime, with all the hues of greens in the pines and the grass, sprinkled with a confetti of wildflowers: violets, red poppies, yellow buttercups, blue irises. In summer, I remember the rows of red roses in the gardens that surrounded our two-story house, and a wood swing that hung from a pink-flowering buckeye tree that later dropped golden-brown nuts on the ground. In the fall, the foliage turned brilliant orange, and then, by November, my world turned a peaceful, pure white again.

I was a little French Heidi and spent more time outside than in. The Four Mountains—part of the Vercors Massif range where World War II French Resistance fighters hid from the Nazis—was my immense playground.

Every Sunday, my family set off on a day trek, a gang of six *en vadrouille*. I wore oversized jeans held up by one of my father's wide leather belts, a long-sleeved men's shirt with the sleeves rolled up, and boots with crampons, my long hair tied messily. I always carried a basket and a knife in case I found anything worth keeping.

As soon as we hit the trail, I tended to run ahead on the steep footpaths to the streams where we hunted for frogs. My parents always shushed me when we spotted a family of marmots—fat mountain squirrels—but I couldn't contain the excitement and screamed. The animals would scatter and disappear. Higher up the mountain, we'd spot deer and chamois—a cross between a goat and an antelope—or nesting hawks. Beyond the tree line, I was looking for edelweiss, the white and yellow mountain flower, growing vertically in the cracks of a rock face.

My love for nature will always keep me grounded. **Because my roots run so deep, I can safely let my head drift into the clouds.**

Four gifts that shaped my life

Looking back, I see how much my parents' guidance and encouragement made me who I am today. They have been my beacon, the lighthouse of my life. She taught me to feed my curiosity and to pursue knowledge and skill. They were never bossy and didn't

fashion books

globe

boucle jacket

sewing machine

tell me what to do. Their education style was to suggest, to guide gently, to throw seeds on the ground and wait to see what grew. In hindsight, I realize how receptive my parents were to all of their daughters' sensibilities. I was born with an intuitive sense of style, but thanks to my parents' encouragement—and their gifts—I developed it.

1. The Globe. When I was six, my parents gave me a globe for my birthday, and along with it, the keys to the world. As much as I loved my family and the healthy lifestyle in Grenoble, the globe ignited my imagination and I couldn't stop dreaming about the different people and cultures beyond the mountains.

I was obsessed with it, and also mystified. If this globe represented the planet we lived on, why weren't we falling off it? My older sister kept saying "The Earth is round," but that didn't help. One day when my mother saw how preoccupied I was by the question, she brought me an orange, delicately picked up an ant in the garden, and put the insect on the fruit. The ant kept running around it without falling off while she turned the orange, and I looked into my mother's eyes, relieved. I will always remember her smile when I finally understood Galileo's discovery. Falling headfirst into the sky off Earth would not be an issue. Once I understood that, nothing would stop me from discovering the other side of the globe.

My curiosity about foreign lands started by a closer examination of the world around me, specifically, of the women in my everyday life. They dressed with casual ruggedness—warm knit scarves, chunky sweaters, and sensible slacks and shoes, to be ready for a day of shopping or trekking on the mountain. The women of Grenoble were sporty, practical, and didn't seem to care about the romance of fashion, or, more likely, they just didn't know about it. Their exposure was limited. Grenoble didn't have any designer or couture stores and there was no Internet back in the '70s.

However, some of them made an effort—certainly my mother, who had a feminine casual style—and I started noticing the distinctions: a woman's perfume, my cousin's see-through blouse, my aunts' makeup. I appreciated the little touches that made a woman stand out. I didn't know it as *sexy* or *seductive* at that age, but I definitely clued in to the effect. I noticed men's style, too, a debonair hat or trench coat, a suit fabric that was more sophisticated, a cashmere scarf—all these details were pure attraction for me.

Curiosity was a way to escape my environment and open new doors of the imagination. I knew that a bigger, fuller, more urban world of style existed, where women dressed to emphasize the silhouette of their bodies, where elegance was prized over practicality. I'd heard about Paris style from my mother. She used to describe the city to me, promising, "We'll go there soon. You'll love it. The history, the art, the museums." I desperately wanted to go to Paris and see how people lived and dressed in the capital. I started wondering what it would be like to make clothes and dress the chicest women all over the world. I'd never heard of a career called "fashion designer" at this time. I just knew that I wanted to be actively part of the glamorous life. Going from French Heidi in Grenoble to *les maisons de couture* in Paris was not a common path. I certainly wasn't born with any connections in the fashion *monde*. There was no logical reason that I'd grow up to have a life of style in Paris and beyond, but I dreamed about it anyway with the conviction that I'd make it happen.

At a very young age, I had the consciousness that Grenoble was just the beginning, the starting point in my life. Even if you're not born in a big city and many generations of your family live in the same place, you're not stuck there. It's your choice to open the boundaries. When the time came, my family was devastated that I wanted to try something else, and said, "You have everything you need right here." But my imagination was too big for Grenoble and my curiosity for discovering the world was burning in my body like a raging fire. The globe had a magic effect on me. It was the gateway to the entire world.

2. The Sewing Machine. My grandmother Mama Manuela had a treadle Singer sewing machine, and it held a place of honor in my mother's bedroom. As a child, I was fascinated by the enormous piece of wood and metal furniture with a moving pedal and spinning wheel. My grandmother had given it to my mother when she was too old to use it, along with other family heirlooms. I didn't care about the jewelry. The sewing machine, a tool she used with so much love, was far more meaningful to me. Grandma could take yards of raw, unfinished fabric and transform them into beautiful drapery. She was skilled at embroidery and knitting, too, and once made a mohair turtleneck of twenty-two colors for me, and a pink crochet bikini I proudly wore all summer on the beach at Saint-Tropez when I was fifteen.

Grandma taught me how to feed the fabric patiently under the needle to make it glide, and how to put the reel with the thread in the shuttle. I took to sewing and could make expert zigzag stitches before I could recite the alphabet.

When I was seven, my mother offered me a sewing machine of my own, a portable Singer that was much smaller than Grandma's. I had never loved any object as much as I loved that little machine. I stayed up late into the night, stitching. Anything that could be put under my needle got sewn. I had no interest in my sisters' maternity games with dolls. My Singer was the only toy that inspired me.

I could spend weekends and late nights sewing together every piece of fabric I found at home, from a handkerchief to a piece of velvet and some furry wool, and with it, I was creating my first patchwork of love.

3. The Little Tweed Jacket. With an inner elegance, my mother favored a casual look of light sweaters, well-cut pants, and low-heeled shoes, but she had two garments that were her special treasures: a beige Yves Saint Laurent silk blouse and a navy Chanel bouclé jacket. I'd tried on the jacket a few times and knew instinctually that it was the real thing, a quality piece with its gold buttons and a chain around the hem. I had a fascination for it, and I thought about it a lot.

One day, when my parents went away for the afternoon, I slid open my mother's closet and took out the jacket. I was ten at the time, working on my sewing, and I was curious about the garment's construction. The temptation was too strong to resist.

I took the masterpiece into my room and carefully opened the black silk lining to explore the inside. I traced the stitching religiously and closely examined the four patch pockets' woven trim. I loved the idea that a jacket could have pockets. They gave it a real attitude. I was nervous but thrilled the entire time to discover the jacket's intimate secrets. Sewing the lining back in took me a few hours. I had to stitch very carefully and delicately to hide the evidence of my explorations.

I was only just putting the jacket back on the hanger when the car wheels crunched on the driveway outside the house. My mother had no clue what I'd done, but a few weeks later, I had to confess. The secret burned inside me and I couldn't keep it in. She wasn't angry at all. In fact, she was touched by my appreciation for something she loved. "You should have told me," she said. "We could have done it together."

In later secret missions, I opened up the lining of a jacket of my father's, too, and came to understand the difference between women's and men's clothing. My father's jacket had a lot of facing inside. It was stiff, rigid, and heavy. The Chanel jacket was decidedly feminine. The sleeve fit close to the arm and had a slight natural curve. The interfacing and silk lining were lavishly soft, and the fabric was smooth and as light as a cardigan. The shoulder pads were small and fluffy. So much miniscule stitching went into each handmade buttonhole. But the most fascinating part was the chain detail at the hem, which lent the garment weight so that it hung on the body perfectly, giving the wearer the Chanel allure.

4. The Biography. Soon after I confessed, Mother brought home a biography of Coco Chanel for me. She was touched by my love for the garment and encouraged me to learn more about it. I read the Chanel book cover to cover, many times. Coco was a marvel, liberating women's silhouettes with unstructured clothes, using soft knits, as supple as skin, from the bouclé jacket, the *petite robe noire* (little black dress), and the *pantalon à pont* (sailor pants). She became my role model of style. Her clothes had functional quality and were carrying a message. She was inspired to bring men's pieces into women's wardrobes to give the working women of the time the allure of strength and independence. After falling in love with Chanel, I became addicted to inspirational books. My family knew what to give me for Christmas and birthdays, and my bedroom became an extension of the Librairie Arthaud, the local bookstore, as I amassed a collection of volumes and magazines about fashion, art, and photography.

My First Fashion Library

Any library—or style—would be enhanced by the addition of these great volumes.

- *Le Temps Chanel* by Edmonde Charles-Roux. It's in French, but what better reason to brush up on your language skills?
- *Poiret* by Andrew Bolton and Harold Koda. Paul Poiret, a Victorian-era French designer, got women out of corsets and into *pantalons*. A revolutionary man, he ushered in the modern era of women's fashion.
- *Madeleine Vionnet* by Pamela Golbin. A biography with exquisite photos about the French designer known as "the Queen of the bias cut," a contemporary of Chanel's, and a pioneer of elegance with softness and movement.
- *Yves Saint Laurent* by Laurence Benaïm. My favorite biography of the master of style.
- *Antonio Lopez: Fashion, Art, Sex and Disco* by Roger Padilha and Mauricio Padilha. Don't you want to flip through this book on the title alone? A collection of the works of a Warhol favorite, this book is about Antonio Lopez, an illustrator who was a major force in art, culture, and fashion from the 1960s to the '80s. He discovered statuesque models Jerry Hall and Grace Jones. His sketches were always colorful, vibrant, and full of energy. In his world, even lingerie was in Technicolor.
- *Guy Bourdin: In Between* by Shelly Verthime and Guy Bourdin. A biography of the late-twentieth-century French fashion photographer and a collection of his bold, surrealistic work.
- *Avedon Photographs: 1947-1977* by Richard Avedon. Thirty years' worth of iconic photographs by the legendary artist, including my favorite portrait of Tina Turner.

- *Helmut Newton: SUMO* by June Newton and Helmut Newton. The ultimate collection of Newton's fashion photography and celebrity portraits in a huge volume of nearly five hundred pages. Its limited-edition publication was an international sensation.
- *Serge Lutens* by Serge Lutens. A collection of images by the French photographer, filmmaker, fashion designer, illustrator, hairstylist, art director, and perfume maker, a renaissance man with a sophisticated vision of style.
- *Shocking Life: The Autobiography of Elsa Schiaparelli* by Elsa Schiaparelli. The Italian designer, a contemporary of Chanel's, describes in her own words how she invented her aesthetic—surrealism, animal prints, newspaper prints, and a shock of pink—and indulged her bottomless curiosity.

And some recent additions:

- *Fashion: A History From the 18th to the 20th Century* by curators from the Kyoto Costume Institute. Three hundred years of fashion, history, and culture as seen in photographs from the collection of the Kyoto Costume Institute.
- *Art and Fashion: The Impact of Art on Fashion and Fashion on Art* by Alice Mackrell. An intellectual exploration of how art and fashion have influenced each other over the centuries, such as Schiaparelli inspired by Dalí, Yves Saint Laurent in collaboration with Picasso, and, more recently, pop artist Sylvie Fleury inspired by luxury packaging.
- *Culture to Catwalk: How World Cultures Influence Fashion* by Kristin Knox. Written by a London-based fashion blogger, aka "the Clothes Whisperer," this book examines the intersection of street clothes and high fashion for a historical and contemporary perspective, with gorgeous photos, thoughtful analysis about the industry, and insightful interviews with designers.

Earliest inspirations

Growing up, I was always on the hunt for style inspiration, and found it in:

- **Erté.** In the corridor that connected our living room and my bedroom hung my parents' collection of lithographs by the Russian-born French artist Erté. He got his start in the art world by working for designer Paul Poiret in the World War I era, but he found his greatest success in the years afterward, illustrating magazine covers of exotic women in elaborate costumes for *Harper's Bazaar, Cosmopolitan, Ladies' Home Journal,* and *Vogue.* Even though I walked down this hallway a few times a day, I never got tired of Erté's sophisticated women silhouetted on a black canvas, striking arabesque poses in dramatic, colorful, rich clothing. Each drape of fabric, flower, fur, and feather detail was drawn with passion and precision.

- *Elle* **magazine.** In France in the late '70s and early '80s, *Elle* was the fashion bible and set the tone for the fashion world and independent women. I would tack the photos and covers—shot by Gilles Bensimon—on my walls instead of pinups of movie stars. It was the era of big hair, red lips, and iconic models like Jerry Hall, Elle Macpherson, and Dayle Haddon. I studied each picture and tried to grab some of that bold elegance to transport me into its Parisian perspective.

- **Les Createurs.** The French designers at the forefront of fashion in 1980 were called Les Createurs. They were as famous as movie stars in France and I admired them all for breaking new ground. **Thierry Mugler**, "the prophet of futurism," was my favorite. He created structured bright-colored clothes with the X silhouette—large shoulders, small waist, and wide legs—in metallic and leather that looked like they came from outer space, a fantasy for the modern imagination. He was the first one to stage a super production fashion show that was more than just models on the runway. **Claude Montana** was known for his bold use of color and soft luxurious fabrics like silk, velvet, cashmere, and thin, drapey leather in sleek, body-conscious, minimalist designs. I remember his black leather short shorts mixed with magenta fur jackets. **Jean-Paul Gaultier**, the rebel, was a master of re-invention. He re-created the *marinière* (blue-and-white stripes) as a ball gown with feathers, hats, socks, and jumpsuits. He brought the corset out from underneath and put it into the limelight in dresses and tops. Who can forget the Gaultier-designed white cone-bra corset worn by Madonna on her *Blonde Ambition* tour? **Azzedine Alaïa**, "the king of cling," created clothes for seduction and transformed a woman into a goddess. He was the first to bring stretch into high fashion, using spandex to create skintight knitted designs that emphasized a woman's curves. He was subtle with revealing skin, too, via pointelle, cutouts, lace, and sheer fabrics. Through the years, he kept his integrity, and up to today, his signature is one of my favorites.

Provocateur of style

My mission to wake the women around me to a world of style and femininity started with my mother, my sisters, and myself. I was my own dress dummy, wrapping and pinning fabrics on my body, hanging chiffon ruffles with safety pins. When I was eleven, long and lean, a tomboy silhouette, I would study myself in the mirror, fitting and shaping my compositions into the ultimate *Parisienne* chic (or, at least, my idea of it). I mixed and matched style combinations, experimenting with color and shape. When I saw an original silhouette in the reflection, I felt happy, like I'd accomplished something new and different. I was in awe that I could alter myself from one look to the next. This treasure was available to me, and everyone, and it filled me with a sense of power. Creating looks was one of my favorite occupations.

At school, I was called an original for wearing platform wood heels, bell-bottom jeans, and striped blouses. During class, I sketched different silhouettes in the margins of notebook pages and made up fabulous stories for the women. I started to look at other girls, imagining how I could improve their appearance and be instrumental in their lives. As it turned out, girls at school and grown women noticed my unique sense of style and confidence, and they started to imitate me and come to me for advice, asking for ideas about how to comb their hair or fit their clothes. I doled out pointers to anyone who asked—tuck in a shirt, try high heels—and, by eleven, I realized I had something valuable to say, and the strength to express it.

Thoughts about how to push the envelope with style filled my head. My parents tried to tamp down my risqué inclinations, afraid that being so adventurous with my look at such an early age would impair my education, so I worked harder in class and on homework to earn my status as a provocateur with style. I bought peace at home with very good grades.

Some of my girlfriends weren't as easily placated as my parents, though. They begged me, "Why can't you be *normal*?" My intention wasn't to embarrass them when we went out as a group. I was having too much fun playing with style and learning about myself along the way. One thing I discovered quickly: I had no interest in a "normal" life. I wanted extraordinary. Being different challenged other people and made them feel uncomfortable. By twelve, I realized that having a look and opinions won me friends—and enemies.

"If you are always trying to be normal, you will never know how amazing you can be"

Maya Angelou

Raising girls

My childhood was idyllic, with a loving home and the beauty of nature at my door. But my mother did not believe in fairy tales. She told my three sisters and me that the weight of responsibility for our lives rested on our own shoulders, and that we shouldn't wait for Prince Charming to come along and take care of us. For her, **independence was a worthy dream and became my first goal.**

My mother, also named Catherine, got married at twenty-two, and she was pregnant soon after. The circumstances of her life made independence impossible and instead of becoming a teacher, her career dream, she was expected to stay home, take care of us, and see to our education.

Although she was happy as a housewife and well pampered by my father, she would have made other choices if she'd been born in a different era. Putting all of her creativity and energy into a family was noble, but it had drawbacks. I think the reason she taught her four daughters to be independent and to make something of our lives was to prove to my father that girls were equal to boys. My mother made sure that he'd be as proud of our accomplishments as he would have been of any son's.

I wasn't aware that girls were supposed to be the weaker sex. I can't imagine four little boys being as fearless as we were growing up. My sisters and I even called each other "brother." I became the leader of my group of friends. I wanted to be in charge, and I was surprised when other girls told me that boys should take the lead and girls should follow. I wasn't made to shrink like a violet, and I held on to my top spot, perfectly comfortable there.

I couldn't relate to princess fairy tales. To be rescued by a prince after he'd had all the adventures? I wanted to have my own. I thank my parents for instilling the values of strength and independence in me, to see myself as the daring one, the hero of my own story. If anyone were going to ride to the rescue to save me, it would be me.

Boys are not taught to be dependent or to wait for Princess Charming. I know firsthand that being raised to be in charge of your life gives a girl confidence. A mother doesn't have to be a living example of the message. Mine was at home, and she told us not to follow in her footsteps. Instead, we would be girls of the twenty-first century. Along with taking advantage of our many options for our own sake, Mom told us, "Men will love you even more if you don't rely on them to live."

I'm very sensitive to girls not having the chance to make their own destiny. To illustrate my concerns I recommend two movies: First, *The Virgin Suicides,* a 1999 film by Sofia Coppola starring Kirsten Dunst, about five sisters in suburban 1970s who were driven to suicide by the repressive family environment. I saw it years ago, and this movie haunts me still. Second, *Mustang,* a 2015 Turkish movie by Deniz Gamze Ergüven, is also about five sisters and their religious parents who stopped them from living a full life. Two were forced into arranged marriages. One killed herself, and only the two littlest ones escaped to find freedom in Istanbul. It's alarming that this situation still goes on today.

As parents, we have to work to prevent such tragedies. I was thrilled about Hillary Clinton's nomination by her party for president. Her "almost" only proved that the dream of equality is attainable, and very close to reality.

Raising boys

When I became a mother, I knew that I had to send a clear message to my son, Oscar, starting very young, not to feel pressured by the role that culture assigns to boys. I encouraged him to explore his creativity and let his imagination take him wherever it wanted to go. As soon as he could hold a crayon, he started drawing on his bedroom walls. I never yelled at him or forbid it. I encouraged him to create. His early scribbles evolved into words and drawings, then the Mickey Mouse stickers, and, as a teenager, graffiti tags. Slowly, his bedroom became a giant canvas where he, and later his friends, expressed themselves: his favorite movie images with Johnny Depp in *Pirates of the Caribbean,* basketball legends like Michael Jordan, Steve Nash, Dwyane Wade, and LeBron James, up to his first graffiti tags about love, sex, and rock 'n' roll. Today, Oscar is an American boy, born in New York and raised with a double culture. He's comfortable in his skin, a basketball champion, compassionate and generous. I trace it back to his toddler graffiti, his freedom of expression. At nineteen, he still marks his walls. Sometimes I go into his room and just look at the record of his imagination. The walls are an inspiration to me, and to him, and a gift for the family.

First creation

When I was thirteen, an original, I wanted to be noticed. The time had come to make an ambitious garment that would do the trick. The family was going on a winter weekend trip to our chalet in Autrans, the capital of cross-country skiing. I knew exactly what I would create for the vacation: a ski jumpsuit.

The outfit represented a real challenge. I'm an aggressive downhill skier, and I really attack the slopes. The garment would have to be warm, waterproof, well constructed, comfortable, and flexible enough to handle every twist and turn. The sleeves and the legs were cut from a sheet of metallic silver vinyl. For the body, I used black nylon, padded with a layer of batting. To give it shape, I added darts and pin tucking to emphasize the waist. To add color, I closed it with a red plastic zipper and put a red elastic belt at the waist, which also underlined a feminine silhouette. To make it practical, I added zipper pockets for my lip balm and lift pass.

The outfit was inspired by Diana Rigg's Emma Peel, the hero of *The Avengers*, whose spy style was a skintight cat suit and sexy boots. When the show came to France, it was called *Chapeau Melon et Bottes de Cuir* ("Derby Hat and Leather Boots"), which speaks directly to the French fixation with fashion. I wanted to incorporate Emma Peel's style into my fall wardrobe, and the sexy jumpsuit with ski boots instead of leather boots was my cat suit moment.

I wore my jumpsuit all winter, carving up the moguls and bursting through a cloud of snow in style. It gave me new wings to become either a racing champion or a disco queen. My confidence in the jumpsuit made skiing even more exciting. **At thirteen, I realized the power of clothes.** Clothes say "Here I am!"—but they're also a way to understand and express yourself. They could change people's views of me and give me more power and joy than I'd have otherwise. **Clothes enhance life.** I went from being just another skier to the star of the slope, turning heads all over the mountain. People stared and stopped in their tracks just to get a look at me. The jumpsuit didn't make me a faster or better skier, but I was unique. My younger sister Helene, also a great skier, couldn't resist the jumpsuit's qualities, and wanted one of her own. I got my first order from her!

Small treasures become big ideas

My childhood house had an attic. I would go treasure hunting in the dusty boxes full of souvenirs, old clothes, and random objects my parents had little use for but didn't want to throw away. When I got older, I took my love of digging through boxes and piles to the open-air flea markets of Grenoble—the Marché Victor Hugo and Marché Saint Bruno. You could find anything there: food, furniture, and, for my purposes, old clothes and fabric, buttons, jewelry, and accessories.

With my mother, I would spend hours sifting through the stalls in search of anything that caught my eye and cost a few francs. I treated every item with great care; each tattered piece of clothing or vintage charm was precious to me because it was rare. With the fabric and buttons, I took to my Singer and experimented, inspired to turn my finds into fashion art.

When I was fourteen, a creative project involved a white Fruit of the Loom T-shirt that I thought was so exotic. It was an American brand, a piece of the American dream of freedom, freshness, and cool we saw in ads for Hollywood Chewing gum, and I wanted to turn it into a French jeweled masterpiece. Whatever precious and meaningful treasures I found at the *marché*—small beads, buttons, patches, crystals, a tiny gold anchor—I'd sew onto the T-shirt. I even found two embroidered gold letters, C and M, and gave them a place of prominence on the front. I bought broken old earrings, took out the pearls, and sewed them onto the shirt to create a necklace along the collar.

The project took a few weekends. When it was done, I put on the embellished T-shirt, rolled up the sleeves—it had a boyfriend fit—and wore it with jeans to dance parties. I felt like a billion-dollar baby, so proud of my supercool Fruit of the Loom. Its uniqueness got so much attention that it inspired my girlfriends to do the same. After a few wears, though, I realized it needed to be washed. I put the shirt in the sink with gentle detergent, and the colors from the patches and beads bled all over. Nowadays, the destroyed look could have been interesting, but at the time, the stains marked the demise of my precious creation and, in despair, I threw it in a box.

That T-shirt could have given birth to an entire collection, but it was my first step. Even at fourteen, I was fascinated by the concept of casual chic, taking an ordinary T-shirt piece and transforming it into an evening treasure.

Iconic Eras of Style

I was fortunate to grow up in the late '70s and '80s when there were so many inspiring musical eras, each with its own icons, character, and look to appreciate and incorporate into my own developing style.

Disco
The disco era was all about glitz and excess. I loved to dance, and with my sisters, we threw parties called *les booms* once a month in our garage. These parties were famous for their stylish décor. I would create a boudoir backdrop with red drapes and candles, perfect for lighting our first cigarettes with an air of mystery. We would send out invitations for theme evenings, like "Saturday Night Fever" and "Studio 54," and spin French hits by Serge Gainsbourg and Claude François as well as American Motown legends Diana Ross and Michael Jackson. We danced and kissed until the wee hours to "Rock with You" and "Upside Down" under homemade disco balls. I made shiny miniskirts

and wore vertiginous heels, or very feminine silk slip dresses unheard of in snowy Grenoble. The whole point was to take bold style risks, experiment and explore, to have fun with fashion.

- **John Travolta's** character Tony Manero in *Saturday Night Fever* wore a waisted white blazer with large lapels, a black shirt, and long trousers that inspired some of my first glittery designs.
- **Diana Ross**, with her big hair and red lips, turned us upside down with awe. On her album cover for *Diana,* she made a pair of jeans and a white T-shirt look achingly chic. I adored her daring décolleté and cutouts, love of color, and feminine silhouette. Always a foxy lady.

Punk

When I visited London for the first time at fifteen with a school exchange program, I explored Carnaby Street and browsed the funky accessories shops, piercing/tattoo salons, and jewelry boutiques that sold safety pin necklaces and spiked bracelets inspired by the Sex Pistols and the Clash. I adored the do-it-yourself rebelliousness of punk style. In a way, I'd had a punk sensibility since childhood, constructing clothes from fabric remnants and repurposing garments.

- **Vivienne Westwood.** The unofficial designer of punk with her slashed T-shirts and spiky blond hair, pale skin, and bruised makeup did a lot to invent the look. I visited her store Sex on Kings Road and bought a "God Save the Queen" T-shirt to wear under a military jacket or a cowboy shirt. Later on, I became a fan of her husband, the composer and musician Malcolm McLaren.
- **Chrissie Hynde.** "I'm gonna use my style, I'm gonna make you notice," she sang in the Pretenders song "Brass in

Pocket," and she rocked the cat eye, teased black hair and uneven chopped bangs, black dress, and black fishnet tights in the video. Hynde's style was—is—provocative alley cat.

New Wave

I've always been fascinated by the mixture of a feminine and masculine silhouette, how to take a man's shirt or trousers and restyle them for a woman. Icons of New Wave took androgyny to the limit, confusing male and female, making it a style of its own.

- **David Bowie.** Bowie had been perfecting the androgynous look since the '70s with *Ziggy Stardust,* and he was personally responsible for the glitter era of men wearing makeup and tight bodysuits. *Let's Dance* was huge in France, and we loved his brilliantly bizarre style.
- **Annie Lennox** of the Eurythmics. Sweet dreams are made of her short-cropped bright-red hair, black suit, men's white shirt and tie, black leather gloves, riding crop, and deep, resonant voice. Although men in makeup was the look of the time, Lennox transfixed her fans by going the other way, a beautiful woman with feminine features in masculine outfits.

Pop

By the mid '80s, dance music was back, MTV was king, and I had my Pop Queens.

- **Sade.** Stylish, sleek hair slicked back, red lips, and gold hoop earrings. Her graphic silhouette was smooth and effortless. She embodied modern sensuality.
- **Madonna.** Her controversial "Like a Virgin" look—the white tulle skirt, corset, lace opera gloves, boy toy belt, and cropped leggings—redefined sexy to a generation of girls who wanted to be a new kind of rebel, sweet and tough.

First Paris fashion show

When I was sixteen, my parents had an apartment in Golfe-Juan, Antibes, where the family could spend summer vacations. With friends, I would go to nearby Saint-Tropez and sell sun visors topless on the beach to make pocket change. I carefully saved every franc; I had plans for the money. I was ready to spread my wings and have my first Parisian adventure by myself.

My goal: to see an Yves Saint Laurent fashion show. By the time I was seventeen, I had enough saved to get there. My parents weren't enthusiastic about the trip. I insisted that I had a safe place to stay and was relentless about how much I wanted to go "for educational purposes," to see museums. I confess today that my parents had no clue about the fact that I wasn't sure about my lodgings, and that I was only going to see a fashion show. Eventually, my mother gave me her blessing, and I set the plan into motion.

I packed for a week with my best clothes, my highest heels, my pocket money, and a piece of paper with the scribbled name of a girlfriend I'd met on the beach in Saint-Tropez who told me to look her up if I were ever in Paris. The ride from Grenoble to the City of Light took seven hours. Luckily, my girlfriend remembered me and had a spare bed for me to sleep in.

I woke up early the next morning and dressed myself for the fashion show in a silk red shirt and black stilettos. YSL was presenting his spring/summer collection at the Louvre's central courtyard, the Cour Carrée. Somehow, I talked my way through the guards at the entrance and found myself inside the square, taking in

the catwalks that had been constructed for the event and all the elegant women who'd come to see the show.

The audience was a true reflection of the Parisian scene. In the first rows were all the fashion editors and the elegant clients of Maison Saint Laurent. (These days, department store buyers, bloggers, and press have replaced clients in the first row.) These women had come dressed to honor the master in two-piece suits with defined waists, shouldered jackets cut in silk or taffeta, and *des escarpins* (high heels). Some wore pencil skirts split on the thighs and hemmed just above the knee in solid, bright colors like fuchsia and grass green, with big bold prints, polka dots, or stripes, an homage to the designer's signature style.

When the show began, I was transported by the dramatic spectacle, full of the joie de vivre often missing on today's runways. The models were smiling, and so was everyone in the audience. The clothes left me breathless. It was the best crash course on tailoring I could have ever taken. Beyond the stunning frocks, the YSL show was a social education. Fashion was not yet the industry it has become, and such events were like salons in the French tradition: places to gather, converse, and educate. I noticed the way the women looked and interacted with each other. **The magic of that day inspired me for years to come.**

I was learning, seeing, and absorbing every detail. I realized I wanted to design clothes at seven. At seventeen, I'd made my first foray into the fashionable world of Paris and stood among the editors, buyers, clients, and models. Being at that show and feeling like part of this world made me never want to leave. It was important to transport myself to the environment that would spur me forward and inspire me forever.

At the end of the show, Mr. Saint Laurent in a slim suit came out to take a bow, which became an indelible memory in my mind. Years later in New York, by total chance, his nephew Laurent Levasseur became the CFO of my company for a time and, on a trip to Paris, he brought me to YSL couture house for a visit. I met Pierre Bergé, cofounder and Mr. Saint Laurent's longtime partner, and, with a lot of emotion, I was introduced to the master himself. He was wearing a black tuxedo suit, a white shirt, and a thin black tie. What I remember most were his eyes behind his dark rectangular signature shades. For a few minutes, I stared at him like I was meeting a legend. I searched his eyes through his glasses to catch a glimmer of his talent. I was moved and tried to imprint his face on my mind forever. When Mr. Saint Laurent passed in 2008, Laurent brought me a bundle of wheat shafts that had been given out to guests at the funeral. I've kept it to remember the master's legacy.

Work in Progress

My next step was to experience more of Paris and continue my education. At eighteen, I went to the ESMOD fashion academy to learn about the construction of clothes and later to the Sorbonne to learn about the history of art. Art and fashion are connected. You can see how style has evolved throughout the centuries in paintings and sculpture. I was curious about everything and soaked up the worlds of knowledge at school like a sponge, spending hours on the construction of a jacket sleeve to achieve the perfect fit.

After graduation, I was impatient to express myself in my own designs, but I wanted to learn even more from mentors. At Dorothée Bis, Jacqueline Jacobson revealed to me the secret of knitwear. With

Louis Féraud, I received an education in color palettes among original paintings by Féraud himself at the Maison de Couture. Observing Emanuel Ungaro taught me all about women's curves and draping.

At twenty-five, I was ready to create my own styles and founded a collective with friends called Cyclopo Loco, a fashion brand based on Rue de la Main d'Or in Bastille. I discovered Paris's nightlife and was inspired by the Paris nightclub scene called the Palace. On June 3, 1981, I saw Prince give one of his first concerts ever to launch the *Dirty Mind* album in France. I remember being blown away by his energy, tunes—the song "Sister" was huge—his ruffled pirate blouse and velvet high-waisted sparkle pants with a big flare. It was a music and style revolution. After hours, we went downstairs to the jet-set club called the Privilege and danced among the night owls dressed up in fabulous eccentric silhouettes. **The era was all about flash and fun, and I was living the extravagant moment.**

Power of Inspiration

The only limit to your dreams is your imagination. If you can envision something, you can make it happen. At twenty, I had a real lightbulb moment about the power of imagination when I saw images of the Bulgarian artist Christo's *Surrounded Islands* artwork wrapping 6.5 million square feet of flamingo-pink polypropylene fabric around eleven small islands in Biscayne Bay in Miami, Florida. It looked like each island was wearing a neon skirt. The project was bigger than life. To achieve his vision, Christo planned for three years. It took millions of dollars, two dozen government permits, hundreds of engineers and workers, and fourteen weeks of installation to bring this new perspective of the world to fruition. Convincing and uniting so many people, dealing with bureaucracies, and overcoming challenges to realize one man's fantasy was a triumph in itself.

In the photos, you can see boats and helicopters circling the bay to admire the seemingly purposeless art. The installation of pink wraps created energy, beauty, and excitement, and it gave a new perspective to the entire world of the neglected islands, formerly covered in garbage. I was so fascinated by the photos in the newspaper that I tore out the sheet and taped it to my bedroom wall. *Surrounding Islands* is a perfect example of the power of a dream and just how far imagination can take you.

I felt the same sense of endless possibility during the Internet revolution in the early 2000s. Men like Apple's Steve Jobs, Google's Larry Page and Sergey Brin, and Facebook's Mark Zuckerberg had a dream of connecting every citizen of the planet in a digital world—a concept that made little sense to most people when they first heard the phrases "World Wide Web" or "smartphone"—and in only a handful of years, they achieved it. I will always remember the first person to show me a BlackBerry in 1997. It was Diane von Furstenberg. I was working at her studio when she showed me this tiny metal box and said, "Look at this. It will change the world. Tomorrow, everyone will have one. And we'll always be connected."

There is no limit to what you can imagine. If you can dream it, no matter how huge, wild, or crazy it might be, you will convince people to share the dream with you, and together, you will make it happen. You can turn any vision into a reality.

My friend, the developer Robert Wennett, lives by this ideal.

In 2008, I received a cold call from an entrepreneur/developer who wanted to show me his new project in Miami and convince me to open a boutique there. I arrived at the Bowery Hotel as planned and discovered this handsome gentleman who intended to convert a square block of parking lot structure into a gigantic luxury shopping destination at the corner of Lincoln and Alton Roads in Miami. I was charmed as I listened to him describe his vision and I decided that sometime soon, I'd visit to see his big dream in progress.

A month later, I happened to be in Miami for the weekend and called Robert. We drove to Lincoln Road, to a dead-end in a very scary area, to see the construction site. Then he showed me a mock-up of the plan, designed by Herzog & de Meuron, the famous Swiss architects who created the Bird's Nest stadium for the Beijing Olympics. The plan was to use the parking lot structure as a skeleton and build an innovative garage/mall out of it in a "house of cards" style. I was very impressed. While we were chatting about the project, he invited me to see the site where his future house would be built, on the roof.

It turned out to be just a bare, neglected rooftop in that dilapidated neighborhood. As we walked across the cement, he said, "Here's the garden. Careful or you'll fall into the pool! Now you're in the living room, and, watch out, we're entering the bedroom."

Was he insane, or brilliant? The man was more in dreamland than in reality. But he took me by storm with the power of his imagination. I said, "The project sounds fantastic and, yes, I'm with you for the boutique. I believe in you. Let me know how I can help."

I introduced him to my friends, the brand owners of Ladurée and MAC cosmetics, and I was happy to see that they signed on to the project, too. Lining up partners and finances took almost ten years, but now he's the developer and owner of the most gorgeous garage/retail space in America, an award-winning structure, a destination for shoppers. Architecture and art fans flock to take pictures and admire it.

Before construction was complete, I sold my company and the new owner stopped the retail expansion—so my boutique at 1111 Lincoln Road, Miami, never happened. But I won an incredible friend whose dreams took a run-down, dead-end block and turned it into the most innovative concept mall in America. My friend Robert is a star! Every time I visit him at his stunning modern home on top of that building, **we stare at the view and toast with champagne to the power of vision.**

live your dreams

As a girl, I dreamed of growing up to express myself, reach my potential (not there yet, but still evolving), and live in harmony with myself and the world. All of my influences helped shape my vision of becoming an independent woman with a full life—a mother, a lover, a friend, a citizen of the planet who embraces culture and diversity—and **the dream is still a work in progress.**

It was a long journey from Grenoble to Paris, Paris to New York, New York to the world. There were thousands of steps and challenges from sewing fabrics to having my clothes represented in more than 350 boutiques in thirty countries, with fourteen stores of my own, and many years in dressing stylish women in foreign lands to having fashion shows in Moscow to opening boutiques in Dubai and Qatar, lunching in Istanbul and dining in Athens the same day for personal appearances. I lived at a hundred miles an hour, carrying my suitcase of ideas.

With a global perspective, I was creating a fashion vocabulary that's strong enough to make my clothes recognizable without having to look at the label. When I was in the thick of developing myself as a women and my career as a designer, I dealt with challenges and successes in the moment, but now, as I look back on my last twenty years, I realize I've been living my childhood vision all along. Lately, new challenges lead me to reboot, and I'm excited by this chance and full of new dreams for the chapters that are just beginning.

I created my own path, and I believe anyone can create hers without being a victim of life. I remember a French friend of mine, Philippe, always dreaming of having a castle in France. He came from a very modest family in Provence, no noble title or lineage, no reason to believe that he could ever have a king's life. But he believed he was royalty, and he put all of his life force into the idea that one day, he would own a castle in France. In the meantime, he developed his career as a writer. A few years ago, at forty, he wrote a popular television series and was able to buy an abandoned castle in Normandy. It was run-down and crumbling. Half of the castle was roofless, no electricity or plumbing. But he restored the mansion to its former glory. A part of it is now a bed-and-breakfast and a rental space for parties. He lives there full-time and has made it his main occupation. The kernel of his dream took twenty years to grow and become his real life.

Between dreams and reality is one word: action. When you wake up every day, ask yourself, "How can I be the best version of myself?" and walk through life with the idea that you are not just dreaming about accomplishment and fulfillment, you are living it. Keep the two ideas—"dream" and "life"—entwined together. You are targeting your actions and building yourself to become the accomplished person you are meant to be.

The American vs. French Dream

I have come to know and appreciate "the American Dream." It's a cultural concept based on three words—freedom, opportunity, and prosperity—which add up to one big word: **success**.

In France, we also have a set of cultural ideals, although we don't call it "the French dream." Our national slogan is "*liberté, egalité, fraternité*," or "freedom, equality, brotherhood," which add up to one big idea: **justice**.

Since I live with one foot in Paris and the other in New York, I have a unique perspective on how each of my two countries' ideals are different, powerful, and a little bit lacking, but that true brilliance lies in a combination of both.

America is all about action. Americans know how to get things done!

France is all about ideas. The French spend a lot of time just thinking.

The American path is pragmatic. They like having a list of ten steps, or a five-year plan; they're always looking ahead and wondering what to do to get what they want. They are focused on outcome. Happiness is success.

The French path is romantic. They feel hemmed in with lists and set goals. They meander in their minds and on the streets, smelling the bread and cheese, sipping wine. They live in the process. Happiness is harmony.

If you take American focus and work ethic, and combine it with the ideas and drama of French romance, you get a glorious synthesis. One arm hugs your dreams, and the other embraces determination.

" style is
a simple way
to say
complicated things"

jean Cocteau

Style allows you to:

- Know who you are . . . and who you're not.
- Send the unspoken messages you want to convey to others.
- Change as you move through different phases of your life.
- Express your creativity.
- Edit your wardrobe. If you have a strong, unique take, you don't need a million options to represent yourself.
- Lead you to your own ideal destiny.

Shape

Your silhouette is the building block of all style. Everything you wear and transmit derives from knowing and understanding your definition, the outline that is you. Your silhouette is the first thing people will notice. At a midnight rendezvous with the streetlight behind you, your lover will know you by your shape.

Studying yourself in the mirror does not make you a narcissist. Your purpose is to look objectively, to understand your body. Imagine yourself outlining your shape with black ink, defining your body. Think of it like the beautiful ink sketches of French illustrator René Gruau.

The magic of knowing your outline: You can emphasize your strengths and forgive your weaknesses. **Elongation is elegance, so always try to create the illusion of length in your silhouette with heels and long lines.**

Movement

Allure is a woman in motion, smiling, jumping, and, most importantly, walking. Your carriage and gait brings your silhouette to life. A feminine walk is feline with a ballerina posture and an elongated neck. When you carry yourself mindfully, with grace, fluidity, and determination, you transmit confidence. In the '70s, one of my favorite walks was Shelley Hack in a gold jumpsuit and high heels, gliding through a chic bar in a classic Charlie perfume ad, accompanied by Bobby Short at the piano. She took long, confident strides with a little bounce, smiling the whole time.

There is nothing wrong with practicing a languid walk and training yourself to sit up straight either in front of a mirror, or by filming yourself to understand how you move and what to adjust. Practice in high heels (not too high, or you might feel uncomfortable) until the glide becomes effortless.

"Life isn't about finding yourself
It's about creating yourself"
Georges Bernard Shaw

Power of style

With style, the possibilities of how to present yourself to the world are endless. Cindy Sherman, the contemporary American artist, explored how looks define a woman's character and her role in society. She staged scenarios of dozens of women's lives—young, old, rich, poor, tragic, glamorous—and captured the moment in a photograph. The surprise of her creations: every photo was a self-portrait. She is the same, but unrecognizable, making each image unique by developing the character with expression, clothes, makeup, and wigs. One woman can be any woman, depending on her style and circumstances.

We are all born with the blank canvas of a face and body, and it's completely up to us to develop a powerful, unique look with style. But you don't want to look like every woman or a clone of a celebrity. The ideal is to create a unique look that transmits your individuality. **Style is memorable.**

I discovered my signature hairstyle—long, dark, and wavy with a middle part—at fifteen after much experimentation. I decided that it was the most flattering, carefree, and sophisticated look for me. I said

"*C'est moi*" to the mirror and have changed it only once, after my son's birth. When Oscar was born, facing maternity inspired me to change my silhouette and I cut my hair short. I knew it was a mistake as soon as I left the salon. I felt stripped of my identity. A change of makeup and new clothes didn't bring back my confidence, so I got extensions. As soon as I had long hair again, my strong sense of self rushed back. Today, my center-part dark hair, red lips, elongated silhouette, and heels (from stiletto pumps to tall suede boots, but always high) make me recognizable at a glance in a crowded room.

Some famous signatures:

Edith Piaf's little black dress. The French chanteuse will be remembered for her throaty singing style as well as her black dresses with V-necks, calling attention to her delicate neck and frail figure.

Karl Lagerfeld's white ponytail. The French fashion designer will be remembered for his contribution to the Maison Chanel, as well as his stark white ponytail, black glasses, slim suiting, and high-collared white shirts.

Anna Wintour's chestnut bob and shades. The former editor in chief of American *Vogue*'s signature style was recognizable in the front row of every fashion show.

Carine Roitfeld's legendary messy hair. The former editor in chief of *CR Magazine* and fashion director of *Harper's Bazaar* is known for her unbrushed and windblown chestnut hair, omnipresent heels and pencil skirt—elegant and chic.

A signature style can be based on the unexpected. **Madonna** created the signature of reinvention. Some of her most famous looks included tattered prom princess; power siren in a corset and whip-it ponytail; glamour queen in diamonds and a taffeta gown; cowgirl with soft waves and a ten-gallon hat; Goth brunette in slashed black leather; English horse lady in jodhpurs, white cravat, and top hat; and the list goes on. **Lady Gaga** has taken the reinvention style to new extremes, intending to surprise and shock with her dramatic apparitions, including a pantsless Little Red Riding Hood, veiled escapee from a Victorian horror movie, razor blade sunglasses, Gaga the Good Witch in a silver hoop dress with a sparkle wand, a black raven feather dress with Frankenstein leather boots and green wig, a dress made of bubbles, a dress made of meat, sexy motorcycle cop, space alien . . . the possibilities are endless. Her signature is provocation.

Once a woman finds her signature, she should commit to it. Not that you are stuck with the same exact hairstyle or perfume from fifteen to eighty, but if your choices are flattering and assert your personality and uniqueness, be loyal to them. When a childhood friend I haven't seen in years tells me, "You haven't changed!" I take that as a high compliment. Of course I've changed! What she really means is that my style is consistent. I have always been working toward being the one I wanted to be.

French It Girls

Some of today's women of style who embody French effortless chic:

Lou Doillon, thirty-four, an actress, singer, and model who is a second-generation It Girl, the daughter of Hermès muse Jane Birkin and movie director Jacques Doillon. Once the face of Givenchy and Chloé, Doillon is tall and slim with long, untamed brown hair and bangs, a mannish look with feminine touches. She wears a designer dress or a T-shirt and jeans with artful casualness; it seems like she discovers style by accident every day as she gets dressed. The overall effect is rock chic.

Charlotte Gainsbourg, forty-five, Lou Doillon's half sister, the daughter of Jane Birkin and Serge Gainsbourg, is an award-winning actress (some of her Hollywood films: *21 Grams*, *I'm Not There*, and *Nymphomania*), a singer (collaborating with Madonna and Beck), and Balenciaga muse. With her long brown hair and fringe, little or no makeup, her style is tomboyish—jeans, boots, a leather jacket, and a men's shirt—making laid-back look classic.

Elisa Sednaoui, twenty-nine, is Christian Louboutin's goddaughter, sister of photographer Stéphane Sednaoui, and Karl Lagerfeld's muse. She's modeled for Chanel, Armani, and Cavalli and appeared in several French films. As a philanthropist, she's created a foundation that sponsors music education for kids. Her style ranges from double-breasted suits, to satin pants, to boho maxi skirts and floppy hats, from sleek to slouch, but with an emphasis on her signature confidence, elongated silhouette, and seductive gaze.

Joséphine de La Baume, thirty-two, is the wife of DJ Mark "Uptown Funk" Ronson, the face (and body) of Agent Provocateur, singer in the band Singtank, and actress in *Kiss of the Damned* and *Johnny English*. Her glamorous style—long ginger hair, sheer tops, stilettos, and fur jackets—is chic sex doll.

Clémence Poésy, thirty-four, is an actress (Fleur Delacour in the Harry Potter movies and Eva Coupeau in *Gossip Girl*) and the face of Chloé's fragrance Love Story. She told *Elle* how she picks her outfits: "I have this sort of big pile of things on my chair and I usually pick the thing that's slightly under the first thing." It's very French to throw on an outfit with the effortless ease of knowing every item fits, like Poésy's favorite Acne jeans and a vintage Chanel jacket. Her style is quality cool.

Myth of French chic

Everything you've heard is true.

- **Discretion.** French designers don't put any obvious labels in a coat. It's hidden in the lining. French women keep their voices low, don't show too much skin, and believe that less is more. Accessories are an exclamation. You don't need to wear ten of them when one or two will make the point.
- **Nonchalance.** They put some effort into their style, but not too much. Their undone hair is flirtatious. A great shirt doesn't need to be perfectly pressed. They find the balance between refinement and negligé.
- **Imperfection.** The French are not looking for perfection. Being obsessed with an unobtainable goal is not a good life, or a good look, and could become boring.
- **Mystery.** French women cultivate mystery, in part by being cinematic. They live as if they're in a movie. When they light a cigarette, sit at a café, cross their legs and sip coffee, they articulate every gesture. And, of course, with the imaginary camera on, they want to look sharp.
- **Simplicity.** If a garment has too many zippers and buttons, it is not French. It's Italian. Simple does not mean casual. Even if they're wearing jeans and a T-shirt, they make sure the jeans are the best for their body and the shirt is fitted, and they add extra flare in the details, like a red lip, statement jewelry, a silk scarf, and heels.
- **Joie de vivre.** The French admire a sense of humor, a

ready smile, a bit of quirkiness, and an appreciation for the small pleasures of life.

- **Quality.** A French woman would rather have one quality piece to wear than a closet full of cheap clothes. And they always have some solid foundation pieces in their wardrobes.

- **Romance.** French women create a little romance with the world in feminine details of lace and silk, embroidery and embellishments, and by revealing skin in a subtle way.

- **Originality.** It's useful to take inspiration from role models and fashion magazines, but, to develop an original style that is totally unique, you can't copy someone else or go to the mall and buy everything on the mannequin. A fashion victim is a follower of trends. Instead, come up with signatures and be innovative. One bold strike leads to more in all areas of your life. Originality is the pathway to realizing your style.

- **Improvisation.** French women are always ready, always surprising, and don't bother making long plans. They would rather be spontaneous and rendezvous at a moment's notice.

- **Loyalty.** The French are faithful to their favorite clothes. They attach deep emotions to them, linking a dress or coat with a special person or experience, taking excellent care of it, and keeping it in their wardrobe forever. The timeless quality of French style comes from the older important pieces in a woman's closet that represent her personal and family history going back to previous generations. Garments and jewelry are always passed down to daughters and granddaughters, gaining meaning and

emotional significance as the years go by. When I wear my grandmother's rings, I feel inspired to talk about her life. Every French person has a story about a tiny village somewhere—say, by the French Alps. Grandma's rings let me carry her memories into my modern life, and my wardrobe.

Create a Seductive Silhouette

I prefer sensual and seductive to sexy. It's whispering rather than shouting, a suggestion rather than a declaration. With that in mind:

- **Don't wear too-tight clothes.** Clothes should skim the body. Constrictive clothes are not flattering. They highlight every bump and could send the wrong message.
- **Emphasize your strengths and forgive your weaknesses.** Find clothes with a shape and structure that emphasize your assets and disguise parts that aren't your best. Remember that a good silhouette starts from the shoulder. If they are beautiful, show them. If they are not, add a little padding to give you more presence.
- **Choose one part of your body to show.** You can suggest a feminine figure without revealing too much of it, and by balancing it. If you show legs, don't show too much décolleté. If you show a deep neckline, choose a longer skirt with a slit. Instead of baring the full arm, show a delicate wrist with elegant three-quarter sleeves. The décolleté is so important to French women that their beauty routine

includes moisturizing the neck, shoulders, and upper chest as carefully as their faces. Style choices to emphasize the décolleté: a V-neck elongates the throat and shows a hint of cleavage; a boatneck highlights the clavicle and suggests sensuality; a slouchy sweater falls off the shoulder; a cowl neck reveals the breastbone.

- **Keep evolving with style.** Style is not the exclusive domain of twenty-year-olds. It ages beautifully, like wine, and becomes richer and more chic with experience. The desire to be seductive doesn't disappear as you get older, and neither should style or your youthful attitude. But by getting older, you have to get more chic.
- **Don't try too hard.** Dare to be undone. I love a men's shirt not perfectly pressed with rolled sleeves for a woman, or a V-neck men's sweater falling off your shoulder. And for an evening dress, try undone messy hair with a touch of lipstick. Elegance should feel easy.

Play with contrasts

Exciting combinations are always provocative, and they go hand in hand with a French woman's unpredictable nature. Let go of rules and open your imagination to the infinite possibilities, the surprise and flare, of mixing things up. Combine pieces in one outfit for:

Day and night. Brigitte Bardot said, "The happiest day of my life was a night." Bring them together by wearing ivory or black lace with a cardigan.

Old and new. A vintage shirt goes well with a new jacket. Or wear estate jewelry with a modern dress.

High and low. Try diamond earrings with a romper, or stiletto heels with shorts and a white shirt.

Summer and winter. French women access their entire wardrobe all year and don't put things in a box for winter. Chiffon skirts with cashmere sweaters, sandals with jeans, and cozy knitwear are always appropriate.

Hard and soft. A leather jacket with a silk camisole or motorcycle boots with a flirty skirt is tough and tender. Wear mannish and feminine clothes together to create sensual tension.

Forever fabrics

Different textiles have their own feel and fall on your body. Experiment with the most flattering fabrics for you and incorporate many of them into a well-rounded wardrobe.

Soft: Satin georgette, silk, and cashmere feel great on the skin and add romance and femininity to an outfit.

Edgy: Leather is one of the most sensual materials to the touch, and indispensable in a woman's wardrobe. A motorcycle jacket is your best companion for a night at the movies or on top of a long dress to the opera.

Dry: Denim can be supple or stiff for more structure. A jacket, a pair of high-waisted jeans, or a jumpsuit look cool and sharp, and a white cotton T-shirt is a must-have.

Sheer: Lace at the top of a camisole or an eyelet-lined dress in nude make the outfit more sensual. Cutouts in any fabric open small, seductive windows. Sheer chiffon and tulle are daring, concealing, and revealing at the same time.

"A dress makes no sense unless it inspires a man to take it off you"

Françoise Sagan

Red Super Power

Color is spice and energy. It's food for the imagination. Instead of just thinking about colors in terms of what's complementary, see them with a romantic eye. Saturated jewel tones are rich and strong. Pastels are soft and tender. Add a color in your wardrobe to send a message about your personality.

Red is the color of seduction, rebellion, heat, and passion. It's my favorite: I wear a touch of it every day on my lips and I have a few bold dashes in my wardrobe. Dare with a splash of red in your:

- Dress
- Blouse
- Coat
- Leather gloves
- Stilettos
- Handbag
- Umbrella

A warning: Red is so powerful, you don't want to overdo it. Play one hue at a time. In summer, I wear an orangey red. In winter, I choose a deeper red with blue, almost burgundy—the Hermès red.

Fire / dress

The red of a poppy is sumptuous. The texture of the petal is soft and so fragile that they begin to wilt as soon as the flower is plucked.

Years ago I was inspired by the poppy to design a dress of layers of crimson silk muslin cut in circles like the corolla of a flower, allowing the fabric to fly with each movement. Suspended by delicate straps of black leather, the dress hung on the body as though on a slender rod. Although the dress didn't make it into the collection I was preparing at the time, it did find a place in my personal wardrobe.

One summer, I was invited to a benefit gala in Southampton, Long Island, and I decided to wear the poppy dress. My partner and I got in a serious argument earlier that evening. When I arrived at the party alone, I moved among the people in my vibrant dress. I was down but my mood lifted and I was feeling empowered by the red color. I started to enjoy myself, laughing and chatting with the other guests.

When my fiancé arrived and saw me glowing in my airy, sensual outfit, he was seduced by the power of red and made every effort to win me back. It was a night of love and torrid reconciliations. I will always associate that dress with devastating emotions and victory.

Future is feminine

For some designers, the jacket stands as the founding element of their collection. For me, the dress is the epitome of the feminine garment, and it holds a very special place in my fashion universe. I usually cut on the bias, which ensures a beautiful fall. My pattern maker and I play with details, shearing, pin tucking, and draping, always in search of a daring, innovative silhouette. I'm looking for transparency or cutouts that reveal tiny islands of skin, but keep the mystery intact. Proportion is the key: A high waist makes your legs look longer. A bias-cut neckline highlights a décolleté. Designing dresses is effortless for me.

Dresses have the power to create miraculous moments. To have a complete wardrobe of them, you need a few little black dresses, to start:

- Cocktail dresses in chiffon or lace
- Working dresses: A-line, boxy, zipped, or button-down
- An evening dress with a bustier top and one with a dramatic deep V
- A few slip dresses cut on the bias in silk for summer with a light cardigan, and in fall on top of a T-shirt with boots

"A girl should be two things: fabulous and classy"
Coco Chanel

Feud for Style

For the French, clothes are emotional. They don't just wear them. They live in them and experience everything—love, sadness, triumph, tragedy—with the memory of their clothes intact. In the end, it's all about the emotions that clothes inspire. If a dress inspires joy, buy it! If it's depressing or disheartening, take it off.

When my customers used to tell me how my clothes make them feel, they talk about "the experience" of putting them on, and the meaning, the texture, the fit, the pleasure, and confidence they inspire. Women have mentioned wearing my dresses on first dates, to weddings, the night they fell in love, and it touches my heart. I met Alicia Keys for the first time at a gala benefit years ago, and when she heard my name, she turned to her husband Swizz Beatz and said, "Yes! Catherine Malandrino! You know my favorite leather jacket covered with studs? It's hers. I feel so strong in it." We started laughing and kissing. I met Beyoncé for the first time at one of Mary J. Blige's birthday dinners. She took me in her arms and said, "You don't even know how many dresses of yours I have in my closet! They make me feel so beautiful!" Her husband Jay Z gave me a high five. It was his way of thanking me for making his wife happy. In 2012, Jennifer Lopez wore my black mesh and leather panels dress—it fit her curves beautifully and gave her a glow of confidence—on *American Idol*. Her determined look was all over the media and interpreted as a powerful answer to her husband Marc Anthony's recent divorce filing. She chose it to show the world that she was hotter than hell despite her troubles. Recently, my friend Kelly Rutherford, one of the *Gossip Girl* stars, gave me a touching compliment. She arrived at an event wearing the famous white cotton blouse with puffy sleeves and shearing that I designed years ago, and she looked chic and stunning in it. "It's my favorite blouse and beautiful clothes never go out of style, we know that," she whispered in my ear with a clinch. I was proud and approved with a big smile. My clothes made all these talented women feel their power *even more*. Dressing friends, women, or celebrities and being appreciated by them is so gratifying for me as a designer, and certainly my highest reward.

Timeless French Wardrobe

What pieces do you need for a basic French wardrobe, and how do you put them together for effortless French style?

Ten Pieces You Need
Silky black slip dress with lace
Little black sheath dress, knee length
Off-white feminine blouse
White men's poplin shirt
Black motorcycle jacket in leather
Trench coat, classic silhouette
Black pencil skirt
Pair of fitted blue jeans
Little black cardigan
Jumpsuit

Six Bold Accessories
Big black leather bag
Evening clutch

Pair of two-and-a-half-inch stiletto heels
Pair of ballerina flats
Pair of dark shades
Printed silk scarf

For work: Combine the blouse, pencil skirt, leather jacket, and heels. Tie the scarf on the handle of your bag for a pop of color.

For a casual date: The silky slip showing the lace and décolleté under the cardigan, plus jeans, a trench coat, and your choice of heels or flats. Add a scarf around the neck to start, and remove it as the date goes on, if appropriate.

For a rendezvous: Combine the little black dress with the motorcycle jacket and heels, plus shades and red lips.

For late night: Combine the lingerie top with the cardigan and the jeans or pencil skirt or the jumpsuit with the jacket, heels, and red lips.

Once in your life, You must wear . . .

Style is confidence you can put on. The right garment can instantly change your attitude and set the tone for the day. You don't have to buy all the items below. You can start by borrowing or renting them, just to see how it feels.

- **Hermès scarf.** Tie it around your neck, around the handle of your bag, or around your waist. It's useful and so extraordinarily chic, you can't help but feel French when you wear it.

- **Chanel bag with a gold chain handle.** Choose a classic one, quilted in soft lambskin leather with hardware. It's such a marvel of proportion, you will feel rich just holding it.
- **Red stilettos.** They make you feel irresistible, a magnet for attention. Go with pointy and classic from Pierre Hardy. Wear a pair, and cross your legs. Every man will catch the movement.
- **Leopard print.** Be a little wild, but not too much! Animal print is great for a scarf or a blouse, but be careful with a full outfit.
- **Black shades** make you more cinematic. You create a character of yourself, a woman of mystery who might have secrets, and you can walk through the scene of your own life with extra flare. Don't choose fully dark black shades, but a smoky lens just to suggest your eyes.
- **Black silk lingerie.** Wear a seductive secret that glides over the skin and gives you a boost all day long.
- **Trench coat.** A classic Burberry. In a trench, heels, and sunglasses, you can go anywhere. Wear it easily open, belted in front, or tied in back for a flattering nipped-waist silhouette.
- **Red lipstick.** The fatal French touch.

"The only real elegance is in the mind If you've got that, the rest really comes from it"

Diana Vreeland

The First time I saw *La Belle et la Bête,* Jean Cocteau's *Beauty and the Beast* (1946), I was ten years old and mesmerized by the enchanted décor of the castle in the south of France, the magical costume design by Christian Bérard and Marcel Escoffier, and how, suddenly, the concept of beauty took a different meaning. At first, the Beast (Jean Marais) frightened me, but, like Belle (Josette Day), I was seduced by his personality, soul, and compassion. Slowly, he became my favorite character when he turned his ugliness into attraction. The idea took deep root, as childhood revelations do, and, as an adult, I was reminded of the transformative power of inner beauty in the 1991 Disney version. It remains my favorite story, emphasizing characters that are rejected from society because of their differences of opinion and free spirit. Belle was strong and independent and didn't bow to social pressure or bullies. She fought back, made her own choices, and stayed positive. Her inner beauty unlocked the kindness and generosity of the Beast. It was a long process, and it eventually transformed them as they fell in love.

Light and effortless beauty

I admire the artistry of makeup in Serge Lutens's photographs, his images of the exquisitely painted models where every brush stroke of eyeliner is as sharp as a diamond cut. But who wants to kiss and touch such a face? You'd be afraid to destroy it or to smudge your hands. The static images in magazines and books of beauty are inspirational and to be admired as works of art, but real beauty emanates from natural looks.

Your face should be an invitation to touch, and your lips, to kiss. Too much makeup is the enemy of the caress.

As a rule, if your routine takes forever and involves precise and painstaking details, you're overworking it. Beauty shouldn't be so hard and should take only a few minutes in front of a mirror.

Clean your skin and wake up the tissues with a great moisturizer, then smooth your skin tone with a light foundation, add a little black mascara, a trace of kohl, a little bit of rose powder on your cheeks, and a touch of red lipstick. It's natural, light, and simple, a look you can wear confidently as you move through your day.

French Face

- **Moisturizer.** Hydrating your skin is a must. I use Crème de la Mer every day on my face, neck, and décolleté.
- **Light coverage.** American woman sometimes put on too much foundation. French women go for transparency. Less makeup is

more natural and sensual. I recommend ultralight SPF 20 foundation like Synchro Skin from Shiseido with a tinted moisturizer like YSL Touche Éclat to add radiance to the skin and remove fatigue from the eyes. Bronzing powder like Terracotta Blush from Guerlain applied with a soft, wide brush from the hairline to the apple of the cheeks gives you a happy glow in any season.

- **Red lips.** Don't go overboard. Heavy liner makes your mouth too stiff and precise, and thick lipstick looks waxy and greasy. Or, if you hate makeup, just run your finger over your lips to bring some red to them like they've been bitten. It's as sensual an application as anything from a tube. Use moisturizer to keep lips soft. I recommend Blistex lip balm and Laura Mercier Joie de Vivre or Chanel Rouge Coco or Tom Ford Red.

- **Dramatic eyes.** Apply black kohl pencil at the roots of the lashes to define the shape of the eyes, top and bottom, and make them appear wider. And for a more dramatic moment, complete with a touch of black shadow on the lid from MAC cosmetics, mascara to lengthen (Hypnôse from Lancôme), and a curler to open the eye. Blondes shouldn't worry about the dark hue. Remember Brigitte Bardot! Black eyeliner was her favorite tool. Use concealer (Touche Eclat by YSL) on difficult mornings.

- **Tousled hair.** When your lover runs his hands in your hair, he shouldn't be blocked by spray and pins. Going undone and a bit wild is more sensual than perfectly straight or stiff hair. Let the wind mess it up. Allow natural tendrils to tumble around the nape of your neck. After a shampoo and rich conditioner, I gently dry and twist my hair in a topknot. When I take out the band, I have soft, natural waves.

- **Expressive brows.** They are important to frame your face and need to be shaped, but I'm not crazy about an overplucked or perfect brow. It creates the same problem as a too-polished face: pretty but not sexy. Respect the natural curve and density, and just clean up around the edges for a brow with personality. Always keep tweezers handy for strays.

- **Chic manicure.** In America, intricately polished nails with 3-D embellishments are sometimes part of the formula for seduction. French women don't object to manicures, but long tips are considered impractical, expensive, and vulgar. They prefer short, rounded nails polished in red or in natural nail polish tones—feminine, elegant, and low maintenance.

"*Aging is an extraordinary process where you become the person you always should have been*"

David Bowie

Silver belle or now?

The sad truth is, gray hair changes your skin tone and ages you before your time. Your features get lost in the ghostly halo. But when you have your original or preferred color, it frames your face and brings out the blush of your cheeks and sparkle of your eyes.

So, unless you go for an extremely chic full silver like the beautiful Linda Fargo, fashion director at Bergdorf Goodman, I recommend dyeing to get rid of the lighter touches. I love gray temples on men, but on women, the process is not flattering and gray strands in dark hair takes you right out of the game. You don't have to go to a salon every month. You can simply buy a box of L'Oréal mousse in a shade that will complement your original color and wash it into your hair. It only takes a half hour every two weeks to keep the color intense.

But if you renounce dyeing, remember that Jean-Paul Gaultier, Chanel, and Gareth Pugh have styled their models with beautiful silver hair on the runway. You can be even more dramatic like Lady Gaga with her full, daring, long silver-gray hair arriving at the 2015 *Vanity Fair* Oscar party in Beverly Hills. But then you have to be ready to go gray all the way.

Forever young

Injecting the face with fillers and toxins to get rid of wrinkles and make the skin smoother is the most common cosmetic procedure in America. These injections can be painful and expensive and you have to keep going back every six months to refresh. Some women are seeing the dermatologist more often than they see their friends. If you are determined to get shots, Botox can help, but don't begin the process until you start to feel discomfort about the lines— sometime after age forty-five or fifty.

We have to do what we can to feel our best, but say "no" to plastic surgery. Tightening the face tends to give women the same cloned look. You lose your uniqueness along with a few wrinkles. We've all seen photos of celebrities who've had work done and changed so much that they're unrecognizable. The eyes or lips that made them famous are gone from uncommonly attractive to age-less and just common.

I prefer women who age gracefully without surgery, or so little you can't even tell. Helen Mirren recently turned seventy and told the *Daily Mail*, "There's a huge pressure on young girls to look a certain way these days. But, as I age, I've lost that incredible insecurity of youth. It's great that the penny has finally dropped." She sat for a close-up portrait that showed every line on her face. Clearly, she wears them proudly. Unlike many of her contemporaries, Mirren's face moves freely to reveal intense emotion. In 2012's *Hitchcock*, she played Alma Reville, the horror legend's wife, a woman who had to keep many of her emotions bottled up. She conveyed the depth of her frustration, anger, fear, and love to the audience with nuanced surface ripples on her regal, natural face. Plastic surgery would have made her performance impossible.

Julianne Moore, fifty-six, once told a reporter, "Cosmetic surgery itself starts to look normal, and we lose track of what a real face is like. I don't know that they really made anybody look younger. I think most of the time they made you look like you've had something done to your face." In 2014's *Still Alice*, Moore won an Oscar for portraying a sharp, intelligent woman descending into the blankness of Alzheimer's, and showing every wrenching emotion along the way with heartbreaking authenticity—again, not possible with a paralyzed forehead.

Aging is an opportunity to emphasize your personality. Some lines are elegant! They should be acknowledged as a good thing. Showing your years is not the end of your life, or of being beautiful. French women inhabit the world of seduction until they die. The older they get, the more substantial they become. They've spent decades building their hearts, minds, and souls. From that deep core, they project the beauty of wisdom, the allure of experience. With age comes softness, grace, and gravity. The superficial luster of youth doesn't compare. Men will be attracted to and fascinated by your substance and assuredness—not just an unlined face.

As time passes, women in their forties and fifties become more of who they are. That profound understanding translates into confidence and peace. In the 2016 Tom Ford show, models Carolyn Murphy (forty-two), Amber Valletta (forty-three), and Liya Kebede (thirty-nine) walked the runway with grace among models half their ages. When I sit next to a twenty-year-old, I feel at ease with who I am and how I look. It's a quiet calm, a certainty. My sense of self is not shaken by young pretty girls. I look at them with a lot of tenderness and joy, thinking about the long journey still ahead of them.

To avoid or postpone injections in the future, I recommend the practice of French women: cleaning and hydrating your skin with quality products every day, wearing light makeup to block the sun, not abusing cigarettes and alcohol, and maintaining a healthy lifestyle. Your skin will stay smooth, soft, and clear into your sixties and seventies, especially if you add on top of your daily routine a nightly dose of love injection! And remember, with all the research on the cell, very soon, we will live to be 120 years old. Fifty will be the new thirty-five!

Beauty of Imperfection

A silhouette that moves, hair that flies, an elongated neck, pale skin, an elegant gesture—this is what French people call beauty, charm, and grace.

America has grown into a new standard of beauty with the Kardashian family and their obsession with perfection as they define

it—nose job, plumped lips, big booty, high hard boobs, stick-straight hair, perfect brows, a cookie-cutter beauty. An American friend told me recently about the custom of girls getting nose jobs the summer between high school and college. The idea is to shave a bump so she can start her new life with a bobbed nose, and no one is the wiser.

The French believe that a prominent nose, or any distinct feature, can be an asset. It's not that they "accept" imperfections or even "embrace" them. They *cultivate* unusual aspects of their features and personalities to create a unique trademark and stand apart.

Maria Callas was born with a prominent nose. Instead of it detracting from her power, she built her life around it. Her singing voice came through it. It gave her a striking profile in photographs. It certainly never stopped anyone from appreciating her beauty, including Greek magnate Aristotle Onassis.

Vanessa Paradis is famous in France for her sense of style and her smile. She happens to have a wide gap between her two front teeth, which the French call *les dents du bonheur* or "lucky teeth." She once said, "Why would I change [them]? I was born with them."

English actress and singer Jane Birkin emphasized her boyish body in jeans and T-shirts, giving her an androgynous charm that was exciting and fresh in the 1960s and '70s when she was the It Girl of Europe. Having a small chest was part of her slim, innocent appearance.

When I moved to New York twenty years ago, it seemed like every woman had a big chest. I am small up top. A New York friend I'd only just met said, "You should get bigger boobs. They'll change your life. I'll give you the name of my surgeon."

For a very short moment, I considered it, and then I came to my senses. My small chest is in proportion with my body. When I pictured my slim silhouette with a great big American chest, it looked totally surreal. I thought, *My life is good! I don't want to change it!* Of course, I hoped that American men would like what they saw when I wore a deep V-neck. My small chest in a half-moon bra was pleasingly unexpected in New York, land of giant boobs. **Difference is an asset for attraction.**

I had a similar experience when I visited my first American dentist. My teeth are a little bit crooked in front. He said, "You can't stay like this. You have to straighten them." After I left his office, I found myself looking at every woman's smile, staring at her perfectly white and straight teeth. I had to remind myself that I'd always loved my teeth. Many times, I've received compliments from my friends about my glorious smile. If my teeth were the same as everyone else, I would lose something charming about myself, so I left my wonderfully imperfect smile alone.

We all want to be loved and feel attractive because of who we are. Our strength is in our individuality and personality, our imperfections and curves, the way we think and speak, and how we present ourselves. In France, they say *"Vive la différence!"* **Imperfections for Americans are pure seduction for French.**

Work out at the gym? NON! Merci!

Very few people go to the gym in France. I tried to work out at a gym a few times in the U.S. and found it to be a discouraging experience. A close room with loud music and sweat is not an inspiring environment to me.

The *art de vivre* or "art of life" in France is about pleasure. The

French apply that to activity. They play sports outside with friends on a pretty day, and have a nice lunch afterward. If a group of girl-friends are together and the sun is shining, they might say, "Let's play tennis!" If it's a snowy week, they might say, "Let's go skiing on the weekend!" If you're with a lover and the leaves are falling from the trees, you might say, "Let's go horseback riding!" You don't play sports just for chiseled abs or a tight rear end. You do it for joy, fun, to share the moment. It's appreciation for nature as well as fitness. French women walk the streets of their city for hours, and the exercise is a side benefit. Instead of going to shop in malls, they go to outside markets, from boutique to boutique, and a journey of shopping is like a day of sports.

Of course, French women want to have a sexy and sensual body. But they have a different idea about what that means compared to the Hollywood standard. The French are at ease with a well-proportioned shape of any size. If a woman has a little belly, she won't devote herself to losing it, hiding it, or squashing it into shapewear. I read once that Kim Kardashian said, "I'm never without my Spanx!" Not a lot of women wear these torture garments in France. Instead, they choose appropriate clothes to forgive the weakness.

Weight and Diet

If a French woman wants to lose weight, she puts a little less food on her plate and is careful with bread and sugar. She doesn't change what she's eating, but she reduces the portions. She doesn't diet drastically because that would mean removing the pleasure of eating. Totally cutting out croissants or butter would be like turning her back on her culture, her deep appreciation and love for the flavor of life. For more on a daily eating routine, read *French Women Don't Get Fat* by Mireille Giuliano.

An American woman could take a cue from the French and, as an alternative to the Paleo or South Beach diets, she could enjoy the occasional patisserie, sweeten her life with a spoonful of sugar, and be comfortable in her skin. She'd be more seductive and so much happier that way. What a tragedy to tell yourself you can't have cake at all. Tiny macarons from Ladurée are delicious in moderation.

Contrary to what you might have heard, not every French woman is thin. They come in all shapes and sizes: round, slim, tall, short. But none of them believe a little extra weight is a huge problem that needs to be solved by suffering. They see everything through the perspective of seduction. If a French woman doesn't feel sexy because of her weight, she eats a little less for a few months to regain her confidence.

I have a close friend who is quite large, thanks to her love for good food and great wine. She doesn't fit into regular sizes. Her husband adores her the way she is and looks at her like she's a larger-than-life goddess. When we go shopping together in Paris, which she loves to do, we walk into Dior and she'll say to the salesperson, "These are my measurements. Make me this dress or this blouse in my size, please." She has all her clothes created for her, and she wears her couture proudly. "The problem isn't that I'm too big," she said. "It's that regular sizes are too small." No, she's not the perfect standard of beauty, but she radiates an ease and confidence that charms everyone she meets, and she emphasizes a beautiful and revealing décolleté that makes her very appealing.

On the other hand, I have another friend who is quite thin and tall. She could be a top model if she chose to be, but her confidence is nonexistent. She complains about her long, elegant legs ("too thin"), her chest ("too small"), her face ("too narrow"), her arms ("too skinny"). Although she is far more beautiful than just about everyone I know, she does not love herself. This phenomenon—pretty girls criticizing themselves harshly—is much more common than you think. Maybe her looks have prevented her from developing herself. She hasn't, actually, accomplished anything that would make her feel proud. Meanwhile, my plus-size friend is always laughing, a big success in her career, and well loved.

Confidence, not size, is the deciding factor in happiness.

Beauty's worst enemies

The most stunning person might possess traits that rob his or her beauty. Jealousy, envy, and anger are not qualities to wear on your face or in your heart.

The two worst enemies of beauty:

- **Bitterness.** A defeated person only sees the negative and blames other people for her unhappiness. She is angry at the world, and hates everything. No matter how conventionally attractive she might be, bitterness makes her ugly. It doesn't age well, either. For me, it's the worst thing that can happen.
- **Stinginess.** There is nothing less attractive than a tight-fisted person. She accepts presents but never gives any. Lack of generosity is antisexy.

Beauty's best friend

Beauty is a way to look at the world. Everywhere you are, if you glance around, you can find something to admire and be inspired by. Start by looking inside yourself to find your most beguiling parts. Your generosity, kindness, and forgiveness are radiant qualities that will make you shine.

A positive spirit is the most important aspect of beauty. Always look on the bright side of life and you'll have a chance at being, becoming, and staying beautiful.

One of the most charming men I've ever known happens to be wheelchair-bound. At forty, he's bursting with life pleasure. He was unhappy for years about the car accident that took his ability to walk when he was twenty-four. But then he was able to reinvent himself into a confident seducer again.

The first time I met him at my friend Michele's country house in East Hampton, I was uncomfortable, but only for a minute. Then he showed his personality by taking a tennis racket and playing a real game on his wheelchair, winning the match against a great player, Michele's husband at the time, on his legs. I developed admiration for his strength and determination. Later, I discovered he was very sportif and went biking with him in Central Park. Nothing stops this man from living his life. He goes swimming and skydiving. His sense of humor, confidence, and beautiful shoulders make him very attractive.

The day he charmed me the most was when he took me to one of the hottest nightclubs in New York at the time, Baby Grand in Tribeca. On his wheelchair but with assurance, he grabbed my hand and brought me onto the dance floor. He started spinning in the chair to the rhythm of the music. It was fantastic. All the women were fascinated by him. We danced all night at the center of the crowd, and I was so attracted to his audacity and confidence, that later, I sat on his lap and kissed him on the lips.

Developing what you've got and making it the best it can be is the key to lifelong beauty. Even if you are given a major challenge like my friend, you can always invent and reinvent yourself into an incredible, beautiful, and seductive person.

seduction

"The very essence of romance is uncertainty"

Oscar Wilde

French women are seductresses.

Every gesture, style choice, and smile has the intention of being alluring, posing a question, creating an air of *je ne sais quoi*. Seduction itself is a mystery. How can you be more romantic, poetic, and dramatic in everything you do, say, wear, feel, and experience? This puzzle is the game of life—*le jeu de la vie*. There is no end to the game, only the joy of playing.

Seductiveness brings color and spice into your day. It creates a thrill, a frisson, that makes any interaction a few shades brighter. For French women, seduction is not a switch to turn on and off. They would never say, "Sometimes, I'm seductive," just as they wouldn't say, "Sometimes, I'm a woman." **Being seductive is being a woman.**

Seduction : Seamless Process

The first person any woman has to seduce is herself.

As a young girl, I made the connection that other people were drawn to me when I felt great about myself and my style. It started when I experimented with hairstyles and clothes in the mirror and surprised myself with how different little changes made me feel. I carried the confidence into the day, and it affected my personality in a very intriguing way. Many of my friends picked up the sense that I had a little secret, and it made them curious about me. Their interest—compounded with my own excitement for life—made me attractive.

Ever since, I've been exploring how being in harmony with yourself can make you irresistible to others. For me, one way to be authentic is to dress well and uphold my style even if I am the only one around to see it. When I get home from work, I change into comfortable but sexy clothes, a lingerie dress or a silk kimono, so that I'm at ease and relaxed, but also seductive, alive in a romance with life.

Being seamlessly yourself brings inner confidence that allows you to shine.

Seduction : Slow Motion

"It's not enough to conquer, one must also know how to seduce," said Voltaire, an expert on the art. To conquer is to overcome quickly. To seduce is to draw out the tension slowly and savor every minute of it.

In the French tradition, seduction is a story that unfolds over time. Compared to the American tradition of the "three-date rule," the French courtship must seem endless. American journalist Elaine Sciolino lived in Paris as a correspondent for *The New York Times* and attempted to unravel the secret of "sexy à la française" in her book *La Seduction: How the French Play the Game of Life*. She beautifully noted the French tendency toward "prolonged sexual play" in a chapter called "It's Not About the Sex." Flirtation can go on for months, even years. The French enjoy the chase more than the catch. They do not "jump into bed" because **romantic torture is exquisite**.

Do's and Don'ts of Seduction

- Do catch the light.
- Do smile, always.
- Do give compliments.
- Do use a restrained and sensual voice.
- Do eat with pleasure and appreciate the flavor, color, and texture of the food.
- Do have a glass of French wine with your meal instead of soda. The color code: red wine with meat, white or pink with fish and poultry. Rosé in summers, and champagne with everything at any time!
- Do stay faithful to a scent that defines you.
- Do go where the night takes you. Being too much in control impedes the chance of love.
- Do make every movement a moment as if your life were a fascinating movie.
- Do create eye contact.
- Don't post too many selfies.
- Don't put makeup on in front of anyone, or you'll betray your beauty secrets.
- Don't get fake nail tips with crazy colors or patterns.
- Don't wear flip-flops! The walking posture in plastic sandals is disastrous. Choose a sporty sneaker or ballet flat instead.
- Don't use too much hair product. Stiff is not sexy.
- Don't spend too much time getting ready. Making others wait is annoying and boring. If you need more time, prepare earlier.

Sensualité

To play the game of seduction, awaken your **five senses**.

Sight

Seduction starts with eye contact, a stealth form of intimacy. It doesn't have to be *coup de foudre*—love at first sight—to be meaningful. Catching the eye of a stranger can be a moment of pleasure that lights up a dull day, a reminder that human attraction is magnetic.

American men are uncomfortable with eye contact. When I first got to New York, I was surprised that they didn't look at me. I felt transparent walking the streets. And then I realized that they aren't comfortable linking eyes because it could be interpreted as a creepy come-on or sexual harassment. In France, to be acknowledged by a man with a sly glance is a compliment, not an aggressive act. When I go back to Europe, I'm happy to connect eyes with men again, and I welcome their smiles.

French women love smoky eye makeup because it creates the perfect window to view the world with just enough shade to allow for secret looks. Eyes are your best ambassadors and powerful weapons. They inspired French surrealist poet Louis Aragon to write a beautiful love poem in the early 1940s to his wife Elsa Triolet. A taste of his devotion:

Les Yeux d'Elsa

Your eyes are so deep that leaning down to drink
I saw all suns mirrored in them
All desperate souls hurled deathward from their brink
Your eyes are so deep my memory is lost there

In the shadow of birds the ocean roars
Then suddenly the day clears and your eyes change
Summer carves the clouds on the angels' pinafore
The sky's never as blue as it is above grain

In vain the winds pursue the azure's griefs
Your eyes are brighter, even through a veil of tears,
And your eyes make the heavens jealous after a shower:
Glass is never so blue as it is when it breaks.

Touch

The old tradition of a man kissing a woman's hand—*le baise-main*—is pure seduction. He bows slightly, cradling her hand like a delicate flower or fragile bird, barely touching his lips to her soft skin as a gesture of devotion. Too bad it's not done often nowadays.

The French do still kiss and touch at every meeting. It's not enough to just say "Bonjour!" and shake hands. They indulge in the sensual ritual called *la bise* (pronounced "la bees"), the double-cheek kiss. Moments into a rendezvous, you are touching, kissing, and discovering his perfume and the roughness, or the softness, of his skin.

One of the most memorable scenes about the seduction of touch was in the movie *The Piano*. Holly Hunter was playing the instrument while Harvey Keitel lay on the floor underneath. He asked her to lift her skirts. She did, and he was transfixed by a rip in her black stockings at the knee. As she poured her heart into the music, he reached for the hole and gently ran his finger around its edges, barely touching her pale white skin. She jolted with their electricity. Unexpected skin contact can be extremely evocative.

La Bise Dos and Don'ts

- Do kiss old friends and family members, as well as complete strangers you are introduced to for the first time.
- Do remove glasses if you both wear them. If you are kissing a man, it's appropriate for him to remove his glasses first.
- Don't make lip-to-cheek contact. It's more a light cheek-to-cheek brush.
- Do *la bise* with both women and men.
- Do it as a sign of affection and respect. Recently, the French president François Hollande went on a TV show about the Elysée Palace lifestyle, and, at a ministry council meeting, he double-kissed every woman in the room. It's hard to imagine an American president doing *la bise* with female cabinet members before calling the meeting to order.

Scent

Parfum is serious, almost religious, in France, where some of the world's most memorable fragrances—Chanel, Hermès, Guerlain, to mention a few—are created. French women fall deeply in love with a single fragrance and will stay loyal to it for years. They might have a short passionate affair with another scent, like a surprise liaison, but they will most likely return to their first love.

My dear friend Veronique Gabai-Pinsky, a master in the *parfumerie* world, is a lover of fragrance, and together we have passionate discussions about the link between scent and seduction. Veronique is the epitome of a stylish French woman, and she was the first ever customer at my flagship Soho boutique in 1998. Since then, she's been my biggest fashion supporter; she still keeps the embroidered sweater she bought almost twenty years ago in her wardrobe as a treasure. Her friendship and loyalty mean a lot to me. We completely agree that wearing a fragrance is an emotional experience, entwined with memories of winter nights under the duvet, sunny days, a scarf in the breeze, the skin of your lover. A woman's scent holds the tenderness of every embrace. Her *parfum* is her most powerful and seductive signature. You'll know her with eyes closed.

I'll always remember the 1974 movie *Parfum de Femme* by Dino Risi, starring Vittorio Gassman. The story of a blind man who was transported by a woman's scent during a passionate tango is irresistible. While I'm dancing I keep in mind the scene and close my eyes to enjoy the perfume of the man whose arms are around me.

The novel *Perfume: The Story of a Murderer* by German Patrick Süskind, set in eighteenth-century Paris, takes a deep dive into the twisted mind of the character Jean-Baptiste Grenouille, an unwanted orphan with a gift: he has an extraordinarily sensitive nose. Using his talent, he becomes a *parfumeur* in Grasse, and later a murderer, killing virgins to collect their scents, and combining them for the ultimate essence of youth and beauty. He sacrifices their lives, and ultimately his own, in the creation of a single transcendent perfume that would send people into fits of rapture. A memorable quote from the novel about the power of perfume:

> Scent is the sister of breath. Together, with breath, it enters human beings who could not defend themselves against

it, not if they wanted to live. And the scent entered into their very core, went directly to their hearts, and decided for good and all between affection and contempt, disgust and lust, love and hate. He who ruled scent ruled the hearts of men.

When I was twelve, my mother took me to the *parfumerie* in Grenoble, just the two of us on a special day together, to find a fragrance I could call my own. My mother's perfume was Nahéma de Guerlain created by Jean Paul Guerlain himself in 1979, a distinctive bouquet of voluptuous roses, and, for me, an ode to my mother's sensibility and beauty. The bottle was in a gold metal basketweave case, and she sprayed a cloud of roses on her silk scarf and neck. For my mother, perfume has always been her touch of luxury. I would soon feel the same.

I sampled different fragrances that day and began a sensual education. My first choice, a creation by Lolita Lempicka, was right for the virgin mountain girl I was then, dreaming about a romantic woman's life. It filled my head with expectations and promises about the future. I started wearing it every day, just a touch behind the ears, and felt like a grown woman with my scent on. In no time, I felt naked without it.

Since then, I've chosen my fragrance by myself or with *mon amoureux*, a romantic mission since we'll enjoy it together (Chanel No. 5 commercials used to say, "Share the fantasy"). Fragrance becomes part of the love story. For some years, I wore Opium by Yves Saint Laurent. I created an entire imaginary world around that sublime oriental scent. During that time, I was in a romance with a young, mysterious Arab man. I associated the glowing red of the bottle with my initial love for him. When the relationship ended, I had to close my affair with Opium as well. Love and perfume are intricately entwined.

These days, I prefer scents that evoke the mystery of the night. My favorites are A La Nuit by Serge Lutens mixed with a few drops of Ambre Sultan, and recently, Fleur d'Oranger, which inspires freshness and youth. If you are inspired to create your own fragrance, go to Le Labo and work with the passionate *parfumeurs* to combine heavenly ingredients—bergamot, rose, neroli, orange blossom, patchouli, iris, jasmine, sandalwood, ylang-ylang—to build a unique formula that suits your personality.

Recently, my son, Oscar, asked me to help him choose a fragrance for himself. He knew how deeply I care about the subject, and I wanted to introduce him to the world of scents so he wouldn't be overwhelmed by the choices. I don't know many American eighteen-year-old men who go perfume shopping with their mother as a rite of passage, but in France, it's almost normal. Perhaps a father might take his son, but usually, a mother loves doing it.

We were in Paris at the time, and we went to a Sephora store together. About a hundred men's fragrances were lined up on a wall and Oscar didn't know which one to try. I said, "Start with the packaging." Perfumes are marketed very carefully to appeal to people based on their fantasies of themselves. The messaging is often aspirational. As a young man or woman is developing and has big dreams for the future, he or she might choose a fragrance that is a daily reminder of what he or she hopes to become. I asked Oscar to look at the boxes and images and let the packaging do its job. He gravitated toward a few bottles that represented worlds he'd like to explore.

The next step is to close your eyes and inhale. With matters of sensuality, trust your heart and your nose, and the instant "yes" or "no" reaction.

Oscar had some trouble. "I can't tell them apart! They're all the same," he said.

"Take your time," I told him. "Concentrate. One might be more smoky, spicy, or grassy. One is like leather or a flower. Which one seems right for you?"

He tried again, and started to identify the differences. I said, "Can you imagine yourself feeling at ease wearing this as you go through your day?"

That helped him narrow down the choices. I asked, "Does the scent make you feel good?"

Oscar wasn't embarrassed by the question, and neither was I for asking it. He had girlfriends. It was the reality of the situation. A man, just like a woman, wants to create romance, and that means choosing a scent that his partner would appreciate. If Oscar understood this at eighteen, he had a head start in learning the power of seduction.

Finally, he chose Sauvage by Dior, with the wild image of Johnny Depp. "Do you like it?" he asked.

I approved of his choice wholeheartedly. He started to wear it every day. Soon after, he came home and said, "Mom, we nailed it! I feel great! Girls love it!"

I experienced a moment with my son. He learned how to please others and to trust his nose. It opened a new world for him, just as my mother had for me all those years ago.

"What Do I Wear to Bed? Chanel No. 5, of Course."

The quote is from Marilyn Monroe, a seductress who understood that a perfume is as essential as a silk evening gown. How do French women apply theirs to the skin to create a romance with the world?

- Spray or dab on the hot spots: behind your ears, on your wrists, and in your hair.
- Put a few drops on your pillow, and on your lover's.
- At home, spray the air and walk into the mist or just let it float down lazily.
- Don't spray your clothes, except perhaps your scarf to add a little something in your movements.
- Your scent shouldn't enter the room before you do. A few drops are enough.

Sound

I believe you can fall in love with the sound and texture of a voice, especially if it's speaking a foreign language or has a charming accent. For American men, I've heard many times that French is a language of poetry, linking words like a love song, each sentence crescendoing with drama and suspenseful pauses.

Voice and words are seductive weapons. Remember the tone from the Golden Age of Hollywood, especially the husky voice and sultry style of Lauren Bacall in her noir thrillers? Her dialogue from *To Have and Have Not*—"You know how to whistle, don't you? Just put your lips together, and blow"—is a complete course in vocal seduction, and a part of her romantic history. *To Have and Have Not* was her first movie with Humphrey Bogart. They fell in love while filming, and married soon after. When he died, she put a whistle in his coffin as a memorial of the famous scene.

Even in the era of texting, short communication, and instant gratification, words can still be magic. Author Tim David wrote about their power in *Magic Words: The Science and Secrets Behind Seven Words That Motivate, Engage, and Influence*. One of those seductive words? "Thanks." Another? Your own name, preferably whispered in your ear by your lover.

If the person you're talking to has to lean slightly forward, it focuses his attention on your lips. Is there anything sexier than a man staring at your mouth while you speak, as if he is transfixed by your words? All the more reason to highlight your lips in red, the color of seduction. A soft voice doesn't mean a mushy one, though. Speak clearly by articulating each beautiful word. If you're bothering to say it, it should matter. Also, learn to appreciate the seductive sound of silence. It's better not to speak at all than to chatter gratingly to fill a conversational void. Better to just stay silent and use body language instead.

Flavor

Even after many years of being a New Yorker, I didn't know that Americans use the phrase "French kiss" to mean the act of tasting a lover's mouth. The first kiss is a culmination of all your senses, the final scene in a five-act play. It starts with the eyes, looking at his lips and creating the desire to taste. It develops as you draw closer to touch and notice each other's scent. It builds with a soft purr or a whispered "yes." And then your lips connect, and as the kiss deepens, you open up to explore each other, alive and in thrall. People talk about provocative tastes like strawberries, oysters, caviar, sea urchin, and champagne, but the most delicious flavor is your lover's mouth.

Baisers de Cinema

The 1988 Italian film *Cinema Paradiso* by Giuseppe Tornatore explored the emotional power of the kiss in the final scene. The story starts in the World War II era, when a priest insisted that the local movie projectionist cut every embrace from the movies played at the cinema. He edited the reels and left the censored scenes on the floor. The projectionist struck up an unlikely friendship with a young boy and let him watch movies from the projection booth. Destiny and tragedy separated the two. When the boy, all grown up and a successful filmmaker, returned to his Sicilian village for the projectionist's funeral, his widow gave him one of the projectionist's film reels. The man watched it and realized it was a spliced-together reel of all the censored kisses. The scene of his watching it was very touching and always brings me to tears. The montage of dramatic kisses included the lips of Jane Russell, Charlie Chaplin, Errol Flynn, Greta Garbo, and Ingrid Bergman, in glorious black-and-white.

If I were to make a reel of my favorite kisses, it would include:

***The Thomas Crown Affair* (1968)**. The scene starts out with Faye Dunaway in a backless, taupe silk dress and Steve McQueen playing chess by a blazing fire. "Do you play?" he asked. "Try me," she replied. As they moved pieces around the board, she absentmindedly touched her arm and her lips and stroked a bishop while he stared, trying to keep his cool. After she put him in check, he lifted her to her feet and said, "Let's play something else." And then their lips met in a tight close-up to the swelling Michel Legrand music. It's the longest kiss scene ever—nearly seven minutes. The sexual tension builds to the limit.

The Notebook (2004). When Ryan Gosling and Rachel McAdams stood with thunder and lightning, he grabbed her and lifted her off her feet, all the emotion of their years of separation and misunderstanding erased in one marvelous kiss in the pouring rain.

Velvet Goldmine (1998). Two fabulous men, Jonathan Rhys Meyers, a glitter rock god in a sparkling suit with a top hat, and Ewan McGregor, in a metallic gold trench coat, locked lips and kissed openmouthed in a close-up for a full twenty seconds at the center of a circus ring in front of the crowd.

Spider-Man (2002). The totally original upside-down kiss between Kirsten Dunst and Tobey Maguire began as he hung from a fire escape in the rain in his Spider-Man costume. She didn't know his identity, but he'd saved her life, and she was indebted to her hero. In a soaking wet dress, she peeled down his mask to reveal just his lips. When the kiss was over, he shot his web and disappeared into the night.

From Here to Eternity (1953). On a beach, Deborah Kerr lay on top of Burt Lancaster's muscular body, wet in their swimsuits under the hot sun, the only two people in the world. The foamy waves crashed around them as they kissed on the shoreline. During a pause, she confessed, incredulous, "I didn't know it could be like this."

Black Swan (2010). After a chaotic night of dancing and drugs, Natalie Portman returned to her girly pink ballerina bedroom to find Mila Kunis (or a hallucination of her). The women rushed into a desperate, frantic kiss that quickly led to shedding clothes, love, and tasting adventures.

Interaction

Seduction is an exchange, a captivating conversation of words and laughter.

Listen Well and Have Something to Say

To be a good listener, make eye contact, and let the other person know you are genuinely, fully present. A seductive woman listens without worrying about her companion's judgment, or how she'll appear. She reacts with honesty in the moment, disarms and charms with a smile.

To be a good talker, use intonation, be generous with your wit, and share your interests. A discussion is a contest of equals that inspires both participants to be at their sharpest. French people are considered *beaux parleurs,* smooth talkers. One of my favorite songs is the flawless duet "Paroles, Paroles," with Dalida answering Alain Delon, "Toujour des mots, rien que des mots . . ." ("Always words, nothing but words . . ."). The French love to delve into their passions and share what they've done, seen, and read because they are seduced by their own interests and want their excitement to spread to others. When you are about to meet someone new, remind yourself of interesting things you've experienced lately. It might be a play or an article in a newspaper, a basketball game you watched with friends, an art exhibit, or a new restaurant you've tried. The discussion might inspire your companion to expand his horizons or to suggest taking you to see a similar exhibit he's appreciated or a play you might both applaud.

I've noticed that in New York people jump into conversations by asking "What do you do for a living?" or "Where do you live?" Money and status come up so often because people are excited about their professional lives and they want to talk about it. In social situations in France, people don't bring up money, careers, or real estate. They consider it vulgar, the opposite of seductive. Lively conversation at a Parisian table is about art, food, travel, music, and sex, subjects that are inherently compelling and inclusive. Except for money matters, the French don't restrict any topic. The entire point of the interaction is to get a reaction. He returns with his opinion, and you are now having an animated exchange. French people love to argue. It gets the blood flowing. Politics, religion, soccer, any subject that can cause a disagreement is open to debate. The conversation might start light, but will quickly go deep. Yes, let's talk about how a celebrity had an affair and who is cheating on whom. It's a favorite French subject.

If you happen to notice that there are things unspoken between you, a seductive woman might steer the conversation toward the intimate by asking a personal question (not "What do you pay in rent?"). You could ask him, "What is that perfume you are wearing?" You just know there's a story there. Coax it out of him.

Les Mots Bleus

A smile, *un sourire*, opens doors and hearts. As you walk toward someone, smile, and you'll see judgment and defenses dissolve. Along with a kind and friendly face, offer *les mots bleus* to seduce strangers and friends alike. In his famous 1975 song, the decadent dandy Christophe sang *"Les mots qu'on dit avec les yeux,"* meaning "the words we say with the eyes." An unspoken suggestion, question, or comment can relay paragraphs using just a glance.

The French also use *les bon mots*, compliments to acknowledge that you appreciate something in another person. I think it's sad that, in the United States in this day and age, saying something nice about someone else is often interpreted as offensive. When President Obama praised the former California attorney general and current U.S. senator Kamala Harris by saying, "She's brilliant, and she's dedicated. She's tough. She also happens to be, by far, the best-looking attorney general in the country," I thought it was beautiful. Unfortunately, his remark was considered by the media to be a sexist gaffe.

There is a big divide between how Americans and the French view compliments. Americans try to separate attractiveness from accomplishment. In France, they are inextricably linked. French people use sensuality to bond with the rest of the world. Seductiveness is not merely a part of who they are, it is the filter through which they empower themselves and relate to others. They smile because it can turn the tide. They speak softly because they want to be heard. Saying nice things will win their favor, which is the intention of seduction.

Atmosphere

A seductive atmosphere, be it flattering lighting, a warm setting, or an air of mystery, creates the mood.

Light

I'm a lover of light. I'm aware of it, natural and artificial, in every setting, in the brightness of the morning and the twilight at dusk. Light creates shadows, elongates lines, and makes everything appear severe or soft. For artists, composition is the study of illumination. Monet adored natural light and was fascinated by how it changed the landscape over the course of the day and the year and in different weather, as well as how light affected colors, textures, and moods. He chased sun- and moonlight most famously in his Giverny studies of water lilies and haystacks, documenting how darkness and light can evoke primal emotions. Italian Renaissance painter Caravaggio is known for the intensity of his "chiaroscuro," the contrast between dark and light, like in *The Inspiration of Saint Matthew,* as a spotlighted angel emerges from a bottomless black background. The American photographer Man Ray (an honorary Parisian) was famous for his nude portraits of his muse and lover Lee Miller, as well as surrealist imagery of elongated silhouettes, hands, and close-ups of eyes and lips. Not only did he explore a timeless black-and-white world of light and shadow; he used light in a technique he created called "solarization." While his film was being developed in a dark room, he'd flash light on the print, making the image part negative, part positive. He was at play with contrast, a magician with light. Shifting light unlocks emotion and expands the limitations of how you see the world.

My favorite window in my apartment overlooks Riverside Park and the Hudson River. I love the crisp, blue morning light of New York. Gazing at the sky first thing from that spot is one of my simple, great pleasures and it adjusts my attitude at the very beginning of each day.

In photographs, lighting is everything. I'm conscious of how it will reflect my mood and shadow the planes of my face. I'm always chasing the light and make sure I catch it.

In a meeting, I try to learn beforehand whether the lighting will be the cold glare of overhead fluorescents or warm with lamps and sconces. The temperature of the room starts with the light. It sets the tone.

At a rendezvous at home, I dim the lights to create mystery or use candles and plant leaves to create shadows. Golden flickers cast a spell and create instant intimacy. Two people in a dark room with only the single flame between them are wrapped in the flattering glow of their own small world. My favorite scented candles are Diptyque's Figuier and Tubéreuse.

Mystery

Subtlety is a matter of what you choose to reveal and what to keep hidden. It's always preferable to hint and suggest, and leave questions unanswered. Make others fill in the blanks about you, but never confirm their beliefs completely. Shrug instead of explaining. Give a sly smile instead of a commitment. Not every time, of course. That would be predictable.

You don't see many famous French people revealing their personal lives on Facebook, Twitter, and Instagram. They value their privacy, and are cultivating mystery. If you are an open book, why would someone be motivated to dig in and learn more about you? There's a fine line between sharing your life and giving away your mystery for likes and comments. Avoid crossing it.

By holding some things back and being careful about what you say, wear, and do, you place a higher value on yourself. It's smarter, more respectful, and far more seductive to wait for the right moment to express your opinions and desires. Baring your soul, like baring your skin, is a gift that's too valuable to give away.

If discretion is one side of the seduction coin, the other side is spontaneity. When a free-spirited woman has the desire to sip a glass of wine at lunch, she just goes for it. It's not that she's flighty and impulsive. She's moved by the moment and has the confidence to say what she wants—and we love her for it.

Consider two women: One puts so much product in her hair that it looks like a motorcycle helmet. The other woman's hair is a mess because she just *took off* a motorcycle helmet after an impromptu ride on the back of her boyfriend's Moto Guzzi. Which woman is seductive? Which woman do you want to know better?

If you are always tightly wound, then you are incapable of letting go. Sex is about surrender and freedom and both require abandon. Seduction is the poetry of life.

Magic

Every morning, I make coffee—a fragrant roast in a French press—and arrange porcelain cups on a silver tray. Two cups, always. The second is for my lover or, if I'm alone, an offering to the universal spirit to help me seize another day.

Create romance in life by infusing it with sensuality. Even the simple act of making coffee can be a sensual, seductive gesture. It doesn't take any time or effort to turn the mundane into the extraordinary. Within five minutes of waking, you could do a few things that set a romantic intention for the day and transform what could be lost time into beauty and grace.

Picasso said, "It is your work in life that is the ultimate seduction." Your life is an empty white canvas. Design it and make it magical.

French Seduction on Film

Dangerous Liaisons (1988) by Stephen Frears with John Malkovich, Glenn Close, and Michelle Pfeiffer. This Oscar-winning film was

je je t'ai
je t'aime je
je t'aime je
ji t'aime je
ji t'aime je t'ai   je t't'aime
ji t'aime je t'aime   je t't'aime je t
je t'aime ji t'aime   je t't'aime ji t'aim
je t'aime ji t'aime je t't'aime je
je t'aime ji t'aime je t't'aime je
je t'aime ji t'aime ji t't'aime je
je t'aime ji t'aime ji t't'aime je
je t'aime ji t'aime ji t't'aime je
je t'aime ji t'aime ji t't'aime je
je t'aime ji t't'aime je t't'ai
je t'aime ji t't'aime je t't'
je t'aime ji t'aime je
le t'aime ji t'aime
le t'aime ji t'ai
le t'aime je t'
le t'aime je
le t'aime
je t'ai
je

based on the eighteenth-century novel *Les liaisons dangereuses* by Choderlos de Laclos about the Marquise de Merteuil, a great lady of society, and the Vicomte de Valmont, her scandalous ex-lover. Together, they set out to corrupt a virtuous and faithful married woman, Madame de Tourvel, for their entertainment, and as a part of their own slow seduction of each other. In the meantime, naive lovers played by very young Uma Thurman and Keanu Reeves are entangled erotically in the plot. In their world, seduction is an art, a manipulation, a high-stakes game that can bring you to life and love, or to death. My dear friend Julie de Noailles, the heir to one of the oldest aristocratic families in France, sometimes reminds me of Glenn Close as Madame de Mertueil, with her intriguing mind, elegance, and beauty.

La Piscine, aka *The Swimming Pool* (1969) by Jacques Deray. Romy Schneider is in love with Alain Delon at their vacation house with a pool in Provence. Her whimsical smile, golden tan skin, and effortless elegance are irresistible to her boyfriend, and to his best friend who drops by unexpectedly. The passionate love triangle sets off suspense, volcanic passions, and violence. A very young Jane Birkin plays the teenage ingénue who is not as innocent as she originally seemed. The sensual tension between four characters ends with the murder in . . . *la piscine.*

A Man and a Woman aka *Un Homme et Une Femme* (1966) by Claude Lelouch, starring Anouk Aimée and Jean-Louis Trintignant. A young widow with a daughter meets a young widower with a son at their children's boarding school in Deauville. She's a script editor for films whose husband, a stunt man, died in a car crash. He's a race car driver whose wife killed herself after his crash at a daylong race at Les Mans. The similarities draw them together—as do their stunning, languid sexuality and the lush scenery—but they have conflicting emotions, visualized by changes from color to black-and-white to sepia. They fall in love and finally embrace, but the memories of their dead spouses haunt their tender lovemaking. It's heartbreaking, but optimistic. The final scene is when the two see each other again on a train station platform, and you get the feeling that although the movie is ending, it's just the beginning of their love story.

Port of Shadows aka *Le Quai des Brumes* (1938) by Marcel Carné with Jean Gabin and Michèle Morgan, written by Jacques Prévert. The French equivalent of *Casablanca*, it's a complex story of two wartime lovers who are pulled apart by forces beyond their control. Jealousy, obsession, and murder take place in the mysterious Le Havre setting. In this dangerous universe, nothing is more important than passion. The tone is pure noir, a dark and erotic mood with hazy streetlights, cobblestone streets, wide-brimmed hats, and cigarettes. The iconic scene is when Jean Gabin and Michèle Morgan are looking into each other's faces and he says, "You have beautiful eyes, you know." She replies, "Kiss me," and they do, pressed passionately against a brick wall.

Sweetest Taboo

In Paris, the nightlife tradition is exotic and erotic, from the Belle Epoque with Toulouse-Lautrec paintings of cancan girls at the Moulin Rouge to the Jazz Age of the 1920s. The toast of Paris in 1925 was Josephine Baker, an American from St. Louis. Her extreme childhood poverty was no match for her talent. At sixteen, she was cast in the Broadway hit *Shuffle Along* as a featured dancer and starred in vaudeville in black face before traveling to the City of Light at nineteen to perform in *La Revue Nègre* at the Théâtre des

Champs-Élysées, an elegant Art Deco *boite de nuit* with bas-relief sculptures of Apollo and the nine muses on its marble façade. Baker shook and shimmied through the *Danse Sauvage* for Parisian audiences obsessed with jazz and mesmerized by her dark, glistening skin, slicked-back black hair, and luscious-lipped smile. Her humor, sensuality, and beauty made her an instant sensation.

As her fame grew, Baker moved up to the Folies Bergère, a legendary Art Deco music hall decorated like a carnival with a turquoise-and-gold grand foyer with enormous candelabras and carousel horses. Baker performed an evocative belly dance in *La Folie du Jour*, a jungle-themed number costarring her pet cheetah. The show was a smash and the "Black Venus" became one of the highest-paid entertainers in Europe, befriending Picasso and Hemingway. Legend has it she received over a thousand marriage proposals. In later years, Baker was the first black woman to star in movies—*Zouzou* and *Princesse Tam-Tam*—and she bought her own castle, Château des Milandes, in southwest France. Although she fought for American civil rights, she lived in her adopted country for the rest of her life, becoming a French citizen, and was made a Chevalier of the Légion d'Honneur by General Charles de Gaulle, the highest honor. She loved Paris and it loved her back, honoring her with Place Josephine Baker, a shady park in Montparnasse, and Piscine Josephine Baker, a futuristic glass-walled pool with a retractable roof on the Seine by the Bastille.

The glamour and sensuality of Josephine Baker lives on in Paris nightlife, with a modern edge. Slow seduction takes center stage every night at Le Crazy Horse, the sanctuary of glamour, the palace of eroticism. Unlike cabarets Moulin Rouge and the Folies Bergère, which still do beautiful but old-fashioned musical comedy reviews, Le Crazy Horse elevates eroticism into art, combining style and sexiness into a very chic experience. The ambassadresses of glamour: the Crazy Girls, nearly nude and almost identical dancers who perform a precisely choreographed elegant striptease that's creative, feminine—and extremely suggestive.

Whenever I go back to Le Crazy Horse, I enjoy immersing in the fantasy atmosphere, and I remember the outstanding performances:

- **Dita Von Teese's Crazy Show** (2015). The American burlesque icon is a regular guest star at Le Crazy Horse. Her show emphasizes three things: her tiny waist trussed in a corset, her glorious ivory skin, and the exotic Zuhair Murad–designed costumes that hug her body and shimmer in the spotlight. She plays the starring role in inviting scenarios, including a bevy of French maids, but the highlight of the night is von Teese alone on stage, dancing intimately with the blue smoke from a cigarette, slowly sharing more and more of herself with an impatient audience.

- **Feu by Christian Louboutin** (2012). Feu means "fire," and this show—created by the famous shoe designer Louboutin, a former assistant at Folies Bergère and a fan of cabaret—lives up to the name. Directed by Bruno Hullin, Feu explores four erotic tableaux, including the bondage-inspired "The Final Fantasy." The performance features incredible six-inch stilettos—silver with ankle straps, glow-in-the-dark green, red-glittered pumps for dominatrix Dorothy, boots with laces that crisscross all the way up the thigh—with the trademark Louboutin red soles. An aerial fabric dancer worked her stilettos into the dance, hanging by her heels. The choreography emphasized the Crazy

Girls' endless legs and dainty feet, for some the most seductive parts of a woman's body. If you missed it, a 3-D
film video of the show is available on Amazon.

- **Desire** (2010). Directed by internationally renowned chore-
ographer Philippe Decouflé and art directed by Ali
Mahdavi, the show is about the animalistic hunger for desires and pleasure with imagery of women as caged leop-
ards and lionesses, a row of legs covered in zebra stripes, a
woman silhouetted like a cat on a fence moving with feline
grace, and nude dancers flowing like serpents caught in a
whirlpool of lust. One costume that caught my eye was a
seductive ballerina in pointe shoes with straps that crept all
the way up her legs, dancing in a spiral of red light that
looked like fire rising from the stage floor. Watching the
spectacle will have you blushing with desire.

- **Arielle Dombasle** (2007). This French singer, actor, and
wife of intellectual Bernard-Henri Lévy was fifty-four
years old when she performed a show, and she looked
amazing in quite revealing costumes. One clever costume was of three black leather gloves that covered only
her delicate areas. She danced with the Crazy Girls, looking as good as any of those young women, and sang her
hit songs with passion and panache. With the magic of
lighting and atmosphere, Dombasle proves that age is just a
number.

"Find someone
who makes
you feel drunk
when you are sober"

J K Huysmans

Being in love is a beautiful chaos. It's like being taken by storm, surfing the world. Even in the rain, a woman in love walks in the sun. She is transformed into Superwoman, as if she could fly. She wakes up grinning, dances through her morning, and sings all day long. When you are madly, passionately in love, every moment is an adventure. Even something as mundane as grocery shopping becomes a magical experience with him.

Being *amoureuse* is the highest source of inspiration and the best time to create. That is one reason I cultivate this state of mind. For any creative person, it opens new ideas and heightens emotions to pour into your work. **Love unlocks the crazy genius in yourself.**

Love is radiant

A love infusion in a very physical sense allows a woman shine brightly from bottom to top. **Sex makes her glow from the inside out.** Her skin is brilliant; her smile lights up her face and the world. Her messy bed hair makes her feel a little wild and alluring. From sex: beauty.

A French couple, friends of mine, have been married for forty years. At a party recently, someone asked the wife how she has stayed so beautiful. Her husband said, "Because I make love to her every night." They laughed, and we could all see the sparkle in their eyes and the joy they found in each other. **Desire is the best remedy.** Losing youthful vigor has nothing to do with getting older, or being pretty or rich enough. Love elevates your spirits and gives you energy. It smooths wrinkles and polishes your skin. Instead of going to the spa or a dermatologist for a Botox injection, get back in bed with a man who loves you. **Infuse the serum of youth.**

Love is tous les jours

In America, I have heard about the custom of "date night." The two people in a couple have busy working lives, and are forced to set aside time once a week or month to rediscover what they love about each other. **I like to think that every night is date night. Every moment you are together can be infused with love.**

Love is Rare

Saying the words *"Je t'aime"* is a declaration of complete devotion. I was surprised that people say "I love you" so easily in America. They will say "I absolutely love her to death," or they end a conversation with "I love you" or "I adore you" even if they're speaking to a friend or acquaintance. Instead of saying "good-bye," they say "Love ya!" The problem is, if you say the three little words too often to too many people, it becomes meaningless.

French people say *"Je t'aime"* only to family, friends, and lovers, *amoureux*. It's too sacred a phrase to throw the word around lightly. **When you speak of love, it should be with reverence.**

Love is nuanced

In both of my home countries, there is a romantic tradition of picking the petals off a daisy while thinking of the man you love. In

America, girls say "He loves me, he loves me not, he loves me . . ." and so on until the daisy is denuded, and the last petal reveals the truth about his passion.

In France, a girl says "He loves me *a little,* he loves me *a lot,* he loves me *passionately,* he loves me *madly,* he doesn't love me at all . . ." and so on.

You notice the difference. In America, it's all or nothing. Black or white. In France, there are many nuances of love. **Playing with the ambiguity is what makes love all-consuming and endlessly fascinating.**

I think American women live in fear of falling out of love and losing control, as if this is a thing that can happen suddenly, like a book falling off the nightstand and hitting the floor with a loud bang. Yes, people do lose love, but the book had been falling in slow motion for some time while they were looking elsewhere.

In France, people respect the unpredictability of love. They watch it closely and pay attention to subtle shifts, and when they notice a change, they react immediately and emotionally. **The French don't love with their brains. They love with their hearts and instincts.** People are imperfect, and expressing raw human emotions—anger, vulnerability, joy, and sadness—is, in itself, seductive and charming.

Love is Therapy

Although romantic love is deep and intense, it can also be fun and childlike. It can make you feel full of ebullience and uncomplicated joy. You want to jump up and down, dance and sing, to put on your brightest dress and run through a field of flowers barefoot, laughing. Love makes you see the world, and the object of your affection, with the wonder of a child. The two of you are on an adventure together, and you never want it to end. Love gives you the feeling that the problems of real life can be managed and helps you put all your troubles into perspective.

Innocent love is captured in the artwork of Niki de Saint Phalle, an artist whose own childhood was not so carefree. At eleven, she was raped by her father. She escaped her home by marrying at eighteen and having a child quickly, and suffered a nervous breakdown in her early twenties due to the pressure of being a young mother and reliving the traumatic events of her past. Her psychologist urged her to create art as a form of therapy. Her paintings and sculptures often featured big, beautiful, bright women dancing and jumping under the sun, or lovers kissing under a pulsing swirling Tree of Love, with the message "Vive l'amour" at the bottom.

Love is Private

In France, love is played close to the vest. What happens between a man and a woman is not something to share with friends and pick apart. **Part of the mystery is keeping your private life a secret.** I don't often talk to my girlfriends about my relationships, and if I do, it's one on one, not in a large group. Some French women might not tell their friends she's fallen in love for many months. What could be more exciting than a secret romance that only the two of you savor together? Part of the tradition of clandestine affairs has to do with kings and courtesans. If too many people knew what was happening in the royal boudoir, heads would roll.

Being Single Is a Chance to Discover Yourself

You are alone? This is not a time to panic, to obsess about an ex, count your flaws, and fly into the hunt for a new man. In America and in France, anywhere in the world, desperation is the enemy of seduction.

Time is precious and freedom is a gift. Use both to discover more about yourself. Go to shows, museums, and exhibitions; take tennis lessons. Dare to travel solo and eat in sushi bars. Being single is a chance to become a fuller, richer person with unique interests, which will make you more attractive and fascinating to the next person who crosses your path. You'll have so much more to talk about, and plenty of ideas for things to do.

French eroticism

In France, eroticism is art. Our music, film, and dance are about love opening a door to a world of imagination to explore together.

Classic Love Songs

My favorite French *chansons d'amour*:
"La Vie En Rose" by Grace Jones
"Ne Me Quitte Pas" by Jacques Brel

"La Bohème" by Charles Aznavour

"Mon Dieu" by Edith Piaf

"Je T'Aime Moi Non Plus" by Jane Birkin and Serge Gainsbourg

"Je Suis Venu Te Dire Que Je M'en Vais" by Serge Gainsbourg

"Ma Plus Belle Histoire D'Amour C'est Vous" by Barbara

"Dis, Quand Reviendras-Tu?" by Barbara

"Ma Préférence" by Julien Clerc

"Message Personnel" by Françoise Hardy

"Les Mots Bleus" by Christophe

"Tu Verras" by Claude Nougaro

"La Declaration d'Amour" by France Gall

"Le Coup de Soleil" by Riccardo Cocciante

"Que Je T'Aime" by Johnny Hallyday

Amour et Danse

I love dance, especially the grace of the artists in contemporary ballet, like Pina Bausch and Marie-Claude Pietragalla. Recently, I was breathless watching *Déesses et Démones* in Paris, the last work of choreography by Blanca Li, that explores women and power through mythology. The spirited gestures were a testament to love and beauty. The French take dance seriously. Whether it's an aristocratic *valse* or a passionate tango, it reflects a proud artistic history and sensuality. It's the soul of romance, and a wonderful reason to be close and stare into your lover's eyes.

Cherish a man who hums in your ear as he twirls you around the kitchen. You live and love within the small space of your bodies moving together, the only two people in the world. There is something masculine and irresistible about a man who takes your hand and brings you to the center of the dance floor, wraps his arm around your waist, and draws you close. Touching hands, cheeks, and bodies, moving together to music, is part of the romance of *la vie en rose*. **When you stop dancing in life, you become old.**

Love on Film

The American erotic movie formula seems to be sex+violence=box office. *Fatal Attraction* tells the story of an *amour fou* between Michael Douglas and Glenn Close that escalates into obsession and murder. In *9 ½ Weeks*, Kim Basinger and Mickey Rourke play strangers who fall into a tempestuous affair, until the escalating sexuality imperils them both.

In comparison, most French erotic movies are evocative and sensual, with themes of sexual discovery, seduction, and breaking taboos.

My favorite erotic movies:

* *Belle de Jour* (1967) by Luis Buñuel. Catherine Deneuve is a housewife by night, and a prostitute in the afternoon.
* *Emmanuelle* (1974) by Just Jaeckin. Sylvia Kristel goes on a journey of sexual discovery in Bangkok.
* *Histoire d'O/The Story of O* (1975) by Just Jaeckin. Corinne Clery goes to a retreat with her lover to learn about sexual perversion.
* *Bilitis* (1977) by David Hamilton. Ingénue Patti D'Arbanville learns about the art of love while on summer vacation.
* *37°2 Le Matin/Betty Blue* (1986) by Jean-Jacques Beineix. A handyman and writer falls in love with a sexually intense woman who slowly goes insane.

- *Les Nuits Fauves/Savage Nights* (1992) by Cyril Collard, based on his real life. He stars as a bisexual HIV-positive filmmaker who becomes involved with a woman and a man. All three players have a taste for self-destruction and erotic adventure.
- *Le Pianiste/The Piano Teacher* (2001) by Michael Haneke. Isabelle Huppert falls in love with a masochistic musician.
- *Happy Few* aka *Four Lovers* (2010) by Antony Cordier. Two couples have an affair with each other, creating a love rectangle.
- *La Vie d'Adèle/Blue Is the Warmest Colour* (2013) by Abdellatif Kechiche. Adèle Exarchopoulos meets blue-haired Léa Seydoux, sparks fly, and the girls' lives are changed forever.
- *Jeune & Jolie/Young & Beautiful* (2013) by François Ozon. A student explores her sexuality by leading a double life as a call girl.
- *Adore* (2013) directed by Anne Fontaine. Naomi Watts and Robin Wright are childhood best friends who, during a seaside vacation, sleep with each other's adult sons.
- *L'Inconnu du Lac/Stranger by the Lake* (2013) by Alain Guiraudie. A man meets two other men at a beach by a lake, befriends one, and takes the other as his lover, circumstances that lead to obsession and murder.
- *Love* (2015) by Gaspar Noé. A beautifully filmed tragic love story (with explicit sex scenes in 3-D!) with imagery inspired by classic paintings.

Nudity: a woman's secret weapon

The French used to go topless on the beach in the late '70s. (It's not fashionable anymore.) But they're not puritanical about nipples and breasts. The sight of a woman with a small chest lying on the beach in Saint-Tropez is just a woman who is at ease with her body. It's part of the glamorous life on the Cote d'Azur, the beauty and freedom of doing whatever feels good under the Mediterranean sun.

But in private, the attitudes are reversed. Some American women judge the strength of their relationships by their comfort walking about nude in front of their partners. I believe that baring yourself completely should be strictly reserved for intimacy, and sometimes not even then.

Creating desire enhances the erotic experience. It's all about longing. He longs to touch you and see you. If you are always nude, while brushing your teeth or having coffee, dressing and undressing in front of him, you sacrifice the power of it. Complete nudity is a woman's precious gift, her last-resort ammunition. Be mindful of when to use it.

What to wear to not be naked

Lingerie is a second skin and a big part of the feminine French wardrobe. Lacy, silky garments are not meant to make you feel girly and flirty. They are about being a woman who enjoys the sensuality of soft fabrics on her skin and the sexual confidence they give her. You can see the effect of black lingerie on a woman in Helmut Newton's famous photo of Catherine Deneuve in a black slip dress, smoking a cigarette.

Lingerie is a caress. It makes a woman feel a bit of romance all day long. As soon as she puts it on, she is in seduction mode. Her secret feminine power is switched on. Having the awareness of her

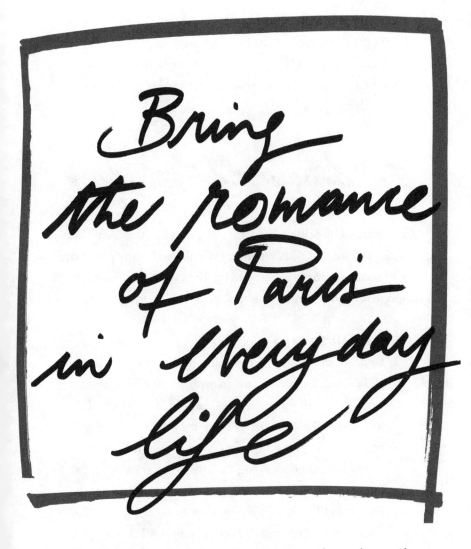

Bring the romance of Paris in every day life

sensuality translates into how she moves, speaks, and acts. She wears a coy grin, an air of mystery, that draw people in.

Mona Lisa's smile? Perhaps her secret was that she was wearing a silk bra.

Lingerie is a wink. Showing a bit of lace on the décolleté from under a men's shirt, or a little bit of bra strap on the shoulder with a cashmere sweater, gives your lover a glimpse of the kind of sensual woman you are. Show peeks during the day to hint of an unpredictable night.

For lingerie Addicts only

I'm fascinated by delicate lingerie from the 1920s, the Great Gatsby era of elegance and extravagance. I've collected many pieces over the years to wear or to be inspired by. To develop your own French lingerie wardrobe, begin with the basics.

Six Lingerie Starters

1. *La petite culotte.* Americans call it panties. Keep it simple and refined. I choose classic colors like white, champagne, ivory, deep red, and, of course, black, in lace and silk. **Culottes or a silk short are far more sexy than a g-string.**

2. *Le soutien-gorge.* Otherwise known as a bra. I have had a very hard time shopping for bras in America. All I can find are push-up bras that plaster the two breasts together and lift them right up in your face. They're also thickly padded to smooth over the nipple. **Visible nipples must make Americans very nervous.** Some women wear "pasties," little pieces of tape, to cover them when wearing a backless dress. In France, the nipple is not hidden or thought of as vulgar. **The silhouette of a real breast is sensual and seductive.** French women prefer delicate lace

or tulle bras that feel sensual on the skin, even in larger sizes with underwire for support. Women with small chests don't wear a bra at all sometimes.

3. *La camisole.* Such a romantic and feminine piece. **Wearing a camisole is easy enchantment.** As always, keep it simple in refined colors (black, ivory, or nude), and look for feminine details like a delicate touch of lace at the décolleté and skinny spaghetti straps. I wear a camisole with everything, from track pants to shorts, under a men's shirt or sweater, and with a cardigan in the fall.

4. **A slip dress** should be elegant, sensual, and refined with a bias cut that allows it to flow around the body, which feels delicious on the skin. **A maxi slip dress that falls to the floor is the height of drama.** You can wear it around the house to feel relaxed and feminine, or with a cozy cardigan to go out to dinner, keeping seduction mode on high.

5. **Fishnet stockings.** In the Belle Epoque of the late 1880s, fishnet tights started to appear on the legs of Moulin Rouge dancers and on prostitutes in the bordellos of Paris. By the 1920s, they were worn by flappers as a statement of rebellion and liberation. In the 1980s, fishnet lost some of their scandalous and controversial reputation and emerged as edgy and cool, appearing on the legs of pop stars like Madonna and on fashion models. Nowadays, nude or black tiny fishnets are pure elegance with a black pencil skirt.

6. **The mule or ballerina.** Don't wear big fuzzy slippers in the shape of a puppy or bulky socks that bunch around the ankles. I prefer ballerina flats, or a mule with a little kitten heel.

Three Lingerie Finishes

1. **A bodysuit in tulle or lace.** You can wear it under a men's shirt or with a cardigan. Don't worry about peeling it down to use the bathroom. There is an opening under the leg that makes it even easier than *la petite culotte*.
2. **A mask.** My sleep mask in black silk and lace can be a prop for a playful night of love, or just help me fall asleep.
3. **A silk kimono.** The word "kimono" used to mean "clothing" in Japan. Over the last thousand plus years, the exotic robe has evolved from an everyday garment into an ornate work of art made of silk crepe with elaborate patterns and embroidery. **The kimono is casual elegance, easy exoticism.** I have a collection of them from Japan—cotton ones from Tokyo, and vintage embroidered silk ones from Kyoto. Nothing is more sensual than wrapping yourself in silk, feeling the easiness of the cut, tying the belt to highlight the feminine waist.

Favorite Lingerie Brands

- For silk slip dresses, camisoles, and half-moon bras: Carine Gilson
- For tulle or lace bodysuits and fishnet tights: Agent Provocateur
- For day-to-night: Maison Close
- For the invisible seams: Eres
- For embroidered tulle garments and silk kimonos: I.D. Sarrieri
- For slip pajama shorts and satin sleep masks: Kiki de Montparnasse
- For satin mules and ballerinas: La Perla

I design
clothes
to create a
little romance
with
the world

Secret to a long, happy relationship

In America, there's a lot of pressure around getting engaged and married: The size of the diamond ring. The announcement in the newspaper. The bridal shower and gift registry. Bachelor and bachelorette parties. And, of course, the perfect wedding itself. The party seems to become the focal point of getting married. For many couples, marriage is the accomplishment, an ending, when it should be the beginning.

In France, people don't rush to the altar, even if they are madly in love. They are more likely *not* to marry, but to live together and share their lives without the piece of paper. **French couples stay unmarried to deepen a commitment.** When you are not obligated to be together, staying in the relationship is a daily choice. However, if you are legally married, it's possible that you'd take things for granted and forget about seduction. This is a big mistake. **A relationship is always a work in progress.** Being unmarried reminds you of your responsibility to create romance and nurture love.

When you're unmarried, you haven't given yourself completely to another person. That apparent sliver of freedom creates a healthy frisson that fans the flames of desire. Marriage is proprietary. **A couple in love does not need to own each other to play at seduction.** Being unmarried keeps the game unpredictable and fresh. It's possible that **by holding a little bit of yourself back, you can make love last.**

A free-spirited woman or man, gay or straight, who doesn't see herself or himself as a conventional, predictable person might consider not getting married, just to see how life unfolds. The places you'll go and the decisions you'll make will be different if you are unbound to another person.

The idea of longtime partnership without marriage is appealing to Americans, too, including Oprah Winfrey. She told interviewer Lorraine Kelly, "I'm not a traditional woman and I haven't had a traditional life, and I think that had Steadman [Graham, her longtime partner] and I gotten married, we certainly wouldn't have stayed married. The very idea of what it means to be a wife and the responsibility and sacrifices that carries—I wouldn't have held that well."

Women have to be confident and secure that their partners will stay because they want to—and that, if the relationship fades, it's not the end of the world. It's a mistake to rely too heavily on someone else for accomplishment, comfort, and security. If you believe marriage is the answer to all your problems, you are putting your happiness in someone else's hands. That is too much pressure for anyone to tolerate. **Emotional dependency prevents you from realizing yourself as an individual. Emotional independence will make you even more attractive to the person you love.**

Is cheating the end of Love?

Some believe that having an affair adds a layer of intrigue to a relationship. It's certainly true that many French men have mistresses. French women take lovers as well. (And some Americans too.) And yet, despite infidelity, long-term relationships and marriages hold together.

Fidelity is a mystery that could always remain unsolved. The

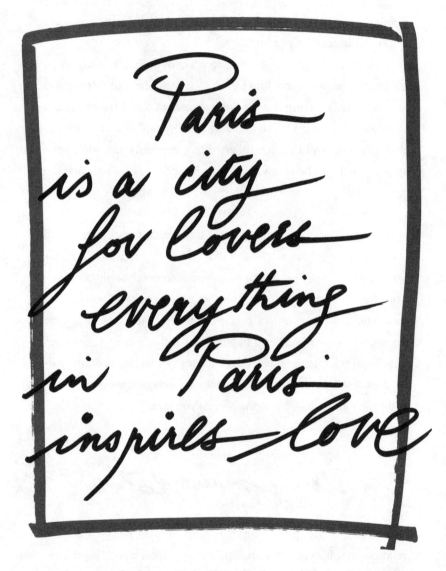

Paris is a city for lovers everything in Paris inspires love

not knowing for sure—"Is he?" "Is she?"—could bring intrigue to a relationship.

Playing with ambiguity inflames passion. For this reason, a man's fidelity is always unknown. He might even pretend that he has a mistress—being unaccountable some of the time, or having impromptu meetings—even if he doesn't have one, to make himself seem more desirable to his lover. The point of the farce is to excite his wife or lover's interest. I recommend the 1988 book *Le Zèbre* by Alexandre Jardin, which illustrates the fight of a man who refuses to lose the passion he once had for his wife after fifteen years of marriage.

Marital affairs used to be an accepted part of French culture. The French have a long history of powerful men who have both wives and lovers. American culture is more puritanical, and does not tolerate it. A classic example of the culture divide was at former French president François Mitterrand's funeral in 1996. His wife Danielle Mitterrand, his legitimate son, his mistress Anne Pingeot, and his illegitimate daughter Mazarine stood together in mourning. Headlines around the globe expressed shock. The two families lived in different wings at the Élysée Palace, the presidential residence, for fourteen years, in a perfect French secret.

Our former president, François Hollande, is very French in never having been married. He had four children with Ségolène Royal, a politician and his partner for twenty-nine years. After that, he was in a relationship with journalist Valérie Trierweiler (twelve years younger than Royal) for a while. Then, he took up with Julie Gayet, an actress (seven years younger than Trierweiler). French people do not have a problem with a man in power who trades in his old lover for a younger one every so often and doesn't marry any of them. It is impossible and nonsensical to judge.

Compare Mr. Hollande's history with the saga of Bill Clinton and Monica Lewinsky. The president had an affair under his desk, and he was impeached by Congress, investigated like a criminal, and hounded by the press. Because of Clinton's fling, his protégé Al

Gore lost a step and was defeated in the next election by George W. Bush. The history of the world was disrupted because of a tryst.

New York vs. Paris Romance

In New York: People date.
In Paris: People flirt.

In New York: Couples strive for openness.
In Paris: Couples have their secrets.

In New York: People hug to say hello.
In Paris: People kiss two times to say *bonjour*.

In New York: Women judge a man "on paper."
In Paris: Women search their hearts about his worthiness.

In New York: Women need to know where they stand in a relationship.
In Paris: Women are captivated by ambiguity.

In New York: Lovers are concerned with their performance.
In Paris: Lovers are steeped in romance.

In New York: Relationships follow a predictable path.
In Paris: Relationships are unpredictable.

Voulez-vous Coucher avec moi ?

A bedroom is an invitation to the fantasy of the night, a place for dreams and sensuality. **The only things that happen in a bed**

should be sex and sleep. It's not where you should watch television, have a snack, or work on the computer. A friend recently told me she was preparing her taxes by organizing all of her papers on her bed. Once the duvet is cleared of bank statements and receipts, she's going to sleep or make love in the same place she was agonizing about her finances? I don't see how that will work.

A bedroom is sacred. I prefer it dressed in white, black, or dark red cotton sheets and a plush duvet with generous pillows. Also, the bed should be low, almost to the floor, so it's only too easy to tumble onto it.

Turn down the lights

Candlelight in the bedroom, like the scent of *parfum* or bubbles in champagne, makes one think of sex, and infuses lovemaking with mystery and magic. **A single scented candle can transport you to exotic places. Less light means more imagination.** You lose your inhibitions in the dark.

On the other hand, too much brightness isn't as erotic. Sex is not an anatomy lesson. Not to say that it's impossible to make love in full sun or a hotly lit room, but the circumstance would have to be just perfect, like the famous love scene from *The Postman Always Rings Twice* (1981) directed by Bob Rafelson, with Jack Nicholson and Jessica Lange. He comes into her house one day, and they start kissing and groping each other on the kitchen table, making love with passion and urgency, keeping their clothes and shoes on, a torrid and intense scene of an afternoon love affair.

Forbidden Entrance

For a seductive woman, the world is her stage. But she also has a *backstage* that only she can access. **French women are careful with their secrets; they dole them out a little at a time.** There are some things they don't like to share. For example, they don't want anyone to know or see their grooming rituals, leg shaving and face cream, the plucking and hair drying, scrubbing and clipping.

It's not about a lack of confidence. I'm sure a man would find it erotic to watch a woman brush her hair. But **romance is about mystery,** and it's more seductive and empowering if he doesn't know what she does privately. **I like having my time alone, to prepare and explore, to be able to experiment. The first person I want to seduce is myself.** So when I do my bathroom rituals and dress in my walk-in closet alone, I am in the process of empowering myself.

Legendary loves

Apart, each partner in a grand passion is special. Together, they are transcendent. Some pairs are so intense, they are a cult of two, or as we say in France, *les couples cultes.*

The Muses: Camille Claudel and Auguste Rodin

In 1884, sculpture student Camille Claudel, nineteen, apprenticed in the workshop of forty-three-year-old Auguste Rodin, then on the verge of becoming the most famous sculptor of his time. Despite the age difference and the fact that Rodin was married, the two artists quickly began a passionate love affair and artistic collaboration. She was his muse, his model, his student. He was her mentor, her muse, her obsession. During their ten years together, they both created incredible works of art in marble and bronze, nudes in motion, that changed the history of sculpture. Rodin wouldn't leave his wife, and that wore on Claudel. She ended a pregnancy and the relationship in 1892. A few years later, Rodin became famous and Claudel suffered a nervous breakdown. She accused him of stealing her ideas and trying to have her killed. She went into seclusion and destroyed many of her sculptures. Shortly after he died in 1917, Claudel broke completely from reality; she was diagnosed with schizophrenia and locked up in a mental institution for the last thirty years of her life. A sad ending for her, but their love made them immortal, and it gave the world the passion of Rodin's *The Kiss,* his famous marble of a couple entwined. The 1989 film *Camille Claudel,* directed by Bruno Nuytten and starring Isabelle Adjani and Gérard Depardieu as the lovers, tells the story of their raging passion.

The Intellectuals: Simone de Beauvoir and Jean-Paul Sartre

He was the father of French existentialism and author of *Being and Nothingness.* She was the mother of modern feminism and author of *The Second Sex.* They met as philosophy students at the Sorbonne in Paris in 1929. Instantly drawn to each other, the intellectual pair rejected conventional rules in relationships, and, instead, lived by their "transparency principle." In effect, they could do whatever and go wherever they wanted, have affairs with whomever they desired, as long as they told each other *everything*. "What we have is an essential love," Sartre wrote to her, "but it is a good idea for us also to experience contingent love affairs." The personal was professional; the free lifestyle was inspiration for their novels. Throughout their five decades together and their *many* affairs, some that lasted years, Sartre and de Beauvoir were faithful to their essential love, always supportive and helpful in their writings and committed to the honesty policy. De Beauvoir outlived him by six years and, after she died in 1986, she was laid to rest next to Sartre in Montparnasse Cemetery in Paris.

Beauty and the Beast: Jean Cocteau and Jean Marais

By the time they met in 1937, Cocteau was already a legendary writer, artist, and filmmaker, and had been through a series of relationships with young men, many of whom died tragically. Marais was twenty-four years younger, a blue-eyed blond and a handsome film actor. He saw an exhibition of Cocteau's drawings, and he set out to meet him. Marais knew Cocteau was attracted to younger men, and he thought that a relationship with the artist could help advance his career. His ulterior motives changed, however, when the couple fell in love. They lived, worked, and traveled openly as a couple, even during World War II in Paris when Nazis rounded up gay men and sent them to concentration camps. Cocteau used Marais in several films, most famously *Beauty and the Beast*. With Marais's help, Cocteau was able to break his addiction to opium. They stayed together until the artist's death in 1963. Marais said, "I bitterly regret not having spent all of my life serving Cocteau instead of worrying about my career."

Crazy Lovers: Simone Signoret and Yves Montand

It was love at first sight in 1949 for Signoret, a movie star (she became the first French actress to win an Oscar for 1959's *Room at the Top*) and Montand, an up-and-coming actor and singer, one of Edith Piaf's protégés. They met in one of my favorite places, La Colombe d'Or Hotel in Saint-Paul-de-Vence. She was there with her then-husband. Montand came to meet a mutual friend. He and Signoret spent some time together and, as she wrote of their first encounter, "in those four days, we had been struck by lightning, and something indiscreet and irreversible had happened." Montand asked her to leave her husband . . . and she did. Just like that. She and her three-year-old daughter moved in with him and they married in 1951. She introduced him to her circle—Picasso, Sartre, Mitterrand—and he fit right in. Soon enough, his fame as a singer grew, and she was his number one groupie. Their mad passion started to fade as Montand transitioned into acting. In 1960, he was cast in *Let's Make Love* with Marilyn Monroe. Montand and Signoret lived in Beverly Hills during the troubled shoot in a bungalow right next door to Monroe and Arthur Miller, her husband at the time. When Signoret and Miller were out of town, Monroe showed up at Montand's house in a mink coat and nothing else. They began an affair that lasted until the end of the shoot. He has said he did it to keep Monroe, famous for her unpredictability and disappearing acts, on schedule. Signoret suffered through his infidelities, began drinking heavily, and gained a lot of weight. Montand has said that they didn't have sex for the last decade of their thirty-six-year marriage, but they stayed together in tenderness and friendship. She died first in 1985 and he was buried at Père Lachaise Cemetery next to her in 1991.

Soul Mates: Françoise Sagan and Peggy Roche

Novelist and screenwriter Sagan's 1954 romance *Bonjour Tristesse* (*Hello Sadness*) was published when she was just eighteen, and it was an instant sensation. She became rich and famous and turned into an enfant terrible and bon vivant, partying with her friends, racing cars, experimenting with drugs. When the money dwindled, she'd just write a new book. During the '50s and '60s, Sagan married and divorced twice, and had a son. In 1970, she met Peggy Roche, a fashion designer, and the women became lovers. Her son Denis Westhoff wrote in his memoir *Sagan et Fils,*

> Between these two women there was a mixture of passion, gentleness, respect and mutual admiration of the kind my mother had not known in the past, and I don't think she experienced after Peggy's death in 1991. Everyone knew about her preference for women [but] we respected each other's privacy and never spoke of the subject openly. Peggy and my mother shared the same apartment, went on vacation together and didn't conceal their relationship; but when my mother met with President [François] Mitterrand, a friend, or with [Jean-Paul] Sartre, a dear and beloved friend, Peggy wasn't invited to join.

The women depended on each other in every way. Roche ran the house and became Sagan's protector and gatekeeper, keeping out the hangers-on, bill collectors, and drug dealers. When the couple moved, as they did often, Roche handled the logistics. Sagan, in turn, financed Roche's (failed) attempts to make it as a player in the fashion world. They had twenty happy years together.

When Roche died, Sagan crumbled. She stopped writing, got more into drugs, was arrested a few times, and, in later years, became embroiled in political scandals. When she died in 2004, she was a drug addict and alcoholic, and a million euros in debt. *Au revoir, tristesse.*

The Other Halves: Yves Saint Laurent and Pierre Bergé

The designer and Bergé met in 1959 and it was a merger of the heart and business. YSL was the artist and the visionary. Bergé was the manager of the company that, under their joint direction, became one of the most successful fashion houses in history. They had the trust to build an empire but their romance ran into trouble in the '70s when Yves wanted to explore life and enjoy his independence. Bergé wanted to own the person—the artist and his soul. Yves suffered from depression and anxiety, and turned to drugs. Their love affair split apart, but they stayed in successful partnership together, continued to collect art, traveled to their beloved Morocco to the Majorelle house and exotic gardens, and stayed close friends until the legend's death in 2008. The art the pair collected in their years together was auctioned off by Christie's in 2009 and brought in $484 million. Don't miss the 2010 documentary *L'Amour Fou* by Pierre Thoretton, or the 2014 movie *Saint Laurent* by Bertrand Bonello.

The Yé-Yé Duo: Francoise Hardy and Jacques Dutronc

At eighteen, singer and guitar player Hardy released the single "Tous Les Garcons et Les Filles" and watched it sell two million copies across Europe in 1961. Not bad for a girl who grew up poor with a critical single mother who didn't support her dreams. Her folksy style—trademark bangs with long brown hair and fresh face and bohemian clothes—made her the cool girl next door and led to friendships with Mick Jagger (he described her as "an ideal woman"), George Harrison, David Bowie, and Bob Dylan, among other icons of the era. She modeled for Yves Saint Laurent and Paco Rabanne, and appeared in movies and on magazine covers. She could have chosen anyone and, after some failed relationships, Hardy picked Jacques Dutronc, the artistic director at her old record label, and writer of some of her early hits. Dutronc was young and handsome, an established singer and later a successful actor in his own right. Although they became lovers in 1967, they didn't marry until 1981. She wrote a bestseller in France called *L'Amour Fou* about their devastating love story of an unbalanced love. Their talent passed to their son Thomas, born in 1973, now a successful jazz musician.

The It Couple: Jane Birkin and Serge Gainsbourg

In 1969, he was the Mick Jagger of France, a singer and playboy, the recent ex-lover of Brigitte Bardot. She was a young English actress who'd been married and divorced by twenty-two. They met while filming *Slogan* (1969). She thought that Gainsbourg, her much older costar, hated her, and she set out to win him over. After having dinner with a group, the two went clubbing and wound up spending the night together. "His face was so much more interesting than any other face I'd ever seen, with extraordinarily sad eyes and a beautiful mouth. He read me his poetry, and it was always a play on words. That was such an unusual trait— to be that romantic and funny," she once said about him. Their song "Je T'Aime . . . Moi Non Plus," with Birkin moaning in ecstasy over his gravel-voiced singing, was so sexually explicit, it was banned by the Pope. Controversy sells: the song became a number one hit across Europe. Their fame exploded, and they became the international It Couple of the '70s. The emotional ups and downs of careers and fame, plus Gainsbourg's alcoholism and repeated infidelities, dulled their passion. After twelve years and one daughter, Charlotte, they parted in 1983 and remained friends and collaborators until he died of a heart attack in 1991. For the movie version, watch 2010's *Gainsbourg: A Heroic Life,* directed by graphic artist Joann Sfar and starring Eric Elmosnino.

The Glamorous Divorcees: Monica Bellucci and Vincent Cassel

The Italian actress and the French actor met on the set of *The Apartment* in 1996 and promptly fell in love. They married a few years later in Monaco and were the toast of Europe. She was one of the world's most beautiful women, and he was one of the continent's most famous actors. The only problem was that she lived in Rome, and he lived in Paris, and they were also often separated by the demands of their careers. But if there is passion in a relationship, distance and fidelity aren't major concerns, as Bellucci explained to the *London Times*: "Passion you can feel for the worst man you ever met. But that has nothing to do with a deeper partnership. In such a one, passion stays, but more important is confidence, respect, knowing a man is not just loyal in a sex way, but that they will be there for you. That is more important than just fidelity." They were together enough for Bellucci to become pregnant at thirty-nine with Deva, now twelve. Leonie came six years later. In 2013, after living separately for some time, the couple divorced amicably. Now Bellucci loves being single. "It feels liberating," she told *Hello!* magazine. "The single woman is a free woman and being single does not mean being alone. I feel very alive, I'm lucky to be in good health, and I have two wonderful daughters who fill my life with such joy." I can testify that they still have a nice relationship. One Sunday last summer, I had lunch next to their happy family table at Le Chalet des Ile in Paris.

The Private Darlings: Marion Cotillard and Guillaume Canet

The two gorgeous, glamorous movie stars acted together in *Love Me If You Dare* in 1998 when Canet was married to Diane Kruger. Several years later, after he and Kruger divorced and Canet had already had affairs with Carla Bruni and Élodie Navarre, he and Cotillard began a fling that turned out to be more serious than either expected. He told *The Guardian*, "One moment, you're moving in a particular direction with a person, then one day, you wake up and say, 'She's the love of my life.'" Since they joined forces personally, they have worked together on the films *The Last Flight*, *Little White Lies*, *Blood Ties*, and the upcoming *Rock 'n' Roll*. Although they are a sensation in France as individuals and as a couple, they keep their relationship mysterious by avoiding the press and hardly ever posing on the red carpet together. Canet and Cotillard have a son named Marcel, born in 2011, and a baby on the way.

"There is only one happiness in life, to love and be loved"
—Georges Sand

History of French Cougars

In America, the acceptability of an older woman and a younger man seemed to have started with Demi Moore and Ashton Kutcher. In France, it's a time-honored tradition for a woman of a certain age to share her passion with someone who admires and respects her independence, experience, wisdom, and sensuality. Right now, a younger man with an older wife is at the seat of power in the French government. Emmanuel Macron, thirty-nine, the former minister of the economy and candidate for president (described as "scary smart" by *The Daily Beast*), met Brigitte Trogneux, fifty-nine, in high school when he was a student and she was his teacher. Twenty years later, they married and Macron became a stepfather to her grown children, and a step-grandfather, in his midthirties.

Other famous women with younger men love matches:

George Sand and Frédéric Chopin

The novelist and essayist born in 1804 was known for breaking boundaries in literature, style, and sex. In her novels, she wrote of a woman's right to sexual passion and true love. Each of her many affairs inspired a book, and she wrote nearly *sixty* of them. **She wore men's clothes, smoked cigars, and seduced a long line of lovers—** artists, poets, musicians, men, women, and, most famously, the novelist Alfred de Musset (seven years her junior), and the pianist and composer Frédéric Chopin (also seven years younger). Her rapacious sexuality made her infamous in her time but she knew the world would one day catch up. "The world will know and understand me someday. But if that day does not arrive, it does not greatly matter. I shall have opened the way for other women," she wrote.

Edith Piaf and Theo Sarapo

Edith Piaf had numerous affairs, some positive and many disastrous. Her great love Marcel Cerdan, a boxing champion, died in a plane crash on his way to see her. The director Claude Lelouche made a movie about their love called *Edith and Marcel*. She had affairs with Yves Montand (whom she discovered), composer Norbert Glanzberg, actor John Garfield, and cyclist André Pousse, among others. Her first marriage to Jacques Pills ended in divorce. Her second husband was another of her discoveries, a hairdresser and singer named Theo Sarapo. Piaf and Sarapo married in 1962 when she was forty-six, and he was twenty-six. They recorded a couple of songs together, and he gave her comfort and affection during the last year of her life.

Marguerite Duras and Yann Andréa Steiner

At the age of sixty-five in 1970, novelist Duras was depressed, alone, exhausted, drinking heavily, and not writing. To distract herself from her depression, she read fan letters. Twenty-seven-year-old Yann Andrea Steiner wrote some that were so flattering and intelligent, Duras savored them, although she didn't write back. One night, she joined a group of friends at a bistro. By chance, Steiner was among them. He introduced himself, and she knew his name from his letters. Nothing happened that night, but Duras was intrigued enough to break her own rule about responding to fan mail with a letter of her own. She confided in him about her depression and alcoholism, which was a great relief. Shortly after that, he visited her at home, and never left. For her, he was a muse and caretaker. He remained her most ardent fan, and transcribed everything she said, including her last words, "I love you. Good-bye."

Erotic Library

- *The 120 Days of Sodom* (1785) by Marquis de Sade. Written while imprisoned in the Bastille, de Sade's story has four wealthy men listening to the tales of four prostitutes for inspiration about sexual torture.
- *Madame Bovary* (1856) by Gustave Flaubert. A bored doctor's wife seeks sexual excitement and finds it with Rodolphe, a land-owner. She has a lot of sex before dying tragically.
- *Chéri* (1920) by Colette. Torrid romance between gigolo Chéri and his older courtesan lover Léa.
- *Ulysses* (1922) by James Joyce. The 736-page story of one day in the life of Leopold Bloom, including love scenes with his wife Molly, and with himself.
- *Lady Chatterley's Lover* (1928) by D. H. Lawrence. The lady takes a lover, the groundskeeper Mellors, who awakens her carnal desires.
- *Tropic of Cancer* (1934) by Henry Miller. Miller's autobiographical account of his sexual adventures in Paris was banned for twenty-seven years due to graphic descriptions of sexual acts.
- *Bonjour Tristesse* (1954) by Françoise Sagan. Coming-of-age story of sexual awakening on the Riviera with many unexpected twists.
- *Story of O* (1954) by Anne Desclos. Beautiful fashion photographer O trains to become a submissive in a secret sex society.

- *Lolita* (1955) by Vladimir Nabokov. Humbert Humbert, an academic pervert with beguiling self-awareness, can't resist Lolita, his preteen stepdaughter.
- *The Ravishing of Lol Stein* (1964) by Marguerite Duras. Voyeurism leads to adultery and other sexual delights.
- *Delta of Venus* (1977) by Anaïs Nin. Posthumously published stories about dominance, incest, pedophilia, homosexuality, and erotic avenues in Paris.
- *Bad Behavior* (1988) by Mary Gaitskill. Stories of spanking, dominance, and submission, which are common themes for the American author.
- *Baise-Moi* (1993) by Virginie Despentes. A fantasy of two young punk women teaming up to rape men and rampage through the night.

Eternal lovers

I've always been inspired by women who believe in love. For some reason, my favorite eternal lovers have names that start with the letter C (like mine), like Coco and Colette.

Les mademoiselles C

Coco: You know all about Coco Chanel the designer, that she liberated women from the corseted silhouette, that she created an empire when women were expected to marry and have babies, and that, at the time of her death in 1971 at the age of eighty-seven, she was one of the wealthiest women of all time. But you might not know about the unfettered adventurism of her romantic life. Some of her lovers:

- **Étienne Balsan** was a textile heir and playboy who lived in a castle. He introduced her to a world of wealth and privilege, diamonds, pearls, lavish clothes. She became his mistress in 1906 when she was twenty-six.
- **Arthur Edward "Boy" Capel.** Also a member of the upper class, Capel was a self-made man, a lover of polo and, apparently, women's fashion. He bankrolled Chanel's first shop in Paris and another in Deauville. The rectangular shape of the Chanel No. 5 bottle was inspired by Capel's omnipresent whiskey flask. He married another woman but continued to see Chanel on the side. He was on his way to a rendezvous with her when he died in a car crash in 1919.
- **Grand Duke Dmitri Pavlovich.** The Russian duke was a member of the imperial Romanov family, and a participant in the murder of his nephew Nicholas's tutor, Rasputin the mystic. Pavlovich managed to escape the Bolshevik revolution and flee to France, where he began an affair with Chanel in 1921.
- **Igor Stravinsky.** Another Russian, Stravinsky was the famous composer of *The Rite of Spring*. They were together during a tempestuous eight months in 1921. A great movie about their relationship, *Coco Chanel & Igor Stravinsky*, was directed by Jan Kounen and starred Anna Mouglalis.
- **Hugh Richard Arthur Grosvenor, 2nd Duke of Westminster.** Moving on to Englishmen, Chanel met the duke and seduced him. He adored her and gave her art, jewels, a house in Mayfair, London, and acreage in Roquebrune-Cap-Martin, France. When their affair began, she was forty. It lasted for ten years.

- **Edward VIII, The Prince of Wales.** As legend has it, the heir to the throne was after Chanel, too, and might have had an affair with her while she was involved with the Duke of Westminster.
- **Pierre Reverdy.** She had a brief fling with the French poet in 1926 and kept up a friendship with him for forty years.
- **Baron Hans Gunther von Dincklage.** During World War II, Chanel, a known anti-Semite, had a romantic relationship with this German officer. They lived at the Hôtel Ritz Paris, a German-occupied building.

Colette: The most famous author of her time, Sidonie-Gabrielle Colette lived and wrote as an independent woman in a man's world. Her novels were always autobiographical and frankly sexual. Whoever she was with inspired her work.

- **Henry Gauthier-Villars.** He was the publisher of her first series, the Claudine novels, and a sexual adventurer. He encouraged her to experiment with her sexuality— including lesbian affairs—and then to write it all down.
- **Mathilde de Morny, the Marquise de Belbeuf.** After Colette and Gauthier-Villars ended their relationship, she moved on to the marquise, an actress. In 1907, during a performance of a pantomime called *Reve d'Egypte,* the two women kissed passionately on stage and were reviled by the crowd. It was long before a lesbian couple could live openly in Paris, so they had to keep their affair a secret for several years.
- **Henry de Jouvenel des Ursins.** Her second husband was an editor at *Le Matin,* a French newspaper. Predictably,

Colette became a journalist during World War I. The two also had a daughter, named after her mother.

- **Bertrand de Jouvenel.** Her stepson was sixteen when they began an affair that inspired *Chéri*, the illicit love between a younger man and an older woman.
- **Maurice Goudeket.** Her third and last husband, also a much younger man who let her be the boss, Maurice inspired Colette to write books that criticized conventional marriage and the role of women in traditional society. Her politics, combined with the sexual content, made her novels controversial, and popular. She protected Goudeket, a Jew, during the Nazi occupation of Paris. After the war, she wrote *Gigi*, the story about a courtesan in training, which turned into a Hollywood movie starting Leslie Caron.

Soeur Emmanuelle, aka **Madeleine Cinquin.** You might not have heard of her, but this Mademoiselle C (for Cinquin) was a national treasure in France. After thirty years in Turkey building schools, and twenty years in Egypt living with impoverished garbage collectors, the Belgian-French nun returned to France in 1993 and became a cause célèbre by going to talk shows to say that women should be able to use contraception, and that priests should be allowed to have sex. The French adored her rebellious spirituality; she made the "most popular people in France" list and became the subject of a movie about her life in 2003. She died in her sleep, at ninety-nine, of natural causes. Her book called *Confessions of a Nun* is a treasure and an endless source of inspiration. She described her lifelong physical attraction to men:

When desire assaulted me, only some outside presence had the power to stop me; otherwise I was powerless against the avidity of pleasure. A penchant for voluptuousness and an obsession for sensuality developed in my flesh, the intensity of which is difficult to describe. The fact that the needle has not left my old woman's body is a source of constant surprise and humiliation. I thought that, with the years, its tip of fire would completely disappear. Not at all.

If she hadn't become a nun, she wrote, she would have been a prostitute. Thanks to her faith, she turned that physical passion into a spiritual devotion to God. Thinking of her saved me a few times from my own temptations.

" it's not where
you take things
from

it's where you
take them
to "

Jean Luc Godard

Life is your creation. You need inspiration to make it what you want. I'm always looking for ways to feed my soul and spark my imagination: art, music, food, travel, culture, conversation. Inspiration is about opening windows, and having the audacity to go through them. When I get an idea, I take it on a journey, developing and refining it until I can use it to make a positive contribution to the world. Life is a work in progress. Get inspired.

In love with life

Some artists are inspired by pain and suffering. Sylvia Plath, the American writer, channeled her agony into her poetry. Judy Garland, the American singer, was tormented by failure in love, became an addict, and poured her hurt and vulnerability into her music. The list of depressed artists, many of whom are French, is endless: Baudelaire, Degas, Gaugin, Matisse, Guy de Maupassant, Ingmar Bergman, Emily Dickinson, Franz Kafka, Gustav Mahler, Jean Seberg, and so on. Even John Lennon, who said "Love is all you need," was moved by his depression to write songs of hope and peace.

But not all artists are inspired by sadness. Vincent van Gogh was the embodiment of the tortured artist, causing his own pain by cutting off his ear and eventually killing himself. And yet, he was inspired by positive emotions. In his letters, he wrote, "[My art] is founded less on anger than on love, founded more on serenity than on passion. It is true that I am often in the greatest misery, but still there is within me a calm, pure harmony and music." Artist Salvador Dalí was inspired by joy when he painted *Leda Atomica,* and by love of self. "Every morning upon awakening, I experience a supreme pleasure: that of being Salvador Dalí," he once said, "and I ask myself, wonderstruck, what prodigious thing will he do today, this Salvador Dalí." Pop artist Jeff Koons, who made giant sculptures of whimsical balloon animals, hearts, and lobsters, told *Art in America* magazine, "What inspires me is feeling. I'm talking about a sense of excitement, of awe and wonder."

It's important to search your own reactions to emotions, and to learn which ones are inspiring for you. Suffering leaves me dry. My contribution to the world is beauty and style. The better I live, the better I am in my work. My designs are meant to make a woman feel confident, feminine, audacious, curious, and adventurous. If I have love and joy in my life, I give it back to women with everything I'm able to create, everywhere in the world.

The Fount of Inspiration

Designers' antennas are permanently up. In search of inspiration, they go to exhibits and shows, eat, travel, explore street- and nightlife. Although the creative process is chaotic and very personal, many designers wind up creating collections with common themes and ideas, season to season. Designers don't hold meetings to say, "The hot color this fall is cobalt!" Although there are trend books by *bureaux de style* in Paris like Promostyl, Groupe Carlin, and NellyRodi, creative designers don't read them. Trends are inadvertently created when designers gorge on the same inspirational food.

Chanel recently showed a Cruise 2017 collection inspired by Cuba, the same year Stella McCartney, Proenza Schouler, and Valentino in Italy came out with their Havana-influenced resort looks. Colorful Caribbean flavor became a hot trend because many designers were inspired by the untapped cultural richness of the newly opened island. They're not copying each other, but they are inspired by this new El Dorado, and each is giving his or her own interpretation.

A similar phenomenon occurred in the fall of 2016, when architectural designs popped up in the collections of Narciso Rodriguez and Chloé. The designers were inspired by the trend of stark glass architecture that had been blooming in New York, like Frank Gehry's IAC Building, a Manhattan building that looks like a pleated, metal skirt, or Zaha Hadid's Galaxy Soho, a multitiered shopping mall in Beijing that looks like a striped keyhole dress. When you live in a culturally abundant place, creative crossover is inevitable.

In 2015, there was a Gustav Klimt exhibit at the Neue Galerie in New York City featuring the portrait of Adele Bloch-Bauer, the "woman in gold." The portrait itself is storied: Confiscated by Nazis, it was recovered by the family after an epic legal battle, and eventually purchased by Ronald Lauder for $135 million. Thousands flocked to the museum to see this masterwork, including every designer in the city. Six months later, several collections were infused with Klimtisms: gold and complex patterns.

No one wants to copy each other, so designers are very protective of their ideas and superstitious about sharing their inspirations with anyone. The feeling is, if you talk about your work, you might jinx it. When I meet with other designers, we talk about a lot of things—business, family, event stress—except our influences. **Creative minds sometimes think alike, but it's more fun when they don't.** My friendships are nourished by our diversity. They come from all different worlds—music, architecture, art—and when we are together, we are free to share everything, and great ideas fly.

"There is always flowers for those who want to see them"
Matisse

World of endless knowledge

Curiosity draws you into the discomfort zone. Follow it into strange worlds where you have to learn and change. If you are inspired by nature, don't just go outside and look at a tree. Make a study of them. Learn their names, roots, leaves, and flowers, and find their unique characteristics. Devote time to seeing and touching as much as you can, asking questions that take you down unpaved avenues of thought and experience. Then design and plant a garden that enhances your life every day.

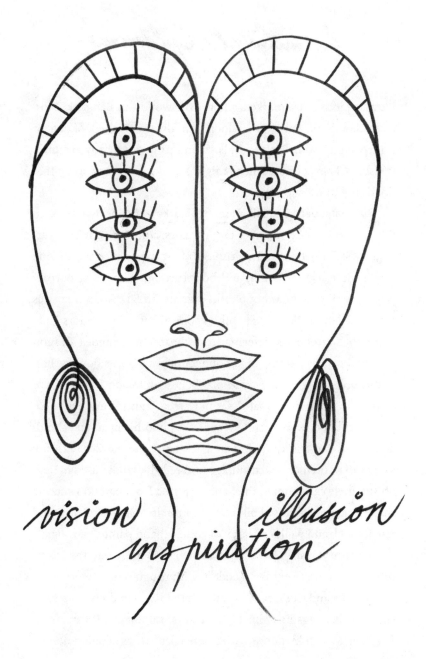

vision   illusion
    inspiration

Inspirational Goldmines

I love exploring flea markets all over the world—in Bangkok, Moscow, New York, Paris, or London. I'm always on the lookout for unexpected and beautiful finds. I tend to gravitate toward little treasures. I never know when I might come across a tiny object that floods my mind with ideas.

The Damnoen Saduak Floating Market outside Bangkok in Ratchaburi is an explosion of bright colors, a hive of activity, a carnival of Thai people and culture. To best experience the unique atmosphere, ride in a long-tail boat through a maze of narrow canals, with thatched-roof booths laden with Silk Road treasures along the banks. Wearing bamboo conical hats, the vendors glide by in both directions, offering fresh meat, cut mangoes, dragon fruit and papayas, dumplings, soup, bunches of lotus flowers, hot-house orchids, golden woven blankets, handmade jewelry, jade elephants. On a riverboat, I sat next to a man selling cut coconuts with a boa constrictor wrapped around his head and shoulders like a cap and cape. I came back from the market with my arms full of orchids, and a vintage umbrella like those used in Buddhist temple ceremonies, the handle crafted from bamboo and the shade made of distressed oil-treated cotton in gold (for royalty) and red (for luck and wellness), and, of course, hand-painted sarongs.

The Izmaylovsky Market in Moscow is a journey into the tsarist Russia of another century. Vendors with rough winter-worn faces in fur vests and Cossack hats sell painted Russian dolls (*matryoshkas*), jeweled eggs in stained-glass colors, military uniforms from Soviet history, gold spoons with enamel depictions of onion-domed churches, beveled crystal decanters, and teacups with bas-relief Madame Bovary types dancing in ball gowns. Babushkas with colorful head scarves tied under the chin talk and laugh with each other from stall to stall, giving the market a friendly vibe. Many of them are selling their own family antiques—furniture, glassware, early editions of Pasternak and Tolstoy—and will tell you long, broken-English stories about them. I found the skin of a lynx and was inspired to design a new print for my collection, an antique vase engraved with lace pattern, and *icones* from a Russian church with incredible gold leaves and hues of blues and greens that became the beginning of a new fall jewel-colored palette.

A few years ago at New York's **Chelsea Flea Market** on West Twenty-fifth Street, all of American history was laid out before you in boxes and stalls: old editions of *Little House on the Prairie* and Philip Roth, Adirondack chairs, taxidermy bison heads, vintage Mickey Mouse toys and antique Tonka trucks, Superman comics, Johnny Cash and Bob Dylan vinyl albums, needlepoint tapestries that say HOME SWEET HOME, Norman Rockwell prints, rusted Coca-Cola signs, Art Deco jewelry, and piles of buffalo nickels. I've made exhilarating finds there—antique gloves and a tattered leather jacket. The most inspiring treasures are usually not necessarily related to fashion. I've come across Danish furniture from the 1960s with seductive clean, bold, round shapes that brought to mind a new graphic pattern. I started playing with it, reimagining it, and before too long, the chairs transformed into a bright new jewelry idea for my collection.

In Paris, **Les Marché aux Puces de Saint-Ouen** is the biggest and best, covering nearly twenty acres with twenty-five hundred stalls and stores in fifteen different *marchés*, each one a journey into its own authentic atmosphere. As a whole, Les Puces ("the fleas") is the crossroads of art and antiques for all of Europe, drawing dealers, artisans, and designers from all over the world who are looking for furniture and art for their homes or their stores, inspiration, or just a fabulous afternoon of shopping and discovery among the maze of streets, covered passageways, pavilions, and cafés. Last time I was at Saint-Ouen, I found an amazing lamp by the famous 1950s French designer Serge Mouille, and a couple of chairs by Jean Prouvé that are now in my Paris apartment.

It would take you a week to walk through all fifteen markets. If you only have a day, I recommend these three:

Le Marché Biron's 220 vendors specialize in French and Asian antiques, design, and art from the eighteenth and nineteenth centuries, like hand-painted ceramics with cranes from Japan, Napoleon III–era mirrors with gilded glazing, Louis XVI–style wood-carved armchairs with silk fabric upholstery, silverware, diamond pins, and brooches. Each stall takes you to a new era, a new country. You can walk through time and space at Le Marché Biron.

Marché Paul Bert Serpette is the most expensive and enormous of the markets, with hundreds of vendors selling antiques from a wide range of periods, from the seventeenth-century empire to midcentury modern, my favorite ones being the late 1950s to the '70s. The stalls are set up like living rooms, crammed with exceptional and rare furniture, mirrors, paintings in elaborate frames, prints, jewelry, tapestries, luggage, ceramics, chandeliers, hardware, and furniture from designers like Pierre Paulin, Pierre Cardin, Jean Royère, Ettore Sottsass, and Olivier Mourgue. I always stop by to see Sylvie Corbelin's selection at her cabinet of curiosities, and visit Clara Lardé at Caverne d'Alibaba. If you can only do just one marché, go here, and browse with antique dealers from all over the world and the occasional celebrity. Don't be surprised if you bump into Bill Gates or Kanye West.

Marché Dauphine offers a more modern experience. It's one of the newer markets. Once a labyrinth of small, dark streets and ramshackle stalls, it's evolved in the last ten years into a modern pavilion with 180 merchants selling high-end space-age furniture, vintage corsets and clothing, furniture from hundreds of years of French history, and, the pièce de résistance, the *carré des libraries,* or booksellers' corner, with first editions of Victor Hugo and Flaubert, old prints and postcards, rare Bibles, Torahs, or antique pornography. For vintage clothes, I can't resist visiting Les Merveilles de Babellou, with their selection of Chanel and Balenciaga, or Chez Sarah at the heart of the passage for the most couture pieces, from delicate lingerie and blouses.

In London, I go to the **Portobello Road flea market,** preferring to arrive early on Sundays, eat a hearty English breakfast in a pub, and then spend the morning exploring the hundreds of stalls to sort through the antique British bits and bobs, gold buttons and lace trimmings, antique phonographs, cameo brooches, Sherlock Holmes novels, Rolling Stones and Beatles memorabilia, vintage fashion from Mary Quant to Burberry, Doc Marten boots in dozens of colors, and Goth costumes that conjure images of Dracula prowling for victims in the West End.

On my first trip to Portobello Road as a teenager (I was on a student exchange program to London), I made an important discovery that became an essential part of my aesthetic: a Victorian blouse. It was white, frilly, classic, fabulous, and made a romantic statement. I started to collect them. Today, I own about thirty vintage blouses, some in better shape than others, but they're all trophies. The full sleeves are dramatic. The cut of the fabric underlines the curve of the chest and accentuates the waistline. The high collar, embroidery, and tapering at the wrists are pure romance. It's easy to imagine a beautiful, delicate, alabaster-skinned English aristocrat wearing them. I also love that they were invented during the reign of Queen Victoria when women's education and voting rights were at the forefront of the cultural conversation, making the blouses both feminine and feminist, moral (covering the neck) and immoral (revealing the skin through the cutworks of a *broderie anglaise*). I always used to integrate Victorian-inspired blouses in my fashion shows. With French guipure lace, folds, pleats, and other details, they require a lot of manual work. Pairing them with houndstooth tweed men's trousers or dyed jeans and heels creates an offbeat silhouette. English romance is in my fashion DNA. For one of my first fashion shows, I chose British model Erin O'Connor to wear a backless Victorian-inspired blouse with distressed men's trouser shorts.

"The main thing is to be moved, to love, to hope, to tremble, to live"
— *Rodin*

Houses of Creativity

In Paris, I have two favorite museums, each devoted to the work of a singularly inspiring artist.

Musée de l'Orangerie. Located in the heart of Paris in the Jardin

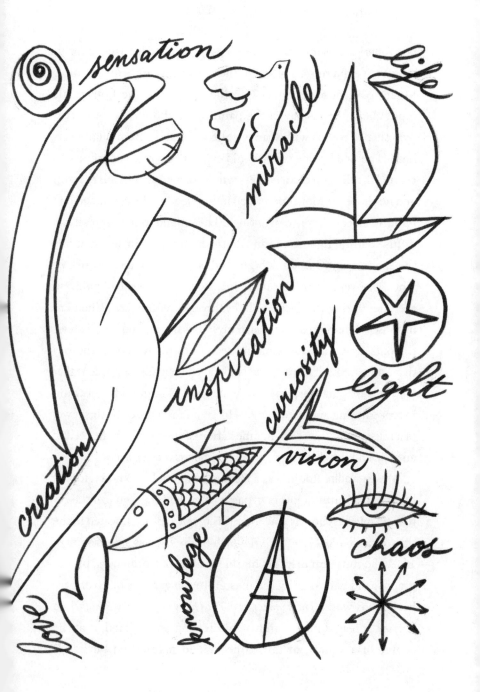

des Tuileries, this museum houses Les Nymphéas de Claude Monet, a series of eight murals of water lilies. Several years before he died, Monet gave head architect Camille Lefèvre of the Louvre his input about the display of the paintings and the concept of two oval-shaped rooms with sparse white walls and natural light overhead. The side-by-side ovals would evoke the symbol of infinity to create "the illusion of an endless whole, of a wave with no horizon and no shore" as Monet described it, for viewing the combined one hundred linear meters of paintings. The unique roof design allows diffuse natural light to illuminate the painting from above. It fills the space when the sun is high, and is more subdued at dusk or when it's overcast, mirroring Monet's own experience of painting the lilies during the cycles of light throughout the day. When I'm in those white rooms, I immerse myself in the art and forget about the outside world. A fascinating secret not many people know is that Monet himself planted and landscaped many of the gardens that were his original inspiration. As he said, "I'm good for nothing except painting and gardening." His creations, housed in this jewel of a museum, is the literal manifestation of starting with the seed of an idea, and watching it grow into a timeless masterpiece.

Musée Rodin. Rodin was a romantic realist, best known for his lifelike sculptures of lovers in passionate embrace. You feel the romantic spirit as soon as you enter this magical place. Located in the ornate castle-like Hôtel Biron, which Rodin used as a workshop in 1908, the museum displays marble sculptures, drawings, photographs, and paintings by the master. In the gardens out front are his famous works *The Thinker* and *The Gates of Hell*. *The Thinker*, in bronze, a seated man with his chin resting on his hand, is at the center of a square of tall, cone-shaped manicured bushes, a monument to Rodin's intellect. When you go inside, you dive into the sensuality of his art. The cold stone marble of *The Kiss* seems warm and alive, soft and rippling like human flesh. Other works are of smoothly muscled bodies emerging from blocks of marble, as if they were freeing themselves from a prison of rock. One touching sculpture is of two hands in the suspended moment before contact. A room is devoted to Camille Claudel, his student and lover. Her ornate works of waltzing couples and lovers clenched tightly echo the romance in Rodin's work—they were clearly inspired by and for each other. A feeling of love and sorrow envelops you as you walk through the history of their passion and heartbreak.

Alive in the dark

A night owl, I love to discover the nightlife in Paris and New York. Walking among *les gens de la nuit* (people of the night) is always fascinating. After-hours New York is a parallel universe for the curious, adventurous, and dangerous. When the mood is right, I enter this world of imagination and larger-than-life personalities, drama, fantasy, and desire. Darkness frees the night owl's spirit and lowers inhibitions. Things they might never do during the day are possibilities, inevitabilities, after midnight.

One of my favorite clubs in Manhattan for a moment was The Box. It's on the Lower East Side where, like a Fellini movie, night comes to life inside its gold walls. Every inch of the front room drips with glamour and decadence with the draping of red velvet couches and booths, dramatic chandeliers hanging from vaulted ceilings, and flexible girls doing acrobatics on hoops hung from the ceiling over the bar, almost close enough to touch. The people who go to The Box are real characters, and I can feel their joy in shedding the weight of their buttoned-up daytime personas to allow their true rebellious natures to be free to dress up (or undress), and go wild.

Venture deeper into the experience in the backroom cabaret to see hedonistic burlesque shows with a predominant bondage theme. One show I saw was like a devil's circus or opening a Pandora's box with all manner of night creatures emerging. A demon in a sheer bodysuit orchestrated the action, while orgiastic dancers onstage writhed to free themselves of a spider's web. One number put the spotlight on a line of women in sexy black cat costumes, with kitten ears, whiskers, and black thigh-high stiletto heels—and nothing else. A bare-chested Indian contortionist coiled himself like a cobra into a glass box. A dominatrix in a red sequined dress cracked her whip as nude men bowed to kiss her stiletto boots. A roman gladiator, Marie Antoinette, and Batman and Robin made cameo appearances in skintight spandex costumes. Unlike a French cabaret with its chic seduction, the New York style is raw, rough, frankly erotic, or violent—and always fascinating.

"To define is to limit"
Oscar Wilde

Masterpiece inside

Don't look at things the way they are, but as what they can become. Being "realistic" puts you in a box. If you are inspired, you can break down the boundaries and see that potential is unlimited. All you need is the spark and the wherewithal to transform into whatever you wish to be.

One day, I was thinking about turning a piece from my collection of antique lingerie into a dress. While playing with it, the dress turned into a coat with lace, a totally new garment that made sense for a woman today. The lingerie had the potential to be a robe, and an even greater potential to be a trench. Its power was unlocked by change.

See yourself as a start with no finish. The road of life keeps on going and you are always evolving. I have a friend (American) who does yoga every day, and one of her favorite sayings is, "Where you start a pose is not where you finish." You might be inspired to realize a dream, but then it changes as you continue to evolve. A yoga pose, an art project, an entire life, is always deepening and transforming. What will happen? What can you become? The mystery of life is what makes it so interesting.

Michelangelo once said, "In every block of marble, I see a statue as plain as though it stood before me, shaped and perfect in attitude and in action. I have only to hew away the rough walls that imprison the lovely apparition to reveal it to the other eyes as mine see it." I just finished a poetic French book named *Pietra Viva* from Leonor de Recondo about Michelangelo's hypothetical journey to Carrere, Italy, in 1505 to find a marble tomb for Pope Julius II, and how he ended up staying there, working the quarry to find the perfect block of marble to make the Pietà. The fabulous novel explores the mystery of creation and the artist's vision with surprising and touching emotions.

Creativity is about discovering the potential of your own raw material. You can look at a block of marble—or yourself—and realize that there is so much to discover and reveal. Any kind of raw material can transcend its original form, become better than it was at the start, and only continue to improve with age. You are the statue hiding in a block of marble. **You are your greatest masterpiece.** Hew away through your rough walls to find your best self.

"You don't make art you find it" Picasso

Unexpected combinations

As I observe the world, I take mental pictures and file them away. My mind is like a library of images. My subconscious weaves them into a beautiful, chaotic patchwork, and, before long, the collage turns into an idea for my work or my life. Every time this happens, I'm humbled and amazed. **The creative process is an everyday miracle.**

When I lived in France I wasn't exposed that much to rap music, but when I got to New York and heard Eminem and 50 Cent for the first time, I was inspired to combine the raw energy of hip-hop with the delicacy of Parisian style, and I came up with my Urban Queen collection of leather stretch T-shirts with inserts of gold and silver lace. Taking elements from different worlds and marrying them together brings about the unexpected. Fusion—in any form, any lifestyle—expands your ideas about what's possible.

Inspiring friendship

Early in my New York life, I saw an American singer in *Glamour* wearing one of my dresses. The quote under the photo said something like, "This dress makes me feel feminine and seductive."

The artist was Mary J. Blige, a superstar, millions of albums sold, multiple Grammy awards won. I was a fan of her *411* album and her new duet with Wyclef Jean "911." It was deeply satisfying that a woman whose voice I admired appreciated how my dress made her feel.

I wrote Mary a note, thanking her and praising her music. At the end, I quickly added that I was celebrating my birthday in a few weeks and that I'd love for her to come to my party. I jotted my cell phone number at the bottom of the note and gave it to a stylist friend we had in common to deliver.

I was very busy preparing a new collection and taking care of Oscar, a baby then, and forgot about the note. The night of my birthday, the party was just getting started when I received a call.

It was the stylist friend. She said, "Mary would love to come to your party." I gave her directions to the venue, a little restaurant in Hell's Kitchen. An hour later, a limo full of boys with gold chains, over-sized jackets, and distressed jeans came in, followed by Mary herself wearing a black jacket and a tightly fitted leather catsuit. What an entrance! Everyone there—fifty of my family and friends—stared with jaws dropped.

I went over to Mary and her friends and gave her the double kiss. Her entourage melted into the crowd, leaving Mary and me alone together. With my accent and her cadence, we had a hard time understanding each other, but we ended up talking all night about music and fashion, how we were both trying to empower women in our own ways. I felt a real connection.

I told her about my upcoming fashion show in Harlem at the Apollo Theater, on the Sunday morning of New York Fashion Week. I had the idea to do the show during church hours, to evoke the elegance of dressing up and the celebratory spirit. I called the collection Hallelujah! and prayed daily that I'd be able to pull it off. I had a lot of audacity and optimism, but no money for top models. Many people told me that no one in the fashion establishment would want to come to Harlem for a show, and never on a Sunday. I shared my ideas about the show with Mary, and she immediately wanted to support me. Not only did she come to see it and talk about it, she joined me onstage, holding my hand.

On September 9, 2001, the street outside the Apollo was packed with limousines and the theater was filled to capacity. The unusual idea of a fashion show in Harlem during church hours caught every-body's attention. It was a big success, and was featured on the cover of *Women's Wear Daily* with strong reviews. Mary was there to share my vision and to inspire other collections. Urban Queen was for her, for strong women who've had ups and downs and want to fight and develop the best of themselves.

Somehow, Mary and I found each other, and I'm so glad we did. Me, coming from the French Alps, Mary, coming from Yonkers. We had different histories, and yet we made a beautiful friendship. Our two worlds collided—fashion and music—and our collaborations have been changing some lives. In 2010, Mary asked me to create a line of T-shirts for charity, and together we put on a joint fashion show at MoMA for Mary's organization Foundation for the Advancement of Women Now (FFAWN). The collection was sold exclusively in Bloomingdale's and Mary raised enough money to pay the college tuitions for thirty high school graduates from the Bronx.

Surround yourself with friends who respect and support your vision, with whom you can share dreams and hold hands. If you are actively pursuing your passion, you'll attract people who have the same character, and you can encourage each other to realize your passions. **Allow time to cultivate your friendships and share your ideas.** The happiest way to construct your dreams is by being part of a vibrant team and to inspire each other to be better people.

Icon Inspiration

These French women are the epitome of beauty, style, and grace. Whenever I need a reference of style, I go back to their finest films.

- **Brigitte Bardot.** Bardot's career started in 1956 in her then-husband Robert Vadim's *And God Created Woman* as a scandalous, liberated young siren in Capri. Her bare legs and a plunging décolleté turned her into an international "sex kitten." In Jean-Luc Godard's 1963 film *Le Mépris,* she asked the tantalizing question "Do you love my ass?" as she posed for photographs, giving voice to her sexual confidence and abandon. I used the George Delerue soundtrack from *Le Mépris* in one of my fashion shows.

- **Anouk Aimée.** In Jacques Demy's 1961 *Lola,* Aimée played an enticing cabaret dancer in a black lace corset, feather boa, cigarette holder, and top hat. In Claude Lelouch's 1966 film *A Man and a Woman,* Aimée's doe eyes, free dark hair, and simple style paired with the unforgettable music by Francis Lai cast a spell of love and intimacy.

- **Romy Schneider.** The French-German actress played a glamorous girl next door in Jacques Deray's 1969 *La Piscine.* Slicked-back hair, bronzed skin, crisp white dresses, and black bikinis heightened the drama as she realized her nice life and relationship were anything but. She showed another side as Lily, a fragile prostitute, in Claude Sautet's *Max et Les Ferrailleurs,* in a black slip dress, a ribbon tied around the neck, and a black patent leather trench coat.

- **Catherine Deneuve.** In 1967's *Belle de Jour* by Luis Buñuel, Deneuve played two parts: a polished, cool housewife in a black coat and pillbox hat, hair in a tight chignon, and a loose-haired prostitute in white lingerie. In 1975's *La Sauvage* by Jean-Paul Rappeneau, Deneuve was accessible and wild on the beach with messy hair and a striped tunic.

- **Françoise Dorléac** was the beautiful sister of Catherine Deneuve, an actress in her own right who died in a car accident on the French Riviera in 1967 at twenty-five. Director François Truffaut called her "Framboise" and thought she was two Hepburns at once, Audrey and Katharine. In Truffaut's *The Soft Skin* (1964), she played a stewardess in love with a businessman, a fragile gamine with doe eyes under a curtain of brunette bangs. In the Bond spoof *That Man from Rio* (1964) by Philippe de Broca, in which she appeared opposite Jean-Paul Belmondo, she danced barefoot on a beach with children in a clinging blue dress, her hair bouncing, smile flashing, pure joie de vivre.

- **Carole Bouquet.** As Melina Havelock in John Glen's 1981 *For Your Eyes Only,* Bouquet played the classic beauty with fine features and elegant carriage to seduce Roger Moore's James Bond. In Luis Buñuel's classic *That Obscure Object of Desire,* she is a glacial beauty, fire and ice, pure seduction.
- **Isabelle Adjani.** In Jean Becker's 1983 thriller *L'Été Meurtrier,* Adjani played a troubled teenager in a provocative white off-the-shoulder ruffled top and short shorts. In 1985, she starred in Luc Besson's *Subway* as a spoiled rich girl. In the famous dinner scene, she wore a huge Mohawk coiffure, which I used on models in my Flag Show.
- **Marion Cotillard.** An Oscar winner in 2007's *La Vie En Rose* by Olivier Dahan, Cotillard captured the fragility of Edith Piaf in *la petite robe noire* and a jaunty sailor cap with a red pom-pom.

Ideas come to life

Creativity is the result of waking up every day and observing the world in search of inspiration. I use all of my tools—curiosity, imagination, and sensuality—to find a spark that grows into an entire collection.

Flag (2001)

The Inspiration: In the eighties my first crush was an eighteen-year-old rocker with a chopper motorbike. I saw him at the school gate when I was sixteen, with his black leather bomber jacket and cowboy boots. He inspired my American dream of rebelliousness, patriotism, and freedom. That dream was shaken when I arrived in New York in 1999, as I watched the presidential election between George W. Bush and Al Gore. Disturbed by the politics, I wanted to reboot the country of my dreams, and came up with the distressed American flag idea. The controversial collection was about shoring up the strength and free spirit of America, while emphasizing women's feminity.

The Collection: The Franco-Americana collection included a New York schoolgirl skirt worn with a scallop-edge leather top, a rockabilly baseball jacket in cashmere worn with a Liberty Statue printed ruffle dress, a three-piece tailored suit paired with a flag print silk blouse, and to emphasize confident femininity, a famous shirtdress in silk stamped with distressed American flags. References include a Jasper Johns's Flag painting and Peter Fonda's stars-and-stripes-painted Harley from *Easy Rider*.

The Show: It opened with Paris Hilton (a new symbol of capitalist America at that time) in a cashmere flag sweater and distressed blue jeans, and ended with Chrystèle Saint-Louis Augustin, a half-black, half-white French couture model and actress, walking the runway totally naked in American flag body painting. The collection turned out to be my breakthrough. My flag dress was in the window of Bergdorf Goodman on September 11, 2001, the day of the terrorist attack. The motif of the distressed stars and stripes struck an emotional chord. Women wore the dress as a symbol of unity and strength. The first celebrity fan was Madonna in her Drowned World tour, then Mary J. Blige, Meryl Streep, Halle Berry, Sharon Stone, and many others. The timing was disturbing—I'd designed the collection a year before—and I had conflicting emotions about people buying my clothes because of that tragedy. But you can't know or plan how your work will be received or why it becomes a success or a failure. You can only create when you feel inspired.

New York Canyon (2002)

The Inspiration: Nourished by a trip out west, I drew a link between the Grand Canyon and the canyons of New York skyscrapers. The silhouettes were inspired by the nineteenth-century gold prospectors of the American West, and the twenty-first-century New Yorkers who bring energy to the city in their hunt for gold. The parallel landscapes of the vertical lines set up the vocabulary of urban looks inspired by cowboy attire, balancing the rugged and soft sides of human nature.

The Collection: Thigh-high cowboy boots with embroidered flowers; lace and voile wool dresses with the skirted silhouette of cowgirls and -boys. Gloves and pants in suede with details of sheering and fringe, taupe, dust, camel color palette, prints of steer heads, and silkscreen tops with the words OUTLAW and WANTED. Pintuck cotton blouses were inserted with lace and tulle to define the feminine cowgirl attitude. My favorite piece was an urban interpretation of an ivory cowboy dress with an asymmetrical ruffled hem and a touch of Victorian flavor worn by rising star Liya Kebede.

The Show: It took place in a Meatpacking District loft, an open, concrete, rough space. The girls walked to a remix of "Walk on the Wild Side" by Lou Reed.

Slam Princess (2003)

The Inspiration: After attending Russell Simmons's *Def Poetry Jam on Broadway,* a show that mixed verse, music, and urban culture, I was touched by the poets who went up onstage and rapped out their lives with eloquence and passion. I loved this new kind of urban rhythm of storytelling, and was inspired by the Bronx roughness combined with the softness of poetry.

The Collection: Velvet mini-dresses with metal studs, leather and lace jumpsuits, studded silk blouses worn with zip cargo pants and chain-embellished cashmere sweaters presented a rough-and-refined aesthetic. The showstopper was a leather motorcycle jacket with five thousand Swarovski crystal and metal studs—every one nailed in by hand. I made only ten of them, each signed and numbered, but the demand was so high, I had to make twenty more. Lenny Kravitz owned one. Demi Moore wore a dress from this collection to the premiere of *Charlie's Angels*. Beyoncé still wears the Elvis motorcycle jacket in silver gray, as well as Alicia Keys in blue leather.

The Show: The show was held in a Broadway theater, and it opened with an artist with a microphone doing a piece of slam poetry about women's strength. Then the first model walked out on the runway, and fell down. The shoes were vertiginously high with a too-narrow platform. I had no idea they were so unstable. (The shoes hadn't arrived until the day before, and we didn't have time for a rehearsal.) The drama kept happening, over and over. Thirty-five looks, eight falls. Every four outfits, a model hit the floor.

The press said the clothes were stunning, but the show was a living nightmare. Backstage, I watched girl after girl tumble, devastated. I didn't know if I should cry or laugh at this tragicomedy on a Broadway stage. Heidi Klum was doing her comeback and one of the show's models. I prayed she didn't fall. That would have been front-page news. Luckily (or not!), she didn't.

Smoking Not Smoking (2004)

The Inspiration: When the law about smoking in public places in New York changed, I missed the drama of smoking, the silhouette of a woman with a cigarette, the cinematic scene of looking at someone through a cloud of smoke, saying "Let's go have a cigarette" with a nonchalant attitude. Yes, we have to be careful about our health, but there is beauty in the gesture, so much sensuality of bringing the cigarette to the mouth that I felt nostalgic about it.

The Collection: A pack of cigarettes—Gitanes, a French brand with a famous silhouette of a tambourine dancer on the blue packet—was the print of the collection. Lean and carefree silhouettes made of layers of silk and tulle evoke the lightness of the smoke. Flowing flower blouses were paired with patrol pants and scalloped necklines embellished romantic dresses. Tailored tuxedo pants in silk were paired with transparent ruffled camisoles. The construction of tailored pieces in draping fabric was a magic contradiction.

The Show: One of my only shows under the tent in Bryant Park. Despite a great production where girls appeared from the smoke of a serpentine runway, I didn't feel that the format was right for me. From then on, I retained my individuality by holding shows in unique spaces that were crafted for the specific theme of a collection.

Party (2005)

The Inspiration: The ambience and humor of Blake Edwards's 1968 movie *The Party,* starring Peter Sellers, about a swank Hollywood bash that turns into a wild night.

The Collection: Hand-crocheted gold-netted top juxtaposed with a pencil skirt in brocade, cotton voile and silk-satin ivory gown ornamented with oversize jewelry, gold lamé caftan and transparent tunic, and a backless harem pant jumpsuit gave a wink to '60s Hollywood fabulousness.

The Show: It was held at my four-thousand-square-foot boutique in the Meatpacking District right before the grand opening. The forty models gathered, talked, and drank champagne among the guests. Each one had an extravagant character to play in her fabulous clothes as she interacted with the guests. White gloved waiters passed flutes of champagne. The atmosphere was like a chic, deliciously sophisticated party, everyone dressed up, drinking and mingling. It was a two-hour presentation as a kind of performance. I was the host and checked in with my guests and ducked off to be interviewed by the press. It was a one-of-a-kind "party" experience, and I have kept the best memories of it.

Metropolis (2007)

The Inspiration: The combination of the futuristic vision in Ridley Scott's 1982 cult movie *Blade Runner,* and a lot of new buildings being raised in New York, gave me the idea of representing femininity in the city of the future.

The Collection: Cylinder collars in outerwear with geometric cutouts and embroideries of metal shapes were worn on top of a silk T-shirt and sheer organza blouse. Liquid jersey dresses were suspended by jewelry chain straps, asymmetrical tops were embellished with mirror pieces, zipped jumpsuits cutouts on the sleeves and sweaters revealed shoulders.

The Show: We built three floors of scaffolding for the models to walk through and pose on so the audience could see all the looks at once. The construction took two days of furious activity. We didn't have enough power to support the lighting and blew out the electricity an hour before the show. We had to run out and find a generator while the girls got ready in a huge, pitch-black room. There's always unexpected drama when you do a show, but somehow, it all comes together in the end, and what was impossible only moments before suddenly becomes reality. The show must go on. Beyoncé, Rihanna, Cate Blanchett, Mena Suvari, and Kerry Washington wore pieces from the Metropolis collection.

La Colombe (2009)

The Inspiration: The village of Saint-Paul-de-Vence, Provence, and its artists Sonia Delaunay, Braque, and Léger. La Colombe d'Or is a famous hotel there, where Yves Montand met his wife Simone Signoret. Artists paid their bills with paintings, and many of the works hang on the walls to this day. I think of it as my secluded hideaway home. Whenever I stay there, I'm transported by the green cypress trees, the pink and orange flowers, and especially the magical, luminous aquamarine sky. I love the hotel so much, I stole the room key and use it as my everyday key chain in New York City.

The Collection: A palette of painterly prints that evokes the poetry, freedom, and vitality of the artist's life in the south of France. Sonia Delaunay–inspired bold prints, jubilant colors in unexpected marriages of saffron, chartreuse, garnet, emerald, turquoise, and purple. The romantic dresses were finished with a petal neckline. The pencil skirts were composed of layers of scalloped organza, and off-the-shoulder poplin blouses were embroidered with colorful seeds of silk. Masculine high-waisted pants and pleated shorts were paired with hand-crocheted cotton tops and mini cardigans. Angie Harmon, Lindsay Lohan, Brooke Shields, Janet Jackson, and Dita Von Teese embraced the collection.

The Show: I chose the Chelsea Art Museum to emphasize the theme of art. We built a giant wall with fresh ivy draping to transport the audience into a Provence garden.

Over the Rainbow (2009)

The Inspiration: Surprise creates desire; the gesture of a hand holding back a curtain; a wing around a waist; an eye with a teardrop. I was inspired by surrealism, the works of Salvador Dalí, and the delicacy of hands, feathers, and clocks. The abstract but feminine concept was a new territory to explore for me, but I enjoyed it.

The Collection: A cinematic collection, net veils on the body to create the illusion of nudity. Black, nude, sky, shafts of fuchsia and violet coupled with metallic accents to embody beauty and mystery. One silk dress's belt was a hand—with a ring on the finger—reaching around the waist, with another hand for an off-the-shoulder strap. A sexy black backless gown, cowl-neck dress embroidered with lips, fitted column dress inserted with fishnets, black tulle blouse with heart-shaped embroidery and paired with leather leggings emphasized the sensual and mysterious woman.

The Show: It took place on the top floor of the Rainbow Room at Rockefeller Center and had the models walk in a circle along the edge of the dance floor. They were styled to give drama to the collection with black, dramatic eyes. Their hair twisted into knots and wrapped with fishnet veils, a look created by the master in the field, Odile Gilbert, who does the hairstyles for all of the Chanel shows. The whole experience was designed to lift you out of reality and take you into other realms.

La Feline (2011)

The Inspiration: The original 1942 horror flick was *La Féline,* but this show was inspired by the 1982 erotic horror film *Cat People* by Paul Schrader, starring Nastassja Kinski and Malcolm McDowell, with music by Giorgio Moroder and lyrics by David Bowie, about a woman who changes into a killer cat by night. I have always been attracted to the cult of the femme fatale and fascinated by eroticism.

The Collection: Fur neck collars in black and midnight blue, sleek ivory and black vinyl pencil skirts, emerald tailored jackets with leather lapels, a patent leather trench coat, complemented lingerie silk dresses and embroidered lace camisole. Dresses with laser-cut and jeweled straps were softened by cashmere shrugs. A cat jumpsuit was accessorized with buckled belt with the word "erotic" in Swarovski crystal. An outerwear jacket with a fur collar inserted with a patent leather bustier was worn with a pencil skirt. The feminine silhouette was soft yet provocative.

The Show: It took place in a Chelsea gallery and was an installation of a row of girls on a concrete runway-cum-catwalk, exploring the world of vice and virtue by night. All the girls wore styled cat-eye makeup and hair slicked back on top, hanging long in the back. The day before the show, we had a drama. Struck by a February snowstorm in New York, the Italian shoes never arrived, and my dear friend Selima walked all over the city to find forty pairs of patent leather stilettos in sizes forty and forty-one (nine and ten in American sizes) in the color of the collection. She went above and beyond and I will never forget her friendship and devotion.

La Marais (2012)

The Inspiration: The 4th arrondissement, the Marais, and the effortless, chic, and bohemian attitude of *la Parisienne* mixed with Lower East Side rebellion.

The Collection: The little black dresses are mini and embellished with studs, piercing, and chains. Graffiti-painted T-shirts and motorcycle jackets were worn with A-lined skirts. Capes in fur were on top of denim dresses. Flowy blouses with balloon sleeves were worn under sleeveless jackets. A model with a chinchilla bomber jacket carried a python tote with the word "Paris" on one side and "New York" on the other, a shout-out to my two favorite cities.

The Show: It was in a cavernous empty space, a former *New York Times* building that was about to be bulldozed and rebuilt as a luxury hotel. I heard late that the most important press editors were stuck for thirty minutes in the elevator. It shut down because it was too heavy and above capacity. I thank my team for not telling me about it the day of the show. I would have had a breakdown! I didn't learn what happened until two days afterward when I received a note from an editor at *Vogue* who wrote, "Great collection, but I almost died in the elevator on my way up."

Cast Iron (2013)

The Inspiration: Art Deco furniture designs, rounded edges, and thin legs, of French legend Émile-Jacques Ruhlmann, who epitomized the glamour of the French Art Deco style of the 1920s.

The Collection: Long, lean, and clean geometric shapes in velvet, leather, and tulle with tonal embroidery for a simple and sleek silhouette. Knit sweater dresses, pine-green lingerie tops with black sheer mesh were paired with romantic bell-shaped skirts. Black and nude lace bodysuit, silver-gray curved-hem jackets, funnel-neck coats, plum cocktail dresses with a square-cut diamond pattern, a burgundy leather car coat with Deco applications and a black python trench coat emphasized rich, dimensional textures. It took weeks to achieve the intricate pattern of hand embroidery of a tulle black dress that was an homage to the Chrysler Building. Despite the outrageous price, Neiman Marcus couldn't resist ordering ten of them. Draped silk gowns and a strapless column dress of black fringe ended the lineup of the show.

The Show: Extraordinary! For once, everything ran smoothly at the show at a Chelsea gallery, and I fully enjoyed the moment.

Goes With the Wind (2014)

The Inspiration: Les Voiles de Saint-Tropez, a sailing race that takes place every September in the Mediterranean. Elegant sails are filled and flutter against blue sky and the ocean spray as the hulls cleave through the water. It's poetic, but it's also a performance. The yachts are racing, and the tension of competition turns poetry into excitement.

The Collection: White-and-blue-striped off-the-shoulder tops are paired with white A-line parachute drawstring skirts. Silk jumpsuits were belted with a sash. Cutout white poplin shirts with balloon sleeves are contrasted with cropped sailor pants. Mini anorak dress with hood and pockets were presented next to striped *mariniere* tops and tunics. Knit sailor sweaters with buttons running down the full sleeve were worn with transparent maxi skirts. Silk shirtdresses were printed with a wave pattern, or little planes and boats that evoked travel. Jersey dresses and tops in shades of blues revealed curves and décolletés. Some silhouettes were finished with white wrapped knit coats, cotton crocheted cardigans, or cropped peacoats.

The Show: It was a sunny day at Pier 92 in New York and wind machines were going full blast to bring movement to the clothes. As chance would have it, a beautiful boat sailed by on the Hudson as the girls were walking, underscoring our seaside naval theme. The show was the picture of tranquility, but I was extremely tense. It was the first day of the new school year, and my son was transported that morning to the hospital with a severe case of pneumonia. On top of that, my new business partners were assisting at the presentation for the first time and we already had strong differences of opinion about the future of the company. Gone With the Wind was my last show under the "Catherine Malandrino" label, the end of the chapter and the beginning of a new era.

"To live
is the rarest
thing in the
world
most people
just exist"

Oscar Wilde

Life is an adventure if you dare to live it on the edge. Playing it safe—in love, in your career, in the places you go and the things you do—is just skimming the surface. You will never learn who you really are and what you're capable of. Being bold and audacious raises you above the crowd, and takes you beyond your own limitations.

The best, most fun way to discover yourself is to, as Eleanor Roosevelt once said, "Do one thing every day that scares you."

An audacious woman spins out onto an empty dance floor.

She travels the world with just a carry-on, a credit card, and a passport.

She will eat almost anything once.

She faces her fears.

She has a need for speed.

She says, "Let's go to Paris or Buenos Aires for the weekend," and actually does it.

She learns from her mistakes, but doesn't dwell on them.

She's ambitious. When someone tells her, "That's a crazy idea," she knows she's on to something.

She puts on red lipstick and stiletto heels, and heads out to conquer the world.

Throw out the rule book

When I was seven months pregnant, I came back to New York from a consulting mission in Japan. I intended to just stop by in the city and then go on to Paris where I was designing my collections for the upcoming Fashion Week, but my doctor told me I was too pregnant to travel and would have to stay in New York.

I gave birth to Oscar on March 2, 1997, and his father toasted his birth in the delivery room with champagne. I stopped working for only a week and then, in a pinch to get everything done, I returned to the studio with the baby in my arms, along with a supernanny and Oscar's crib to put next to my desk for his naps. I carried my baby boy around the studio or let others hold him, especially beautiful girls. Poor baby grew up in the arms of top models like Chrystèle Saint-Louis Augustin and Liya Kebede. Somehow, we pulled the collection together in New York, and showed it there.

It worked for me, and as I already said, I was inspired by the chaos. The excitement affected the collection's spirited designs and I built on the success. Flying from challenge to challenge gave me Wonder Woman energy and our new company was growing fast.

The most important rule for an exciting life: Throw out the rule book. It was written a long time ago by someone else, and it doesn't apply to you and today's life. You are unique, and only you can find your path. There is no right or wrong way to do things. There is only hard work, determination, and dreams to guide you toward your vision of achievement.

Instinct is a Strength

After the success of my early fashion shows, my partner and I decided to open our first retail store on Broome Street in Soho, New York. Back in 2001, it was a not-so-nice block on the edge of a cool neighborhood, but definitely not in the heart of it. When we told people about renting the storefront there, they said, "Don't sink all of your money on that street." But we put everything we had into the store and the collection and we didn't have a choice but to make it work.

Fortune smiles on risk takers. Two or three months after we opened, Patricia Field, the stylist for *Sex and the City,* walked by my boutique and must have really liked the colorful fantasy display in the window of ultrafeminine and light red and yellow dresses. She set up a meeting with me and said, "I love your collection. I love the aesthetic of the store. Let's film a scene in there."

Sarah Jessica Parker and the rest of the cast, along with a huge crew, descended on the boutique. In the three- or four-minute scene, the actors walked around the store, went in and out of the fitting rooms, tried on yellow, blue, and orange dresses, and delivered their funny, witty lines. The show aired two weeks later, and the next morning, the line of young women outside the store went around the block. Broome Street was such a hit that we made enough money to open another boutique in East Hampton, in the Meatpacking District, and another thirteen more, one after the other, in the years to follow.

In 2005, the Meatpacking District was a wreck, nothing but abandoned warehouses with broken windows and wholesale meat and fish markets. But I had a feeling, and I have learned to listen to

202 • Catherine Malandrino

my heart. We opened our second NYC store there. I wasn't the only one who noticed the area's potential. Jeffrey was also audacious and opened a store there a few months before we did.

I first discovered the Meatpacking District years earlier, when my partner brought me to 675 Hudson Street for a surprise adventure. It was November 25, on St. Catherine's Night. In France, on St. Catherine's Day, the tradition is for unmarried women to wear elaborate hats and pray to God to send them a husband. The prayer depends on your age. If you're under twenty-five, you pray for a kind, handsome, rich man. If you're over thirty, the prayer is, "Send me whoever you got, God, and I'll settle!" We were thirty and dating and celebrated this day ironically. I dressed in pure, virginal white.

We headed out the door and he said, "I'm taking you to a place you'll remember forever." The mystery was exciting. We took a taxi to the far West Side, and we got out at a run-down building that was very dirty and grubby. We walked down narrow stairs into a dimly lit room, with a bar, tables . . . and naked men handcuffed to the stone walls. Dominatrixes in black leather corsets and Goth makeup cracked their whips to make groveling submissives kiss the sharp tips of their thigh-high stiletto boots. People were bound with chains, locked in cages, and wore fetching dog collars. Couples would slip out of the main dungeon into private salons where the house rules—no oral sex, no penetration—were surely broken. And there I was, in the Meatpacking District, in this grungy, bondage emporium of whips, chains, and leather, dressed like Snow White in the heart of downtown New York!

The place was the Vault, the famous downtown S&M club. My partner was right: It was a memorable night. I came to associate the ramshackle neighborhood with the exciting, weird, rough edge of the city.

I observed the neighborhood in the years after, and happened to notice the corner storefront at 652 Hudson Street, only a block away from the Vault, was for rent. It had crumbling brick walls and the sidewalk out front was destroyed, but I was sure the space had a lot of soul and great memories. People said, "You can't open a store there. It'll never work!" Of course, we signed a ten-year lease.

The spirit of New York is so powerful, life and excitement always spread to the dark, strange corners many people don't dare to go. Our Hudson Street boutique, and all the others, was designed by my talented friend Christophe Pillet and looked more like a poetic installation of mirrors and curves. The "summer rain" chandelier of eight hundred "drops" of Murano glass brightened the distressed tone of the neighborhood. Around the same time, some fabulous restaurants like Pastis opened and drew raves from critics and crowds. The High Line park was designed. Warehouses were converted into cool office spaces for tech companies. The Meatpacking District transformed into a dynamic neighborhood, and is, today, a major commercial center of the city.

If we'd listened to everyone who said "You're crazy!" we would still be searching for the perfect location. **Don't hold out for perfect or you'll wind up waiting forever** for a location, a job, a man, a life. **Trust your instincts to realize your passion, and improve what you can get.**

If you hear a voice within you say, "you cannot paint" then by all means paint, and that voice will be silenced"
Vincent Van Gogh

Need for Speed

Skiing

As soon as I could walk, my parents put me on skis. Skiing is second nature for every kid who grows up at the foot of the French Alps. Opportunity is one thing, but to excel, you have to develop the inner quality of adventurousness and fearlessness and great technique. I was one of the risk takers, and went on to ski competitively. I was never afraid of falling. If you push your limits, you will eat snow, and you'll learn. Then you get back up, and progress.

Skiing has always been about speed for me, and I feel empowered by the adrenaline rush. When I'm standing at the top of the slope, I stare it down for a moment, and then attack it dynamically and aggressively, living in the pure joy of the moment.

When approaching a mogul, a little hill carved into the slope, you have to lean your weight to one side to cut around it, which causes you to rise onto the sharp edge of the skis. You are connected to the ground on a razor's edge. Riding it at full speed, knowing that with one wrong move, you could crash, is what it means to be alive. Living on the brink of danger is pure excitement. When I'm skiing, I push myself breathless, making faster, sharper turns, taking higher moguls, until I get the feeling that I have risen out of ordinary life and entered a cold world of silence and infinite pleasure.

Being aggressive on the slope doesn't mean I lose my feminine style. Even at thirty miles an hour, I ski like a woman and use my body to take the curves with grace. It's like a dance with the mountain. Like all tangos, it's most exciting when you are pressed very close to your partner. He might surprise you with a dip or spin—or an unexpected patch of ice—making your heart leap into your throat and your legs wobble. I avoid tracks made by other skiers, and seek out those rough patches, the ungroomed terrain, so I can blaze new trails through the pines. A woman who dares to push herself to race on the edge of her fear will have more confidence and exude radiance. That après-ski rosy glow on her cheeks comes from within.

My Favorite Slope

If you ever get the chance to ski in the French Alps, I recommend Les 3 Vallées

Courchevel. A French resort at the heart of the Three Valleys—Meribel, les Menuires, and Val Thorens, linked together by lifts and ridge trails—it is the largest ski area in the world. The scenery stretches from Mont Blanc in the north to the Ecrins in the south with a fabulous view of the Swiss and Italian Alps. From the valley floor to the glacier, people enjoy all forms of skiing and snowboarding. The Combe Saulire red slope is one of the most sensational rides for a gentle cruise with spectacular views. On top of the hill, don't forget to take a picture with a giant white bear sculpture from the French artist Richard Orlinski who, in 2014, brought art to the top of the mountain.

In the village at 1,850 meters up on the edge of the ski tracks, hidden in the pines, you will find the most haute couture chalet called Le Cheval Blanc, decorated with sensuality. Soft warm fabrics like cashmere, sheepskin, fur, and leather contrast with shining bronze and brushed brass fixtures. A sleeker option in the village is Le K2, with a dozen separate chalets with modern décor in gray slate and chrome contrasting with plush red and ivory velvets and fur. You will be

206 · Catherine Malandrino

surprised by the sophistication of the design. To continue the glamour on the slope, have champagne and caviar and enjoy the music at the Cap Horn restaurant, located near the altiport (for landing small planes between two slopes at the top of the mountain), and higher up, at 2,732 meters, taste the specialty of the mountain at Le Panoramic restaurant: hot melted cheese with black truffles and cured ham.

A few years ago in 2008, Christian Lacroix designed an exceptional ski set called Courchevel in limited edition that comes with a travel trunk. Only ten units were produced for a mere $67,000 each.

Courchevel is the most glamorous resort of the Alps, but I love it because of the diversity of the trails and the quality the village has to offer. For a friendly, beautiful address, go see my friend Christophe at Le Bel Air located on the slope at 1,650 meters and have a lunch of a simple salad with Gruyère and nuts, followed by organic roasted chicken with *gratin dauphinois* and blackberry *tarte* from the Alps. The atmosphere is warm and authentic and you will be welcomed with love and taste.

Kitesurfing

A couple years ago, I went on a vacation to the Dominican Republic. I was invited by the New York pediatrician star and childhood friend Michel Cohen, and I thought I'd just enjoy the sun and rum drinks while lying on the beach. He took me to his favorite secret spot near Cabarete named Encuentro Beach, a delightful place with yellow sand and shallow water. What made this stretch of gently curving shoreline extraordinary was the sight of dozens of surfers skimming the ocean surface with colorful forty-foot U-shaped canopy kites attached to their waist harnesses by hundred-foot-long cords. It looked like a sea of flying butterflies.

As soon as I saw the dozens of rainbow nylon kites, the acrobatics of the kitesurfers, and the pure magic of capturing the wind to fly across the ocean, I had to try it. Empowered by my friend Michel, a master in the sport, I signed up for a few lessons.

In the morning, I started out just by getting used to having an enormous kite hooked onto a waist harness. The first time my kite caught the wind, it lifted me onto my toes and forced me to run down the beach as if weightless, the sand soft and hot under my feet. I learned how to manipulate the kite's handle to steer it around the face of a figurative clock in the sky to the optimal points at nine and three o'clock. If you go outside that zone, the wind is too strong. The relax point is at twelve o'clock.

After two days of running the beach with the kite, I was ready to add the surfboard. It reminded me of a snowboard; it was shorter than a regular surfboard, with two attached booties pointed sideways. I hooked my kite to my harness, directed it up in the air, and then sat on the beach in the shallows to put the board on my feet. The trick was to get the kite at nine o'clock and let it lift you out of the water and upright on the board, and then just glide on the surface of the water. If you leaned too far forward or backward, you'd wipe out.

I waited, half-submerged, until my kite was in the right position. I pulled down on the handle to lift myself up slowly, but the wind was so strong, I sprang out of the water really fast. So fast, in fact, that I was pulled right out of my bikini bottom. I was concentrating so hard on not falling, I didn't even realize I was kitesurfing bottomless! My instructor watched me from the beach, laughing hysterically. When I realized what had happened, I let go of the kite and jumped into deeper water. I couldn't find my bottom anywhere, and had to come out of the ocean covering myself with seaweed. It was hilarious.

The next day, I played it safe and wore a one-piece bathing suit.

By the end of the week, I was kitesurfing, and I was starting to feel the pleasure of the wind. I'm no expert . . . yet. I'm far from done with this sport. My next goal is to learn how to launch myself into the air like the pros, and glide like a butterfly.

Skydiving

Despite my affection for birds and my dream of flying, I have had a lifelong fear of heights. I don't even like to stand at the window of a tall building. I start shaking and feel like I'll get sucked into the void.

As I got older, the fear only intensified. I had to do something to overcome this terror and bring myself to a higher level of consciousness that would have an impact on all areas of my life.

The most extreme test of my acrophobia would be to jump out of an airplane. If I could do that, then nothing could ever scare me again, and, should I survive the fall, I'd grow from the experience. I wasn't going to do it to impress anyone. It would be a personal journey to go beyond myself, and push past the boundaries that existed only in my mind. I chose April 22, my forty-fifth birthday, to do it.

My partner; my son, Oscar; and I drove upstate to Saratoga Skydiving Adventures, about two hours from New York City. On the way there, I wasn't afraid at all, and just enjoyed the sunny drive in our vintage '89 Aston Martin convertible. At the airplane hangar, the atmosphere instantly seduced me: the line of Cessna planes, parachutes unfurling in the wind, the ropes and sets of lines, the shiny metal hooks and equipment laid out on the cement floor. I was impressed by the instructors' concentration as they checked and re-checked the equipment, and very relieved to see how seriously they took the responsibility.

My fear level rose a bit when I read the contract that said I wouldn't sue the company if I died; broke my back, legs, or arms; or had a heart attack. The language was extreme, but everyone had to agree to the terms before they let you on the plane. After I signed, I paid five hundred dollars for the privilege of facing my biggest fear, and then all the skydivers were asked to watch a short film that explained what we were about to do. It covered all the safety procedures, and made it clear that if you didn't follow them *exactly*, the jump might be the last thing you ever did.

The film definitely raised my blood pressure—and my son's. (My partner wondered why he had pay five hundred dollars to witness such a terrible experience.) Oscar said, "Mommy, don't do it. Look at what could happen!" Seeing his concern gave me pause, but I was committed. I suggested jokingly that Oscar join me. But he answered seriously, "I'll come back when I'm eighteen."

I put on my orange zipped-front jumpsuit and was strapped into my red-and-blue-nylon parachute pack. The two other jumpers, three instructors, and I got on the plane. For the tandem jump, an instructor would be strapped to my back the whole way down.

The plane took off. The other people were talking excitedly, but I stayed silent as I looked out the windows and concentrated on clearing my mind. I thought I'd be more nervous, but the jump was still theoretical at that point.

As we climbed to fourteen thousand feet above ground level, and the landscape disappeared under clouds, the instructors coached us again about the procedures. For a while before the parachute opened, they said, we'd free fall with our arms stretched out in front like Superwoman.

"How long is the free fall?" I asked.

"About a minute," said my instructor. "But it'll feel a lot longer."

"How fast?"

"One hundred and twenty miles per hour."

My nerves kicked in suddenly, and my life flashed before my eyes. I went back to Grenoble, and suddenly I saw all the ones I loved in a kaleidoscope of faces in my mind.

Without warning, the instructor violently, terrifyingly, slid the plane door open. Cool air hit my face. The little houses, farms, even the clouds, seemed toys. In a speeding heartbeat, the jump became all too real.

"Let's hook in," said my instructor.

The moment of reckoning. It was time for strength and bravery.

He checked my equipment. Thank God the instructor was . . . wow . . . a very attractive man. He came up behind me and hooked us together. I loved that part of the experience. This man and I, in our orange jumpsuits and goggles, were attached with bondage gear. I was momentarily distracted from the stress of jumping by the sexiness of him plastered against me, his front to my back. We must have looked like we were about to do something incredible together—and we were. We didn't know each other at all, but we might *die* together. But if we survived, we'd fly through the sky and test my bravery to the highest level. My life was in his hands, and the vulnerability and trust I felt were romantic as hell.

"Ready?" he asked. I must have nodded. The anticipation was almost unbearable. My blood racing, he took hold of my hand as we stepped into position at the lip of the open door. The wind was strong and it wasn't easy to stand against it with shaking knees. A green "jump light" by the door turned on, and the instructor said, "Go!" My muscles twitching with nervous energy, I mustered my courage, bent my knees, and leapt into thin air. That split second of throwing myself out of the plane was the most surreal moment of my life. Every cell in my body was on full alert. My heart was pounding; my hands were sweating. It reminded me of other times I'd jumped into the unknown, when I opened my stores and put on a show. But those risky business moves wouldn't have killed me if something went wrong. In this situation, hurtling through space, plummeting to Earth, I might experience a hard landing that you couldn't walk away from. I had to go above my fear *right now* and believe that I would survive.

As soon as you are free from the plane and powerless to the forces of gravity, the wind takes your breath. I had to struggle to make my lungs work. Eyes watering, ears roaring, we fell through sky and clouds at "terminal velocity," 120 miles per hour. Moving that fast, time slowed and every fraction of a second stretched out excruciatingly. I went through a few stages, from terror to amazement to joy. The power of the wind, the speed, the sound, the weight of the instructor on top of me were all exhilarating, but we were so high up, no one could have heard my delighted screams.

I was supposed to stretch my arms forward like Superwoman so the instructor could steer our fall, but I felt compelled to put my arms out to the side, to fly like a bird. He tried to pull my arms in front, but I kept them out. We fell together like we were strapped to a cross.

It seemed to go on for days, weeks, before he took my hand and put it on the parachute release handle. I gave it a firm tug, and the fabric exploded out of the pack above us, yanking us sharply into space, like we might go all the way back into the plane. The force was tremendous—it's actually two or three Gs—and, so overwhelmed by the sudden change in altitude, I had to close my eyes and actually lost consciousness for a few seconds. When I came back, we were spiraling through the air, slower, around thirty miles an hour. The roar in my ears was gone, replaced by silence. My eyes cleared, and I could see the ground, inching closer, but far enough away to look unreal, like an abstract painting of bright colors—greens, browns, blues, yellows.

The view was beautiful, and I had the awareness that I was going above my fear, but the final descent wasn't peaceful and calming. I started thinking again about the landing or worse, and praying that I'd come out of this in one piece.

It took over five minutes to arrive back on Earth. We hit the ground at a run, but when we came to a stop and the instructor disconnected from me, I fell down in the grass. I didn't want to move. I lay there for ten minutes, thanking God for the strength to get through it and that I'd survived. I wanted to kiss the ground, but I couldn't lift my head. Oscar and his father were watching the landing from a distance. Oscar told me later that when I didn't get up, he was really worried and thought I was hurt. But it was pure pleasure. My emotions were too bright to move, and I had tears on my cheeks from joy and relief.

My head was spinning and I took a few shaky steps. I felt drunk and was speechless for an hour. We got back in the Aston Martin to return to the city. The experience behind me, happiness and fulfillment washed over me, and stayed with me for the rest of the day.

I was proud of myself. I did something that I thought was impossible for me, and became stronger than ever because I did it. It was like I grew up at forty-five years old. Fear of anything—heights, failure—was something from a previous life.

When you jump out of a plane, you are coming very close to death. Your rational mind might be aware of the statistics that skydiving is safe. But your survivalist mind is screaming at you not to do it. Falling from a great height goes against every instinct you have, but it's a thrill unlike any other. Once in your life, do it anyway, and challenge fear itself.

A Challenging Journey

Success is easy. Everyone knows how to handle success, and it usually includes celebration and champagne. As wonderful as victory is, it doesn't make you grow. It makes you enjoy. How you handle challenges is far more complicated. If you deal with it well, it's an evolution.

If you dwell on the "what ifs," you might get stuck and seethe. Allowing failure to turn into bitterness is the worst thing that can happen. Every human being's work in life is to not feel defeated. The day you stop dreaming, you're old. Reconstructing your dreams might take a while, but there is no time or age limit. Starting over might mean reinventing yourself and finding a new way to realize new goals, supported by more life experience to guide you.

Reboot Instructions

Behind the glamour of fashion, there are a lot of practical situations and complications. It's not just creating beautiful clothes, especially for the designers with their own labels. It's about aligning interest between the creative process and business opportunities—and sharing the same vision for the brand.

In my personal experience, I had to make choices. It didn't work out the way I had wished, and I needed to take a new direction in my career.

Here is my advice about how to reboot:

Questions

Take a moment to ask simple questions to remind yourself who you are.

What is your DNA?
What are your strengths?
What are your blind spots?
What is your power?
What are your unique, intrinsic qualities?

Love

Rebuild your confidence by surrounding yourself with love. Love has the best healing power. Love from your friends, family, companion, and even the unconditional love from your pets.

Humility

Humility is a strength.

Be aware of your limitations, weaknesses, and mistakes.

And:

- Listen
- Learn
- Join
- Connect
- Share
- Give

Perspective

After chaos, regrouping is about getting actual distance, and it can take months. Go outside your life and gain a fresh perspective on it. With time, the fog of daily problems will lift, and your new path forward will become clear again.

Enterprising spirit

When you are ready to undertake challenges and endorse responsibilities . . .

When you are not afraid of new projects . . .

When you are energetic and have restored imagination and initiative . . .

When you have a strong desire for achievement again . . .

Then you are ready to reinvent yourself.

. . .

Discuss your dreams with people:

Who care about you and know you well.

Who you admire and respect.

Who you trust to be honest with you about your strengths and weaknesses.

By talking with them, they can help you gauge your skills and realize your vision.

Set goals and take actions

Life is a long journey and the breaks give you the opportunity to live something different, meet new people, and contribute to fresh human adventures. Then, with a smile, open the new chapter as a chance.

One of the most incredible entrepreneurs is Richard Branson, founder of the Virgin Group, an enormous business that encompasses hundreds of companies. A self-made man, he started in college by founding a magazine, then opened a record store that grew into a chain of megastores, then created a recording label, a rail company, an airline. Currently, he's devoting his attentions to private space tourism with Virgin Galactic to take thousands of explorers, literally, out of this world. Along with his businesses, Branson has set speed records for air balloon and sea travel, and he's used his influence and funds for humanitarian justice, combating global poverty and climate change and ridding the planet of nuclear weapons.

Branson's road to success hasn't been smooth. He's dealt with failures (e.g., Virgin Cola, Virgin Digital, and Virgin Cars, to mention just a few), botched speed record attempts, and tragedies, like the Mojave Desert crash of the VSS *Enterprise* in 2014 that resulted in a pilot's death. Despite difficulties he continues pushing forward, taking risks, and expanding his reach across the world and into the next, for the betterment of us all.

The entrepreneurial spirit is defined by vision, to go where few have gone before. Inner daring allows you to realize your dreams, reach farther, and push past existing limits into the great unknown.

Being authentic

Authenticity gets you to harmony, although you might have to take some frightening risks along the way. I deeply love my parents and sisters in France. But I knew that to be myself, to realize my personality, I would have to spread my wings and fly. I was eighteen when I separated from my family and the region where I was born to study. Sometimes it was painful and I felt terrible homesickness—still do. But I knew leaving was necessary in order to live the life I'd envisioned, with all its successes and challenges. I always go back to Grenoble, like a migrating bird that returns to his nest, to find the strength to fly higher on my own again.

To be an authentic, harmonious woman:

- **Accept yourself** and go where your heart takes you.
- **Emphasize your strengths**, and be on the lookout for new ones to nurture as they emerge.
- **Forgive your weaknesses.** We all have same. They are part of who we are. Face them and progress.

- **Develop your passion** and make money with it. It doesn't matter if that leads to a tiny start-up or a billion-dollar company. The blooming of your passion makes work a pleasure.
- **Create a network** of equally authentic friends and colleagues, and be generous about connecting people.

Je ne regrette rien

I don't regret anything, including the choices I made that ended badly. I wanted to live them, and I would have regretted them if I didn't try. In life, you only regret the things you *haven't* done, so don't waste time and energy regretting . . .

- **Mistakes.** They're yesterday's news. All that matters is what you do today and tomorrow.
- **Lost love.** Be happy for the best time you had together, and in the knowledge that you'll find love again sometime.
- **Aging.** You earned each line on your personal journey. If you live life to the fullest, you'll earn many more.

Surround yourself with good vibes

Over the years, with fame and experiences, I've made tons of friends and acquaintances all over the world. But when I'm going through a hard time, I seek out only my most meaningful friendships and the people who shine positive energy on me. My few, true friends don't care about wealth and power, beauty, or any superficial measure of success. They only want what's best for me, and the feeling is mutual. If you can surround yourself with generous, supportive love, you can survive anything.

Mary J. Blige gave me this advice: "Surround yourself with good vibes people." Clueing in to how people affect you is a strength to develop. If a friend is encouraging and supportive and loves you for your personality, put your arms around her. If she's motivated by ego, status, and insecurity, undermines your success, and feels happy when you fail, dare to dump her along with all bad vibes people in your life.

Good Vibes vs. Bad Vibes People

Good vibes: "That's fantastic! I'm so happy for you!"
Bad vibes: "Why don't things like that happen to me?"

Good vibes: "You worked hard. You deserve your success."
Bad vibes: "Some people have all the luck."

Good vibes: "Things might look bad now, but they'll turn around."
Bad vibes: "Life sucks and then you die."

Good vibes: "You would be beautiful in jeans and a T-shirt."
Bad vibes: "Are you seriously going to wear *that*?"

Good vibes: "What can I do to help?"
Bad vibes: "I'm crazy busy right now. I'll check in with you later."

Dare to travel

When you are away from the comforts of home, you learn new things about who you are and what you can do, especially by traveling alone. When you don't know the culture, you have to be audacious, adventurous, and confident enough to explore a new city with built-in uncertainty.

Brazil

My trip to Rio de Janeiro was a spontaneous decision. Right before, I'd been invited to São Paulo to visit a mall development. When my retail director, Kevin, and I arrived, we were alarmed to learn that we'd have to travel from the airport and for the whole trip in an armored car with bodyguards surrounding us at all times. When we finished our business in São Paulo, we couldn't resist hopping on a plane to see the beaches at Copacabana in Rio.

I heard about the Hotel Fasano, designed by Philippe Starck, that overlooked Ipanema Beach and its famous black-and-white wave-patterned sidewalk that captivated my imagination and reminded me of "The Girl from Ipanema," the song most famously interpreted by Astrud Gilberto. I booked a room there.

On the first day in Rio, I took a little mountain train to the top of Corcovado to see the ninety-eight-foot-tall statue of Christ the Redeemer, one of the Seven Wonders of the World. It was a foggy day, and I didn't expect to find such a huge crowd. Everyone stood at the base of the statute like we were gathered on a cloud at the feet of God. All of these people, from all different faiths and walks of life, had made the journey to the same spot, to pray to a majestic and generous statue with arms wide open. The vibes were so positive and loving, I was overtaken by a powerful feeling. It can only be described as a religious experience.

The following morning on the rooftop terrace at the hotel, a striking woman, deeply tanned, blond, ageless, in a colorful bathing suit with a huge presence sat next to me. We started to chat, and it turned out she was a fashion designer, too, the queen of bathing suits in Brazil, Lenny Niemeyer, the daughter-in-law of Oscar Niemeyer, my favorite architect who designed, among other projects, Brasilia. Lenny's designs had appeared in the top international fashion magazines and were seen all over the beach below our hotel. Of course I'd heard of her, and she knew my work, too. We became instant friends.

In five days' time, Brazil would celebrate Carnival, a hedonistic bacchanalia of excess before the forty-day abstinence of Lent. People couldn't wait for the official party to begin, and were out in force on the beach. We could hear the samba music all the way up on the hotel roof. We looked down and saw that there was a rehearsal for a Carnival parade going on, with musicians and dancers in exotic costumes. Lenny and I had to be part of the decadent celebration, so we went down to the beach. My new friend took my hand, and we dove into the crowd.

So many bodies with tanned skin covered in a sheen of sweat and glitter, muscular men's torsos, women in sequined bikinis with strands of beads bouncing on their taut bare bellies and hips. The costumes were awe-inspiring: bikini tops that looked like breasts dipped in diamonds; jeweled g-strings; sequined thigh-high boots; huge plumages of colorful feathers on their backs; elaborate headpieces dripping with jewels, rainbow feathers, and sequins; sparkling hanging earrings that somehow stayed on while the women danced furiously; red lips, glittered eyelids, extended dark lashes like butterflies.

"Samba music moves people because its rhythm is like a heartbeat," Lenny told me, and I felt what she meant deep in my chest. In our T-shirts and jeans, no jewelry, we immersed ourselves in the hysteria, the enormous magical opera of humanity moving to the beat of the drums.

For a moment, I felt like I was in the movie *City of God* by Fernando Meirelles and Katia Lund, caught up in the same violent, frantic energy as the characters immersed in the slums and gangs of Rio. We'd plunged into a sea of glistening sexy bodies, men with scars on their faces, gyrating limbs, shaking breasts and hips, music, my thumping chest, bumping into people, losing my footing, losing sight of Lenny, dancing with a new stranger every few minutes. It was raw, rough, euphoric. I didn't know if the man I was dancing with might try to kiss me or pull a knife on me. The crowd moved and I went with it, not knowing where I was going or what would happen next. It was scary, but vibrant. Sweat poured down our faces and glitter got in our eyes, but the energy was addicting.

The parade stretched from dusk to dawn, and we danced until all hours. It was so unexpected, such a lucky, joyous way to take in the color of Brazil. I got to experience what the Rio Carnival was all about, right there on ground level, in the dust and heat, with Lenny.

The following day, some of the people we met dancing took us to the Samba School's center of preparation for the parade. It was an enormous concrete garage, guarded to prevent rivals from taking a sneak peek of the costumes and floats. The room reeked of carpenter's glue, with hammers banging and drills whirring everywhere. Papier-mâché figures and stray feathers lay discarded on the floor. The empty costumes reminded me of giant, sleeping, mythical birds of blue and red, green and gold. The dazzling headpieces were much heavier than I thought, and solidly constructed, to stay on while during samba dance competitions. The whole scene made me think of the chaos before a fashion show when everything is a crazy, confused mess and you are terrified that it'll never be ready on time, but, with a concerted team effort, the magic comes together, right as the music starts.

China

To make an important decision with my potential Chinese partners, I had to go to Beijing. The timing was difficult and nobody from New York could go with me, so I went alone to the other side of the world.

A friend introduced me to David Tang, a mogul and entrepreneur who'd restored a former royal palace built by the twenty-fourth son of the Kangxi emperor in the seventeenth century, and turned it into a boutique hotel called the China Club. I stayed in this hidden gem located on a *hutong,* an alley off a main street. The hotel was spread out over 100,000 square feet, with multiple courtyards connected by traditional single-story Qing dynasty pavilions, a restaurant, fourteen dining rooms (converted from ancient opium parlors and concubine apartments), secret bars, cigar rooms, a banquet hall, and three-story palaces of guest rooms and suites.

My room was an Orientalist vision of glowing lanterns, shining dark wood floors, the faint scent of jasmine in the air, hand-painted silk lotus flowers on red wallpaper, and curtains embroidered with butterflies. The low Chinese bed was covered with velvet pillows and embroidered sheets, with sheer curtains hanging around it for privacy. The room was a romantic painting, a play of shadow and soft light, and I was part of the art. It was like I'd entered the moody world of Wong Kar-wai's 2000 movie *In the Mood for Love,* with its sensual, sumptuous atmosphere. The transparent silk screens and curtains inspired a seductive and unsettling fantasy of being watched as I dressed and undressed. A concubine in her lair of lush fabrics and rich colors, silhouetted by the curtains, the emperor watching silently from the shadows, waiting for the right moment to make his presence known.

It was a very sexy room. I regretted not having my lover with me to share the experience.

Wintertime is not the tourist season and, with such discreet service, it seemed like I was the only guest at the huge hotel. I didn't see anyone else for my entire stay. As I walked through the windowless, eerily silent hallways, it felt like I was descending into the underworld. There was so much intrigue and mystery and a soupçon of fear in this ancient palace, I found myself deeply attracted to it.

I woke up at 6:00 A.M. to visit the walled Forbidden City, former imperial home to Ming dynasty emperors, now a world heritage site famous for its gilded palaces with the distinctive tiered roofs, and collections of ancient Chinese art. I entered through the Meridian Gate, crossed the Golden Stream toward the Gate of Supreme Harmony, through calligraphy, painting, and ceramics galleries, to the heart of the Forbidden City and its hundreds of well-preserved buildings that were, for five hundred years, forbidden to everyone but the royal family, servants, and armies. The main attraction is the Hall of Supreme Harmony, the palace that dates back to 1406 and looms high at the center of the city. It's the inspiration for every imperial palace scene in the movies, with massive red columns; intricately painted walls in gold, blues, and greens;

long intimidating halls; enormous gongs; and an imposing Dragon Throne with wood snakes carved into the hand rests. From there, the emperor wielded his power, making visitors kowtow or bow nine times to him.

I stood in front of the throne and could see it all, the elegant, silent women of the court with lacquered hair and golden threaded kimonos, supplicating men on their knees, begging the emperor for mercy, the tine of swords, the scent of tea and jasmine, the hypnotic plinking of a pipa, the bird song of a flute. I was completely alone in the room and in this fantasy, with no one to distract me from the drifting of my imagination.

Between my underworld hotel and the empty Forbidden City, it was like I was floating through a ghost world. I'd been wishing I had someone with me, but then I realized I was more intrigued by the experience of being by myself immersed in a journey back in Chinese history.

In Brazil, my trip had been about making connections, expressiveness, and melding with humanity. I was empowered by the feeling that I could effortlessly become a part of any culture I visited.

In Beijing, the trip was about disconnection, an exploration of solitude. When you travel, you discover the world and yourself.

James and me

The first time I saw the most original man I know, I was going to a fashion show in Moscow at the department store TsUM. He was sitting in the front row, staring closely at the clothes and beautiful models. I noticed his allure in his cowboy hat, shoulder-length white hair, and deeply tanned face. He was wearing distressed tight jeans, python cowboy boots, and an amazing fringed ivory leather jacket covered in metallic spikes. His style was so unique, I couldn't have missed him. I was fascinated.

Two days later at the airport's caviar bar, he appeared again and sat down right next to me. He congratulated me on my show and gave me his business card, which was just as intriguing as the man himself. It read, "James Goldstein: Fashion. Architecture. Basketball." He said, "Next time you're in Los Angeles, give me a call." I looked at him, smiling with surprise, and then he left.

Three months later, I was in Los Angeles working on the opening of my new boutique on Melrose Place. His card was still in my wallet, and with an excess of confidence, I dared to call him. James said, "I remember you. Come to my house tomorrow night at 7:00 P.M. sharp."

I hung up thinking I'd never go. How daring he was. I didn't know him, after all. But the next day, I received a text from him with his address in Beverly Hills and, spontaneously, I decided to go. I needed to know more about this curious man.

I called for a car to take me there. On the way, I was very nervous and called my friend Jenny. "If you don't hear from me by midnight, call the cops and have them go to his house!" I said, and gave her the address.

I arrived at his modest entryway and rang the bell. He opened the door in a similar wardrobe I'd seen him in three months earlier—cowboy hat and boots, leather and jeans.

He said, "You're late. It's 7:15 P.M."

Before I could respond, he grabbed my hand and, without another word, yanked me forcibly into the most incredible living room

I could ever imagine, with glass walls showing views of the light of Los Angeles, a triangular concrete waffle roof, a long, orange leather couch, a large bar, and a pool on the terrace. I recognized the space from *The Big Lebowski* (it was Jackie Treehorn's modern palace), and realized that I was in the iconic house designed by John Lautner that appeared on the covers of design and architecture magazines.

I barely had time to take it in, though. James pulled me out of the house and into the private tropical jungle planted around the mansion. He was still silent, gripping my hand firmly. So surprised by his behavior, I was speechless. We went through a Bernar Venet metal sculpture and an artistic garden at the speed of a rocket, and he kept pulling me along.

I didn't know if I was living a dream or a nightmare. In sandals with heels, I could barely walk through the jungle leaves, but James couldn't care less. He didn't slow down. If anything, he rushed forward. Suddenly, in the middle of the trees, built into the side of the canyon, we came to a giant concrete cube. The door slid open. He pushed me inside and followed close behind. The door closed instantly.

I thought, *Oh, God, I'm trapped in a dark room with this cuckoo crazy strange man.* I couldn't believe the situation I'd put myself into. My curiosity usually pushed me to the edge, but this time, it could be fatal. I was certain I'd fallen into the hands of a maniac who would kill me and cut me into pieces before burying me in his lavish garden.

"Lay on the bed," he told me with a determined voice. In the middle of the dark room, no windows, was a white leather bed on the floor.

I thought, *He wants to rape me, too, before killing me and cutting me up.*

"Hurry up!" he said.

I fixed him in the eye, gave him a doubtful look, and then, mustering my courage, I lay on the bed. It could be one of the last things I ever did.

He positioned himself behind me. My heart was beating fast, and I was paralyzed, imagining everything that could happen. If I died, at least it would not be an ordinary death, I thought.

From behind me, he said, "Now watch."

Suddenly, a part of the wall slid open and I saw the blue sky with the most intriguing palette of sundown. Then the walls and ceiling started changing from red to blue and pink, and all shades of purple. The sky was onstage for me only. Disarmed and fascinated by the poetic vision, tears of emotion were running from my eyes. I had chills and was not even able to say a word. The unique experience lasted less than half an hour. It was so intense that it felt like I'd had a full night of pleasure.

When it was over, I stood up in the dark and whispered, "James, it was fantastic."

He answered me with an ear-to-ear smile and said in a soft voice, "You arrived late and missed the beginning of the show. Next time, it'll be even better."

The cube was an installation by artist James Turrell, a sky space called Above Horizon that is preprogrammed to begin each day at dawn and dusk. No wonder he was in such a hurry to get me there to see it. (Look up his house and the installation online. It's a modern masterpiece and marvel.)

He held my hand and we walked calmly back through the jungle and into the house. He ordered me a car and I went back to my hotel. On the way, I called my friend Jenny and said, "I'm alive, and I just had the most incredible experience with the most original man I've ever known."

I've visited James a few times at his house, and have run into him at Fashion Week in Paris and New York and at parties in Saint-Tropez. Every time we meet, I learn more about him. He goes to every important basketball game and is the number one fan of the NBA and collaborated with Lautner on the design of his home (which he recently bequeathed to the Los Angeles County Museum of Art), and hosted parties at his canyon-side, gravity-defying space for celebs and pop stars. Whenever I see him, we share a moment of tender complicity, and I just adore his originality and character.

Diane and me

Diane von Furstenberg is an inspiring example of a woman who has dared to live, and taken all kinds of risks to realize herself and her dreams. She's embraced life through good times and bad—and she's always been able to bounce back to bigger moments.

Her story is a fascinating journey about success, failure, love and pain, and superstardom. The daughter of a Holocaust survivor, she married a German prince (a fascinating contradiction there), started her own design company as a single mother, became a very successful woman in fashion before thirty, had several great loves, fought cancer for years, lost and rebuilt a business empire, traveled the world, created the look that defined an era, and has been a kind and generous woman throughout. Her full life story is chronicled in her latest book, *The Woman I Wanted to Be.*

I met Diane in 1998, through our mutual friend Susan Falk. Diane had come back to New York from Paris to relaunch her iconic wrap dress, and she wanted to meet with me to discuss a possible collaboration. I'd just returned from Paris myself and was curious to meet *the* Diane von Furstenberg, a woman who carried herself with all the glamour of Andy Warhol's Factory and Studio 54. I remember being very intrigued in the elevator on the way up to her suite at the Carlyle Hotel where she was living at the time. The door opened, and the first image was diva Diane lounging on the sofa bed in a print wrap dress, with her long legs stretched up, her arm extended, and her generous dark hair on one shoulder. She was impressive and seductive. I immediately admired her obvious confidence.

She invited me to sit next to her on the divan and we started talking in French, sharing our life experiences as women and designers. In the middle of the conversation, she showed me her iconic wrap dress next to the sofa and said, *"Deshabille-toi et essaie la."* Strip.

I was wearing a simple black dress and stilettos. I stood up, undressed right there in front of her, with my black bra and pantyhose, and tied on the leopard-print jersey dress. I turned to look at myself in the mirror on the wall, and said, "I do feel like a woman."

She gave me a huge smile. She was thrilled by my reaction, and at the end of our conversation, she proposed to me the position of senior designer to create all the dresses (besides the wrap) for the new collections.

In the days to come, I went to her studio townhouse and found her to be an impressive woman at work. She was an icon, an inspiration, a boss, a mother, a lover, and, soon, a mentor to me. I just needed to look at her to feel inspired. We shared ideas and vision. I tried my best to get into her mind and express her aesthetic with the collection. She introduced me to the New York fashion scene, and we traveled to Paris Fashion Week a few times together. She was an amazing friend, and remains one today.

After a few years with Diane, I felt the need to express my own world. With much satisfaction for what we had done together and a certain sadness, I left DVF to create my own company.

We stayed close and she always showed me a lot of affection at dinners and fashion events. When I was in trouble in my career, she was one of the first people I went to for advice. As the president of the Council for Fashion Designers of America (CFDA) and as a woman of accomplishment, she would have valuable insight, I knew. Her heart and mind were always open to me. After our conversation, and before I left her studio, she went into a jewel box behind her desk and took out an antique silver coin. She dropped it in my hand and told me that on top of everything else she would do for me, we can always use a little bit of luck. I was very touched by her desire to help. Her support has been continuous and through our many phone calls and texts, she always does what she can for me. I hope she realizes how much I appreciate her.

Diane inspired me to transform my scars into stars.

Effortless confidence

Confidence, like French style, is effortless. To feel alive with self-assurance . . .

- **Smile at people.** As you walk toward someone, remind yourself to smile. It opens your energy to others and erases the fear of being judged.

- **Be spontaneous.** Make an instant decision—where to eat, what to buy—and surprise everyone, including yourself.

- **Free your hair.** Take it out of the clips, barrettes, and spray, and let it fly loose and crazy. Free hair unties your spirit.

- **Put on red lipstick.** Confidence in a lick.

- **Put your hand in your pocket.** It changes your posture and makes you feel strong, steady, and ready for anything.

- **Walk in high heels.** You know your legs look fabulous when you do. Heels give your confidence and height a boost.

- **Wear your glasses** if you need them. You gain ten points of IQ as soon as you put them on. Glasses are another prop, a way to draw attention to your hands and eyes, to look and feel suddenly smarter. To look and feel suddenly sexier, take your glasses *off.*

- **Lower your voice.** Shouting is a sign of insecurity. Loud voices are desperate to be heard. A soft voice says you don't need volume to draw attention. There's power in silence, too. A shrug or dramatic expression says, "I'm so confident, I don't need to speak to make my point."

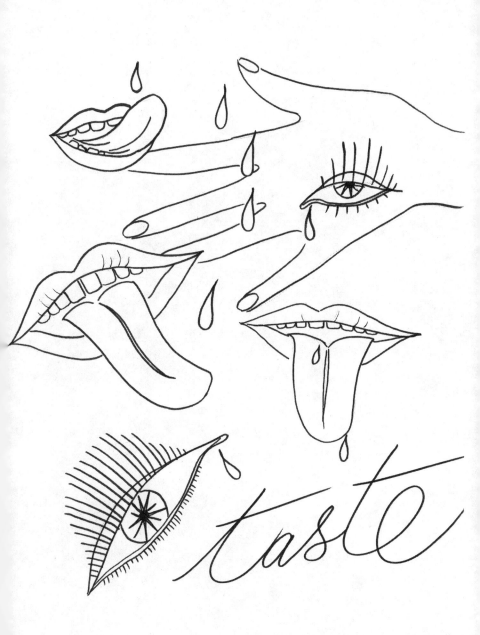

"Beware the girls who don't like wine, truffles, cheese, and music"

Colette

Life is too short to drink bad wine. In France, drinking good wine and eating good food is a huge part of the culture. Every French person grows up with an appreciation of food and learns how to cook. The method itself is similar to the French wardrobe style: **Keep it simple, effortless, make the most of what you've got, and emphasize quality over quantity.**

Americans seem to be more open to the adventure of eating than ever before. Twenty years ago, when I first arrived, burgers and French fries were the only flavors people knew of my native cuisine. But an appreciation for food as more than nourishment or comfort has developed here. It's a fantastic shift. The French chef Laurent Tourondel knows it well.

Food is family

The secret of French cuisine is not just in the recipes, it's in the full journey. It starts with preparing food together and sitting down to a beautifully set table with people you love, taking your time to enjoy it and talking for many friendly hours about the food and about wine, art, politics, sports, and sex. Sharing the pleasure makes the experience even more exciting. The TV, computers, and phones are off. The entertainment is the food and the conversation. Along with nourishing the body, you are strengthening relationships. **Bonding over food is the salt of life.**

For the French, cooking isn't a job or a chore, something that the stressed mother rushes home to throw in the microwave in ten minutes or less, even if sometimes that happens. The work is light because it's shared by the whole family. One person does the chopping. Another trims the chicken. Another makes the vinaigrette. Another opens the wine. The room is alive with a natural rhythm. As you prepare, you're talking and bonding. Time spent in the kitchen is effortless. Magic is made along with the food. Maybe that's why, in a French home, in the end, you always find yourself sitting around an animated table.

A love of good food—*gourmandise*—has always been an important element of my life. Growing up, my parents, sisters, and I used to hunt for ingredients in the countryside, *la cueillette*. We carried large wicker baskets and filled them with wild blackberries or gooseberries that my mother would later cook into pies and tarts. We took the time to find the right mushrooms, chanterelles with golden caps like tiny open umbrellas, or horns of plenty, hidden gems in a moss case buried under the rocks. We'd fill the baskets with walnuts from our own tree. The walnuts of Vinay, a village between Grenoble and Valence, are a regional delicacy, renowned for their ivory kernels and golden shells.

My mother transformed our harvest into delicious dishes we would share in the evening, gathered around a beautifully laid table dressed with linen, porcelain, and silverware. This was the idea of a perfect Sunday night. We took the time to sit down and listen to each other's stories. Sharing meals was always a *merveilleux moment* for the six of us.

I exported this good habit to my hectic New York life, and for many years, I would sit down *en famille* and spend the evening enjoying the food and each other. Talking is a big part of the joy of cooking. In an isolated kitchen, the cook is cut off and alone. So when I moved into my New York apartment, the first thing I did was to tear down half of the wall between the kitchen and the living room to create a bar so we could have a long open space for interacting.

Tonight, I'm cooking a meal for Oscar and a few of his friends. I'm making something hearty and generous that will take them back in time to the aromatic warmth of the kitchens of childhood. It's a rustic French meal: a roasted chicken with *gratin dauphinois* (potato baked with Gruyère, cream, and parsley). Everyone will help. We'll all pick up a knife and stand shoulder to shoulder, chopping. A glass of wine is always nearby—not a Château Margaux every night, but a nice Bordeaux. We'll make the table look as creative as the food, with stem wineglasses and tumblers for water, sets of plates for each course, silverware, cloth napkins, and colorful placemats. My tall pepper grinder is made of olive tree wood from Provence, and every item on the table tells a story. It takes a little more time to set up. But you get so much in return for the visual pleasure of the table to share food and love.

Food is romance

One of the best ways to show your devotion is to put your heart and soul into cooking *un pot au feu*—a beef stew, the ultimate comfort food—and serve it to someone you adore. A couple feels more in love when they come home from a hard day of work, open a bottle of wine together, and put some olives and nuts in a dish to start the evening on a romantic note. You can achieve a wonderful moment just with simple pasta or fried eggs. **Any night can go from ordinary to extraordinary with attention and fresh ingredients.**

Love is necessary for making some French dishes. If you're not motivated by deep emotion, who would have the patience to make a sophisticated dish? The French cook for the pleasure of eating, and for the joy of seeing others relish their food. They can be reserved about expressing their feelings with words, so, often, **the French say "*Je t'aime*" through food and wine.**

The French Paradox

You've probably heard the phrase "the French paradox" about how the French eat real butter, real cream, real sugar, bread, wine, cheese, and still manage to stay so slim. Meanwhile, Americans eat fake butter, low-fat cream (how can such a thing exist?), Diet Coke, substitute sugar, and light beer, try to limit bread and cheese, and they still struggle with excess weight.

The reasons French people stay relatively slender is simple: They love food! They don't look at it as something to fear, regret, or feel guilty about. In America, food seems to be connected to the wrong emotions, and that leads to unhealthy psychological attitudes and overeating. It's sad how food can cause so much pain. Eating is one of life's most accessible pleasures.

Eating "fake" foods can't be good for you. It compromises proper digestion and metabolism and can increase appetite and weight gain. It shouldn't be "lite." It should be fresh, natural, and delicious.

The French also don't seem to struggle with appetite. They eat more slowly than Americans and have smaller portions. The idea is to take little bites, small samples to have new adventures with food. You don't have to eat an entire plate of *foie gras* to experience the creaminess or three full courses and a basket of bread to feel full. A classic French dinner is two small courses, a piece of baguette, a glass of wine, some cheese and fruit, and a *petit café* to end it. The meal unfolds over hours of conversation and laughter with much time to digest.

The French palate prefers salty to sweet. They indulge in cakes, chocolate, or a pastry on a Sunday afternoon, or very occasionally with afternoon coffee or tea once or twice during the week. Portions are light and delicate: a small apple or strawberry tart or one or two macarons, and that's it. If you use real, fresh, high-quality ingredients, a taste is enough to fill you with pleasure and satisfy your appetite and soul.

Enjoy food more, take your time savoring it, and you'll wind up eating less and feeling lighter.

"Dining is always a great artistic opportunity" Frank Lloyd Wright

Create an imaginative plate

My New York friends order in dinner three or four nights a week. Friends with kids order in pizza at least once a week. I order Italian or Chinese takeout once or twice a year. At home, I'd always rather make my own food.

Cooking gives you a moment of creativity and relaxation. It's a time to slow down, to experiment and go wild. The French are always trying to invent new tastes and dishes. What new combinations, textures, and flavors can you create and share? A cook is somehow an artist, and food is the medium, whether it's my favorite chef, Guy Martin of Le Grand Véfour in Paris, or *maman* at home in her own kitchen.

Everyone who loves food can make a little magic with it. All you need is the spirit of adventure and a hunger for experimentation. I invent my own recipes so that I can taste new things and use my imagination. **In the kitchen, you can feed your body and soul at the same time.**

Sometimes, opening the fridge is an opportunity to create something from nothing. Pasta, grating the ends of four different cheeses, and a nice piece of butter becomes "Pates aux 4 Fromages." Or I make what I call "the composition," putting a fried egg in the center of the plate, a bit of ham on the side, a piece of tomato, and whatever is left in the fridge. The most important aspect is that the final composition is colorful, fresh, and *appetissant*—it stokes the appetite, and brings about one of my favorite sexy French expressions, *l'eau à la bouche,* water to the mouth.

Many evenings each week, I make a creative salad and combine ingredients together, like a can of tuna, corn, lettuces, eggs, tomatoes, anchovies, olives, and a touch a cilantro, whatever ingredients will be rich, bright, colorful, and a joy to eat. A bowl of greens really can be a vehicle for creative expression . . . and don't forget the dressing.

The Perfect Vinaigrette

1. Put a spoonful of Dijon mustard in a bowl.
2. Add either balsamic vinegar or fresh lemon juice. I prefer more mustard than acid, so I just dribble the vinegar. I don't use measuring cups. I taste, and turn, and taste again. Play with the quantities until it's right for you. Mix mustard and acid until blended.
3. Add cold pressed extra-virgin olive oil. Mix until tangy and creamy.
4. Add salt and pepper to taste.

Favorite ingredient

Eggs. Eggs are at the top of the list, along with butter, in French cuisine. You can't make a quiche or a soufflé without them. I always try to have chicken, quail, or fish eggs in my fridge.

Croque madame. This ham and cheese sandwich with a fried egg on top is a national treasure. (A croque monsieur is the same sandwich, minus the egg.) I use *pain Poilâne,* a rich brown bread. Cut one long slice and grill it until slightly crispy. Put béchamel sauce (butter, flour, and milk whisked over heat), Dijon mustard, ham, and Gruyère cheese on the bread, and grill it again in the oven. While the cheese is melting, fry an egg sunny-side up in real butter. Put the egg on top of the sandwich, and finish with more cheese on top. On a colorful plate, a sunny-side-up egg always reminds me of a pop art painting.

Salmon roe omelet. I combine two kinds of eggs when I make this dish. First, I break chicken or quail eggs in a bowl and turn them

delice
et
desir

with milk for a long time. I cook the egg mixture until it's soft, and then I put cheese and orange salmon eggs on top. The salmon eggs are pretty and pink, and add a salty explosion in the mouth.

Pasta à la boutargue, a simple dish from the south of France. Cook pasta to taste. Meanwhile, sauté chopped garlic in olive oil. Add lemon juice. Combine the pasta with the garlic and oil, and then add thin slices of boutargue (dried and salted mullet roe) and lemon zest with more oil and grated cheese, if you like. **A fun moment to share: two people eating their way along a single piece of spaghetti toward a kiss à la** *Lady and the Tramp.*

Caviar (salt-cured sturgeon eggs) is a special moment of elegance, served with a mother-of-pearl spoon. Put the tin of caviar on ice, spoon it onto triangles of thin toast, add sour cream and a zest of lemon, and then sip a frosty glass of vodka or champagne. **A glamorous moment to share: eating caviar out of the mouth of your lover.**

Nothing magical happens with a plastic fork

In New York, I see people walking down the street, eating a slice of pizza off a paper plate and women eating salads out of plastic containers. You will never see this in Paris. Eating and drinking on the street is not seductive or elegant. My mother says, **"In life, we all do the same thing, but the way we are doing it makes all the difference."** The French take pleasure in sitting for a meal and eating off a porcelain plate with a real fork. If you eat quickly while you're standing or walking, you are not savoring every bite. You barely taste it at all.

Even if we do order in food (those once-in-a-blue-moon occasions), we take the food out of the containers and put it on the table on porcelain platters and plates with silverware and wineglasses. The idea is to enjoy an elegant moment. I'd feel miserable if I ate off a paper plate. **The French food experience is another way to create a little romance with the world.** There is no magic in a plastic fork. You could be savoring a meal created by Eric Ripert or Alain Ducasse, but on a paper plate, the sensuality of the moment is ruined. Contrarily, if you ate a simple roasted chicken and a salad on a bone-white china plate with a silver fork, you have created an experience for pleasure.

Food shopping for inspiration

Food shopping is a daily adventure in France. You don't order food online or only go to a big store. Real food lovers take their bag or straw basket and stroll store to store to collect ingredients for the next day or two.

The *boulangerie* for freshly baked bread.
The *fromagerie* for cheese.
The *boucherie* for meats.
The *patisserie* for desserts.
The *marché* for fresh fruits and vegetables.

Usually, the shops are all within walking distance. Going from one to the other does take some time, but seeing the food is part of the creativity of cooking. You are inspired to make your meal based on what looks good and is fresh that day. You have a personal interaction with your butcher, your baker. (I miss these kinds of friendships in New York.) When you are with your lover, shopping for a meal you'll invent, prepare, and enjoy together can be exquisitely romantic. **While you are walking from shop to shop, you are building up an appetite for food and love.**

What I appreciate most about the shops in America: they're open 24-7. In Paris, stores close at 7:00 P.M. In New York, you can say "Let's go shopping!" at any day and any time. When I fly back to New York from Paris, I'm often jet-lagged and wake up at 4:00 A.M.—the best time to shop. Walking through an empty supermarket is a surreal experience, no crowds, no rush. I can just wander down the aisles and take it all in.

American vs. French Food Styles

American: Order takeout.
French: Cook easily at home.

American: Eat in front of a screen.
French: Eat and talk at the table.

American: Fine dining is commercial.
French: Fine dining is cultural.

American: Leftovers are put in a doggie bag . . . presumably for the *dog?*
French: Leftovers are eaten for lunch the next day, by people.

American: At a restaurant, say a general, "The food is amazing."
French: At a restaurant, comment specifically about every recipe.

American: Competitive eating: fifty hot dogs in fifteen minutes.
French: Appreciative eating: thirty minutes to eat a single croissant.

American: Individual foods for one person, like a hamburger.
French: Communal foods to be shared by the whole table.

American: Eat quickly because you're "starving."
French: Eat slowly and enjoy every bite.

American: Go to Starbucks for coffee to go in a paper cup.
French: Sit at a café and drink out of a porcelain cup.

American: Have three meals a day plus two snacks, plus two American coffees.
French: Three meals a day, no snacks, plus one espresso.

Petit Déjeuner

At a New York brunch—an American concept—my friend will order a Bloody Mary, eggs Benedict with a side of home fries, coffee, and a piece of pie for dessert. Breakfast in France is a small meal, a croissant and coffee, or toast and jam with a fruit salad and tea, something simple and light. Coffee isn't seen as a cure for sleepiness, like a drug. It's a little bit of elegance in a porcelain cup, a little bit of sweetness on a silver sugar spoon. Caffeine is part of the pleasure, but it's nothing compared to coffee's aroma and flavor.

What is more romantic than breakfast at a café in Paris? Imagine lifting a tiny *tasse* to your lips, nibbling at a fresh, warm croissant, observing Parisian style, and feeling the atmosphere around you. **On the weekend, a light breakfast on a café terrace captures the essence of Paris.** For breakfast inspiration, look to Café de Flore and Les Deux Magots. Separated by the tiny, narrow Rue Saint Benoit (also home of a temple of the nightclub Le Montana), the two famous cafés are the best of friendly rivals.

Terrace Wars

Going to a café in Paris isn't so much about the food. You will find similar menus at all of them. The qualities to look for are a café's ambience, location, and history.

Café de Flore and Les Deux Magots, two nineteenth-century cafés along Boulevard Saint-Germain, make up two points of the triangle (the third is Brasserie Lipp) that mark the borders of Place Saint-Germain, the neighborhood known as the epicenter of Parisian intellectual life where luminaries would gather at one or the other of these cafés to talk about art, literature, and philosophy.

As is the nature of Paris, one café was fashionable while the other was not, until tastes changed. In the first half of the twentieth century, the elites—Ernest Hemingway, James Joyce, Oscar Wilde, Camus, Sartre, Simone de Beauvoir, Picasso—preferred Les Deux Magots to talk, brood, and drink. Café de Flore was out of favor because decades before, it was the favorite spot of the leaders of the French right-wing political party. But as Les Deux

Magot's popularity grew in the 1940s and '50s, it became too crowded for the artists. They were driven across the street into the formerly shunned Café de Flore. By the 1960s, Café de Flore was the fashionable place where the stars of the day—Brigitte Bardot, Jean-Paul Belmondo, Jean Seberg—gathered, leaving Les Deux Magots to the tourists.

In his 1996 essay "A Tale of Two Cafes" in *The New Yorker,* Adam Gopnik chronicled the shifting popularity between the cafés. As a fashionable friend of his explained, "The relationship between the modishness of the Flore and the unmodishness of the Deux Magots isn't just *possibly* arbitrary. It's *necessarily* arbitrary. If you place any two things side by side, one will become fashionable and the other will not. . . . It's the nature of desire to choose, and to choose *absolutely*. That's the mythological lesson of the great choice among the beauties: they are all beautiful—they are goddesses—and yet a man must choose. And what was the chooser's name? Paris."

I choose Café de Flore. It's the ultimate place to sit outside in the early morning or inside on the first floor for more intimacy, to order an espresso and watch *le tout* Paris go by.

Café de Flore
Founded in 1873
White awning with green lettering
Waiters in black and white
Red leather booths
Home of the Prix de Flore literary award since 1994
Setting for movies and TV shows (including *Absolutely Fabulous*)
Inspiration for art, movies, and books

Les Deux Magots
Founded in 1887
Green awning with white lettering
Waiters in white and black

Brown leather booths
Home of the Deux Magots literary prize since 1933
Setting for movies and TV shows (including *Inception*)
Inspiration for art, movies, and books

to be

Parisienne

Four-Hour lunch

The cliché is that the French take a four-hour lunch every day.
Well, not *every* day, but on weekends and vacations, certainly.

Lingering over the afternoon meal is an unselfish pleasure, the spice of life. You are taking time to enjoy food, your companions, and the moment. Sitting at a table with friends for a while is not lost time when you could (or should) be doing other things, like getting back to work. It's how you strengthen your relationships and nourish the soul. Lunch is a window of pleasure that restores your energy. Afterward, you can work again and feel inspired by your conversation. **Losing time for Americans is nurturing the soul for the French.**

The French don't feel guilty about having wine at lunch on occasion. They say, "Let's have champagne! Let's celebrate the good time we're having on this beautiful afternoon." Americans save champagne for birthdays and New Year's Eve, but the French have it whenever they want a taste of fabulous to make a good moment unforgettable.

Any opportunity to add spice and style to life should be taken. Don't be a victim of the system that prioritizes denial over pleasure. The purpose of life is to make it colorful, pleasurable, stylish, and exquisite, as often and in as many ways as possible. **The French ideal is to integrate taste, love, and flavor into your everyday life.**

American vs. French Sandwich

In America, you can get a lobster BLT with:

Two large pieces of toasted bread with butter
Lobster and crab meat

Two strips of crispy bacon
Two slices of tomato
A lettuce leaf
A side of coleslaw
A lemon wedge
French fries and ketchup

For the same amount in euros in France, you can get a classic sandwich with:

A baguette sliced down the middle the long way with butter
A couple slices of ham
Some Gruyère cheese
And that's it

For the French palate, the American version has too many flavors mixed together, and it's just too big. If you took all the elements separately, though, in smaller portions, it would be delicious. My French method for enjoying an American style sandwich: ask for it to be served deconstructed with all the ingredients arranged on the plate. Enjoy!

Christmas dinner

Every year, I cross the ocean and go back to Grenoble to spend holiday time with my parents and sisters. I was born Catholic, but Christmas isn't so much about religion for us. It's a family celebration. (Incidentally, I love Pope Francis. He is a visionary and a fabulous leader to reform the church today.)

After weeks of anticipation, I'm never disappointed by my parents' home at the holidays. The Christmas tree lights up the living room. The fire in the hearth keeps the house warm, even in the French Alps. Much of our time is spent in the kitchen, four or five hours in a row, either preparing dinner or eating it. Sometimes, my sisters and I escape to ski at Alpe d'Huez where my family has a chalet, or to the domain of *Les Trois Vallées* by Courchevel for a family race on the slope. But often, it's more fun to stay at home with our extended family, catching up on what we've been doing all year. Bundled up next to each other on the sofa next to the fireplace, we spend hours telling our stories, laughing, and remembering how much we love each other.

The highlight is Christmas dinner. The night is about family, food, and elegance. My father wears a tuxedo. My mother wears a long black dress and diamonds. My sisters and I rival each other with creativity. We like to astonish and surprise with our outfits. Of course, all of the women—my mother, sisters, and nieces—wear something that I've designed in the past. I realize how much my clothes were carrying ageless and timeless qualities. It's an honor and a pleasure for me to be part of the ritual, and to dress different body types across a few generations (from age eleven to eighty). I might wear one of my signature Victorian blouses with a pencil skirt, or a long-sleeved chiffon dress, or a tailored tuxedo. Even my son, always in jeans, wears black pants, a white shirt, and a jacket for the night. **In a French family on Christmas night, everyone must shine.**

The house is a marvel that evening, with large round white porcelain vases holding generous bouquets of holly with red berries bought at Christmas markets. In the hallway, a branch of mistletoe hangs from the chandelier as a symbol of happiness and immortality. Classical music plays as we sit down at the long dinner table dressed with gilded tableware on a white embroidered linen tablecloth, lit with a candelabra. The Christmas tree is decorated with gold bows and glass ornaments by my mother and nieces. It's the refined setting for a joyous night.

Le Menu de Noël

Aperitif de Noël

Blinis de saumon fumé et œufs de lompe (little pancakes with smoked salmon and lumpfish roe)

Verrines d'asperges et d'avocat au homard et Champagne brut Krug (asparagus, avocado, and lobster served in a glass, and a glass of fancy champagne)

Foie gras de canard avec pain toasté et purée de figues et Vin de Sauternes (duck foie gras on toast with a purée of figs, and a glass of sweet white wine)

Chapon au four farci au foie gras et Bourgogne rouge Côte de Beaune (capon—a castrated rooster—stuffed with foie gras, and a glass of red wine)

Homard roti au beurre de crevette et Chardonnay blanc Pouilly Montrachet (broiled lobster and shrimp with butter, and a glass of dry white wine)

Plateau de fromages des alpages et fruits secs, noix, noisettes, dates, et pruneaux, et Bordeaux rouge Chateau Margaux (a cheese board with local selections of nuts and dried dates and prunes, and some fancy red wine)

> Buche de Noël à la vanille et buche glacée au chocolat et Champagne rose Ruinart (a vanilla and chocolate Christmas log cake, and pink champagne!)

Gastronomie à la Française

The French are audacious about eating. They will try anything and never play it safe. This is why eating is sexy—the risk and adventure can get your heart beating. The objective of French cuisine is to take any ingredient and make it delicious. Every bite has aroma, texture, flavor, and is a delight to the eye. Some French dishes might seem strange, but if you give them a try, you might fall madly in love.

Les Cuisses de Grenouilles, aka frog legs. Deep fried with garlic and parsley, frog legs are compared to chicken, but the flavor is more delicate and delicious. In Paris, go to Roger La Grenouille, Roger the Frog (6th arrondissement), for the best experience.

Les Escargots, aka snails. Cooked in garlic and butter in a special dish, you use a *pince d'escargot* utensil to hold the shell, and a tiny fork to pull it out. For traditional *l'escargot de Bourgogne*, go to Au Doux Raisin (5th arrondissement), Paname (18th arrondissement), or L'Escargot Montorgueil (8th arrondissement).

Le Rognon de Veau, aka veal kidneys. Sautéed in butter with mushrooms and shallots and then simmered in red wine and beef broth, veal kidneys are a rustic dish made elegant. Try it at L'Auberge Dab (16th arrondissement).

Le Lapin à la Moutarde, aka rabbit in mustard sauce. The cuts of rabbit are covered in Dijon, browned in butter, and simmered in white wine. Try them at Le Jaja (4th arrondissement) or L'Epicure (8th arrondissement).

Foie Gras, aka the liver of a young goose or duck. To enlarge the organ up to ten times its normal size, the bird is force-fed a mash of corn and fat, a process called *gavage,* for about two weeks. *Gavage* is controversial, and some people refuse to eat foie gras. But if you do, it's a luxurious, singularly rich eating experience. A chef can prepare it a hundred ways: grilled, roasted, sautéed, turned into a mousse or a paté. A traditional dish is a seared medallion of foie gras, served with toast and a fig jelly. Go to Le Bistro des Oies (10th arrondissement) and order the house special goose plate and foie gras for the ultimate experience.

Les Tripes à la Mode de Caen originated in Normandy in the middle ages. It's a slow-cooked beef stew made with carrots, celery, onions, fresh herbs, an ox or calf foot, cider and apple brandy, and the main ingredient: the lining of the first or second stomach of a cow. For an authentic taste of this ancient dish, go to Le Pharamond (1st arrondissement), a restaurant that's served authentic Norman tripe stew since 1879.

Joues de Boeuf Confites, aka beef cheeks. Since a cow chews constantly, the cheek muscle would be tough if it were grilled or seared. French chefs prefer to braise beef cheeks in red wine for hours to turn it into a tender, succulent morsel. Go to Bistro Richelieu (1st arrondissement).

Boudin Noir, aka blood sausage. One of the many types of French *saucisson,* the *boudin noir* is a mixture of pork, pig blood, apple, and onions. You can find it in many forms: cured or dried to slice and eat, or fresh to cook in butter. For the best *boudin à* *la lyonnaise,* go to Alain Ducasse's Aux Lyonnais (2nd arrondisse-ment).

Le Fromage. There are 247 different kinds of French cheese with an almost unimaginable variety of texture, taste, age, *parfum,* and fermentation. Some cheeses are rich, or sharp, or stinky, but each is unique and the pride of its region. In Normandy and Brittany, they love Camembert. In Alsace and Lorraine, Le Brouère. In Auvergne, Roquefort. Cheese pairs with wine so well that, on most vineyard tours, you'll be treated with *fromage* pairings as you sip. My favorite cheeses are Comte and Roquefort with grapes.

Easy to Love

Les Crêpes. Thin dough stuffed and folded with anything (Nutella, fruit, cream, ham, cheese) are elegant pockets of goodness. In Bretagne, crepes are a staple of life, made in every kitchen on a special pan. Crêpes Suzette, a classic of sweetness and drama, is smothered in caramelized butter, orange zest, and Grand Marnier, and served *flambé* at the table. My favorite crepes are sprinkled with a few drops of lemon juice and sugar.

Le Pain. A famous French bread maker, Lionel Poilâne, once said, "Bread deals with living things, with giving life, with growth, with the seed, the grain that nurtures. It is not coincidence that we say bread is the staff of life." Chef Poilâne's shops are dotted all over Paris and well worth a visit. The smell when you walk inside is heavenly. The French eat freshly baked bread at every meal. In New York in the '90s, finding a good baguette was like climbing Mount Everest. But, lately, thanks to Maison Kayser, you can find a *boulangerie* here with savoir faire. Any *boulangerie* in Paris has an incredible selection *du pain*: baguettes are long, thin, and crusty; croissants are buttery and flakey; boules are round and hearty; brioches are light and cakey.

Les Macarons are brightly colored sandwich cookies, lighter than air, made of meringue (egg white and sugar), and flavored with almond, caramel, chocolate, nuts, vanilla, honey, and fruits. The creamy center is made of ganache, jelly or buttercream, also flavored. You can buy a rainbow of macarons in a box and have a few with coffee or tea, or as a nice treat. For the ultimate experience, go to the Ladurée pastry shop on the Champs-Élysées or in Saint-Germain, the temple of macarons in Paris. And trust Elisabeth Holder Raberin, president of Ladurée USA, the daughter of the company owner, who's told me that their recipe is the best-kept secret of the family. Ladurée has opened in America, in Soho, Madison Avenue, and Miami.

Warning :

Don't say

Bon appétit

Although the phrase is spoken at nearly every French restaurant in America and many in France as a way to say "Start eating and enjoy," it's not considered polite. It actually means "good digestion," or that the food you are about to eat is healthy for the intestines, not the most appetizing start for a sensual eating experience. Just know that if you say it at a real French table, you will sound common. The sign that it's time to begin is when the hostess smiles and picks up her fork, and then we can say, *"Bonne dégustation."*

Parisienne treats

- Ice cream at Berthillon
- Bread at Poilâne bakeries
- Macarons at Ladurée
- Caramels at Le Fouquet's
- Oysters at Mollard
- Steak tartare (raw beef) at Alain Ducasse's Le Relais Plaza
- Fish dishes at the brasserie Marius et Jeannette
- Roast quail at Chez L'Ami Louis
- Cheeses at Fromagerie Sanders
- Pastries at Carette
- Chocolate at Pierre Hermé
- Crepes at La Crêperie de Josselin
- Caviar at Le Maison du Caviar or Caviar Kaspia
- Breakfast at Café de Flore or Les Deux Magots
- Dinner at Guy Martin's Le Grand Véfour

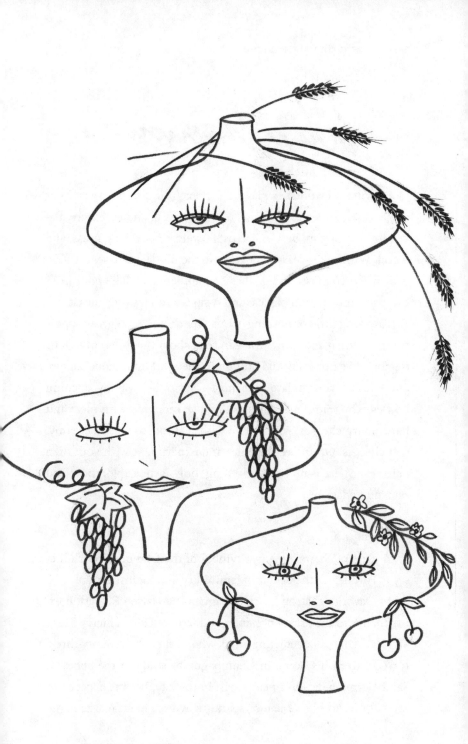

Wine memories

Good wine is a world in a glass. The French *vin* vocabulary is about elegance and finesse, perfume, textures of silk and cashmere, flavors of spice, plum, berries, citrus, flowers, nuts, honey, grass, and wood. Wine takes years to develop in the bottle, but it's worth the wait when you taste the quality and authenticity. The pour is an exquisite anticipation of pleasure. A sip is a full journey into it.

Knowing little or nothing about French wine is a great opportunity to learn and grow. You can read about the different *terroirs* (regions) like Bordeaux and Burgundy, the Loire and Rhône valleys, and educate your palate in a most pleasurable way by opening bottles. The traditional rules are simple: red wine with meat and hard, sharp cheeses; white wine with seafood, fowl, and creamy, soft cheeses. Or ignore the rules and experiment with your own pairings. There is no right or wrong, only taste, exploration, and recommendations.

Champagne

A glass of champagne is a symbol of the fabulous French lifestyle. For me, it's the nectar of femininity and sophistication.

My favorite château for champagne is **La Maison Ruinart**. It exists thanks to the prescience and good taste of Dom Thierry Ruinart (1657–1709), a Benedictine monk who, at the age of twenty-three, traveled from his home in Champagne to study in the abbey at Saint-Germain-des-Prés near Paris. In the city, he was exposed to art, culture, and *vin de mousse,* sparkling wine, a new favorite in the court of Louis XV. Dom Thierry came home to visit his family at their vineyards and told them about this new wine with bubbles. They started making their own. Eventually, Dom Thierry's nephew Nicolas founded Maison Ruinart in 1729, the first established château of Champagne. The first year, they produced 170 bottles. By 1761, they were making 36,000. In 1768, Claude Ruinart bought eight kilometers of an underground chalk quarry in nearby Reims and turned it into a cave to age and store bottles. During World War I, the *crayères* were flooded. During World War II, they were raided by Nazis. But they are still used today, and they look just like they did hundreds of years ago. You can take a tour, descending thirty-eight meters down white stone steps into tunnels burrowed in white chalk, a labyrinth of cool caves lined with thousands of bottles of champagne.

Ruinart Blanc de Blanc is for lovers. The gold luminous sparkles taste like almonds or freshly baked brioche with a bit of honey. A sip puts you instantly into seduction mode. The texture is like velvet in the mouth, soft and rich, an invitation like a woman crossing her legs. Toasting champagne with your *amoureux* is a sensual celebration. Each bubble is a world of fantasy.

Vin Blanc

I associate white wine, especially **Montrachet**, with ancient traditions. Many of the Montrachet wines date back to medieval times. The Château de Chassagne-Montrachet in Beaune was originally constructed in the eleventh century. The grapes are thought to have been planted in the ninth century. The ambience of the grounds, the vineyards, the wineries, the castle itself, and the cellars exude Old World charm and are an oasis of tranquility. You can walk among the rose gardens and rows of grapevines or tour owner Michel Picard's ancient stonewall cellar, which houses one thousand barrels of wine. In the tasting room, stand at upturned wooden barrels, and sample a section of Burgundy wines and ripe cheeses to go with them.

White wine is for drinking, and eating. When I open a bottle of ten-year-old **Chassagne-Montrachet** or **Puligny-Montrachet**, I always pair it with certain flavors: the September harvest of fresh game birds, *blanquette de veau* (a rich veal stew), or Brie and Camembert. I associate Montrachet with tastes of autumn, cool nights, cold wine, and warm, rich food.

Vin Rouge

Opening a bottle of red wine from Bordeaux means one thing: a family celebration around a large table. For such an important night, you need a great wine. I have a deep appreciation for **Château Cheval Blanc**, House of the White Horse. The winery itself is a marvel designed by architect Christian de Portzamparc, and looks from the outside like a modern art museum. Two enormous white concrete wave-shaped walls rise from the landscape like the bones of a whale out of a green sea. The view from the roof overlooks the romantic 1871 country house and endless expanse of vineyards. Inside, the winery is clean and modern, with fifty-two teardrop-shaped white concrete vats and shining silver spouts, and a barrel room of white concrete columns instead of old stone arches. Everything about it says "modern," but the grapevines are centuries old. New and old creates a unique, special blend.

Château Cheval Blanc is a smooth, velvety combination of exotic flavors, spice, smoke, and cherries. As rich as it is, it's also light and fresh. A bottle from 1947 has been called the best wine ever made (a bottle sold at Christie's for over $300,000), but any vintage since 2009 will be excellent. When my family—in Grenoble or New York—is celebrating a birthday, anniversary, or any special night, we open a bottle of it. The *puissant,* deep flavor with a touch of prune is perfect with pheasant, duck, squab, or any hearty dish with the perfume of truffles.

Rosé

Nearly all the world's rosé is made in Provence. I will always associate pink wine with a summer party on the beach, joie de vivre, and the good life in Saint-Tropez. My two favorites are **Château Minuty** and **Bertaud Belieu.**

Entering Château Minuty is like driving into a dream: you discover white and pink peonies that line the driveway, a lovingly restored nineteenth-century three-story manor house with a sculptured façade, and a stone terrace that overlooks a garden of palm trees and hydrangeas, the scent of the sea in the air.

Three years ago, Oscar, then sixteen, came with me to Château Minuty to buy some rosé wine. We went down in the caves—where the wine is aged and stored—to the tasting room where several bottles were open and ready to be sampled. I said, "Oscar, you can try a little bit of wine to get an idea of which one you like best." Just as I was telling him this, a friend of mine arrived. We started talking about our vacation plans, food, wine, and before I knew it, half an hour had gone by. Then, behind my back, I heard the sound of a glass breaking. I spun around to see Oscar stumbling; he had dropped his glass on the tasting table. He said, "Mom, I was just trying the wine, like you told me."

There'd been fifteen bottles on the table.

"You're drunk!" I said. "You're not supposed to drink it all! Just a little sip!"

I had to take him home where he went directly to bed. I think it was his first experience getting a little drunk—with his mother in a wine cave. I'll always think of how hilarious he was when I open a bottle of **Minuty Prestige Rosé**. Its light and citrus notes, and intense floral aroma, velvet and fresh, are perfect for tucking your trashed son into bed on a summer day.

But my favorite is Bertaud Belieu's vineyard of rolling rows of grapes, which stretches out for dozens of acres in front of an old stone winery with impressive Grecian columns, Gothic buttresses, and high-arched dramatic green double doors. The adjacent buildings for pressing and barreling are beautiful examples of old-style Saint-Tropez garrison architecture with a certain Spanish flare: two-story structures, sandy, orange stone walls, terra-cotta shingled roofs, and small shuttered windows. The vineyard and winery are so romantic and cinematic, that Leonardo DiCaprio chose Domaine Bertaud Belieu for the location of his annual July fundraiser for his namesake foundation to sponsor climate change and ecological preservation projects in Saint-Tropez. It draws speakers and performers like Cate Blanchett, Marion Cotillard, Philippe Cousteau Jr., Penelope Cruz, Robert De Niro, Jonah Hill, Kate Hudson, Scarlett Johansson, Tobey Maguire, Edward Norton, Kevin Spacey, Charlize Theron, and many more.

If you aren't invited to Leo's bash, the second best time to visit Bertaud Belieu is mid-August to mid-September, the "cold harvest" season. In the middle of the night, when the air is cool and the grapes are bursting with freshness and flavor, growers cut the clusters by moonlight, placing them gently into baskets before bringing them into the winery to be destemmed and pressed. This process creates a brightness of color and flavor you can't find anywhere else in the world. **Bertaud Belieu Côtes de Provence Prestige**

Rosé is precious and delicate, like sunshine in a glass with strawberry notes—light, crisp, pink, and perfect.

The two estates are so close to the water, you can go there to buy a bottle and then take it to the beach with you. As soon as I arrive in the south of France each July, I stop at a château and buy a few cases for the season. We celebrate summer every day with a glass of rosé.

Louis XIII Cognac experience

In the summer of 2016 in Saint-Tropez, I went by chance to have my first Louis XIII Rémy Martin Cognac tasting experience. The beverage from the region of Cognac is made with grapes that are fermented for five days, distilled, and aged in oak casks for long periods. Louis XIII cognac is aged for a hundred years; it's a blend of twelve hundred eaux-de-vie preserved in a baccarat crystal. A bottle costs four thousand dollars.

At a friend's house, I was offered a crystal glass with the precious nectar by a handsome blond gentleman named Ludovic du Plessis, the executive director of the brand.

From a distance, the aroma was delicate with jasmine and flowers, but up close, I got prune and fig, even honey. I didn't know how to savor it properly, and asked for some advice. He looked me in the eye and said with a sensual voice, "You should put a few drops on your lips first, feel all the aroma, and then taste a little bit on your mouth."

The advice made me a little uncomfortable, and I asked, "Should we dim the lights first?"

We all smiled, and then tried the cognac. The experience of drinking the rich, dark-amber brandy was unique, unforgettable. The delicious taste in my mouth lasted for an hour, time I spent in a very enlightening conversation.

Recently, I realized that in Rihanna's 2015 song "Bitch Better Have My Money," she refers to Louis XIII! The cognac brand made a film with John Malkovich and Robert Rodriguez called *100 Years*, which was then put into a time capsule, not to be opened or seen until 2115. My host for the tasting, Ludovic, initiated this brilliant, so very French, idea.

Unique restaurant adventures

Only in Paris . . .

In a private area where the server knocks on the door before entering. **Lapérouse** (6th arrondissement) dates back to 1766, and the décor takes you back to that pre-Revolutionary baroque splendor of the gilded age of kings and queens. The storied restaurant has many private salons for a cozy dinner without interruption, unless you permit it.

In a medieval chapel. The main room at **La Table des Gourmets** (4th arrondissement) is the first floor of a twelfth-century chapel, with dramatic arched ceilings, long tables, seductive candlelight reflecting on the stone walls, and a reverent ambience. Dining in a nine-hundred-year-old church, in the center of Paris, is a religious experience.

At a salon dating back to the eighteenth century. 1728 (8th arrondissement) was built in that year as a hotel, and it's been restored to its original, opulent glory as a modern restaurant. You can dine in several salons, all romantic with Renaissance art covering the gilded walls, red and purple velvet chairs, and intimate tables for two with a harp melody.

In the middle of a flea market. Marché aux Puces de Saint-Ouen (18th arrondissement) is a sprawling antiques/flea market with a maze of stalls selling just about everything—furniture, clothes, hardware, statues, paintings, and so much more. Take a break from browsing at **Ma Cocotte**, a Philippe Starck open-kitchen modern restaurant that offers a refreshing change of pace from the hectic markets, but my favorite bistro at the flea market is **Le Péricole**. Its walls are covered with hundreds of posters of the front pages from *Paris Match*. Sophie Marceau once ate right next to me and under the cover with her picture on it.

"A day without laughter is a day wasted"

charlie Chaplin

Joie *de vivre* means "joy of living." It's about catching moments of pleasure that change your day. You don't need money or success or to be in any particular place to feel it. **Joie de vivre is opening your eyes to the magic of small things.** It's accessible and effortless. This might be the widest culture divide between America and France: Americans believe that accomplishment leads to happiness. The French believe that happiness *is* the accomplishment. Every day is an opportunity to embrace the wonder and joy of being alive. Joie de vivre is like being blind and then suddenly seeing the world for the first time, every time, and it takes only a few seconds to appreciate the green leaves moving in the wind, or clouds running across the sky. What kills the joy of life is habit. Freshness, discovering the world anew every day, keeps you young and joyful.

Rise and Shine

Every spring and summer morning, I look outside my window onto Riverside Drive on the Upper West Side to check in with the peregrine falcons that live at eye level in a tree across the street, one of only sixteen nesting pairs in the entire city. Seeing them out my window adds a thrill of romance and poetry in my life. In late February, I start looking out for their return to New York and, when I spot them for the first time each year, it's like seeing old, dear friends after too long apart.

Ride in Style

If you use an adventurous way to travel through the day—even if it's just from home to work and back home again or on weekend promenades—it can be an exciting new way to interact with the world that will bring you joy.

- **By blade.** Rollerblades become popular when I first arrived in Manhattan in 1997, and I started skating all over the city with my headphones on, my hair loose and streaming behind me, feeling free. (No, I didn't wear a helmet; it would have ruined my loose hair style.) For a few minutes, I felt like I was Heather Graham skating through life in 1997's *Boogie Nights* by Paul Thomas Anderson.
- **By boat.** I did take the water taxi in summertime to get around New York instead of a regular yellow cab or Uber. I ride on the upper deck, the wind in my face, stopping at different piers to discover a fresh perspective of Manhattan from the river. And soon, we'll have Uber-boat!

- **By bicycle.** I'm always superhappy and energized by discovering New York on a bicycle, whether it's pedaling
though the busy streets of the Lower East Side or on a
marathon ride along the Hudson River from the George
Washington Bridge to the Brooklyn Bridge with music in
my ears, my favorite exercise.
- **By vintage car.** I used to drive a 1989 Aston Martin convertible, La Volante, a James Bond model. Sliding into
the ivory leather seat of my cognac vintage car transported me to the glamorous era. I drove it more than ten
years in the streets of New York. I always remember the
moment in Southampton when my companion and I were
assisting at an auction of antique cars. After I declared my
love for the Aston Martin, my partner raised his hand and,
a few hours later, gave me the keys to my dream car. I
used it many summers for the ride from Manhattan to
East Hampton, where I had a boutique on Newtown Lane.
When I'm in Saint-Tropez, I drive my first car, a well-cared-
for 1985 Mini Cooper that I bought in my twenties with
my summer savings. While I'm in the village in the summer, I love going to the beach with my little Mini.

Petal Power

Bringing home a bouquet is a sweet moment of poetry. Even
sweeter is when a bouquet arrives unexpectedly for you. At my
apartment, I prefer white roses and stalks of iris, named after the

Goddess of Rainbows, with blue, purple, and lavender hues which evoke elegance and royalty, or in the country meadow, the white daisy with its open friendly face and yellow heart is my favorite. I love the perfume of jasmine, Persian for "a gift from God," a star-shaped flower that only opens at dark; it has a soulful, sweet, bewitching fragrance that enchants your night.

I have a special affection for **le muguet, lily of the valley.** The delicate white bellflower is part of a French ritual that I've loved since childhood. The first day of May, the French version of Labor Day, is called La Fête du Travail, and it's a work holiday. It's also La Fête du Muguet, a day to give lily of the valley sprigs to the people you love to wish them good luck and a joyous year. The tradition began in 1561 when King Charles IX gave them to the ladies of his court to celebrate the coming of spring. For many years on the first of May, early in the morning, my parents, three sisters, and I, dressed in raincoats and rain boots, walked in the woods on a treasure hunt to find the lucky sprigs, only just emerged. May first is the only day of the year when it's legal throughout France to sell flowers on the street without a permit in order to honor this ancient tradition, and you'll find lily of the valley at every street corner.

When May first came around my first year in New York, I thought I'd share the tradition with my American friends and offer them the precious sprig of white bells, but I couldn't find lily of the valley anywhere. I was devastated. May Day without *le muguet* made me so homesick. I have since found a French florist in New York (L'Olivier Floral Atelier) that delivers a bunch of my *porte bonheur,* my lucky charm, to me each year on May first. With lily of the valley, I remember my family roots and cultural tradition and celebrate the coming of spring. For a delicate perfume with this scent, I recommend Diorissimo by Dior and the Lily of the Valley Diptyque candle.

The white **Casablanca lily** is the flower of Saint-Tropez, and as soon as I arrive each summer, I go to *place des lice* for the Saturday village market and take home a big bunch in my arms. A single stalk has five or six flowers, each the size of a hand, with a *suave* and captivating scent. When I get home, I put my treasures in vases around the house, and it quickly fills with the *parfum* of Saint-Tropez. If you want to keep the joy with you, I recommend the perfume Lys Mediterranee by Frederic Malle and Un Lys by Serge Lutens.

I also admire the erotic power of the **calla lily** shape. The flower was a favorite subject of Robert Mapplethorpe, who highlighted the fleshy stem, white sheath, and erect spike called a spadix (pronounced spay-*dicks*) in classic photographs. Guy Bourdin explored a similar theme in a bold photograph with posing nude women with anthurium flowers between their legs, fleshy red sheaths, and a prominent pink spadix.

The Power of Yellow

Yellow is the color of joy. Catch glimmers of gold to brighten your life.

- **A sunny day.** Open yourself to the bright yellow sun in a cloudless sky.
- **A fresh egg.** Next year, in Saint-Tropez, I'm going to get a hen. Forget an Hermès bag. Going to the coop and eating a fresh egg every morning, still warm, is what I call luxury.
- **Butter.** The most important ingredient in French cuisine. Just picture a dollop of butter melting on a piece of golden toast, and you feel warm and cozy inside.

- **Baby ducks.** I was twenty-four when I bought four fluffy baby ducks at the Quai de la Mégisserie—a charming flower and pet market in the middle of Paris—put them in boxes with a bow, and went around to my best friends to give them as Easter gifts. Seeing the look on my friends' faces when they opened the box was a moment of pure joy. I kept one for myself. The duck lived with me in my studio for four months, until it become a young handsome duck, and then I took him by train to Grenoble and gave him to my mother.
- **A bright yellow dress.** I understand. It's difficult to wear. The color looks best on dark or tan skin, like the beautiful model Alek Wek in a yellow dress in the 2013 Pirelli Calendar. I designed a sparkled slip dress with a yellow wave motif for Rihanna in 2008 and she rocked it.
- **Sunflowers.** At the end of summer, the long drive from Manhattan to Easthampton, Long Island, is rewarded with an incredible sight: fields of sunflowers appear on either side of the highway, stretching for acres with thousands of happy flower faces. Sunflowers capture the sun and brighten your life. On my way back to the city, I always stop at a farm stand to take a big bouquet of *tournesol* home with me.
- **Mimosas.** Every February, mimosas, the tiny golden pom-poms, burst into bloom on trees in Provence, growing wild in such tremendous quantities that they fill the mountain air with a delicate, fluffy scent. La Route du Mimosa, or the Mimosa Trail, is an eighty-mile route through villages in Provence that celebrate the new blooms every February and March with festivals and parades. At the end of the trail is the village of Grasse, home to a large *parfumerie* where the flowers are turned into a unique perfume, Les Fleurs de Provence Mimosa by Molinard. I also recommend Amarige from Givenchy and the delightful Mimosa candle by Diptyque.
- **American mimosas.** A cocktail of orange juice and champagne. Joy in a flute.

Cocorico!

Americans seem to get tremendous joy from their dogs and cats. Karl Lagerfeld, too, is devoted to his cat Choupette, an all-white lady with her own Twitter account and two nannies. I don't have an animal in my life right now, but I have sweet memories of a vacation three years ago in Saint-Tropez when I did.

I was doing a lot of gardening that summer. I needed to get back in touch with nature by playing in the dirt. It's always been one of my joys, waking early to dig and plant and watch new flowers bud and bloom. Put in patience and effort, and, in return, you're rewarded with organic beauty.

While in the garden, I listened to the music of nature, the singing of the birds, and dreamed about how wonderful it would be to wake up with the *chant du coq*, the call of a rooster, like farmers do in the countryside. The "cocorico" (in America, it's "cock-a-doodle-do") would signal the beginning of a joyful new morning with an authentic country *réveil*.

Soon after, I was at the *marché du village* and, as I was wandering to find fresh eggs, completely by chance, I met a farmer and heard the song of a rooster, a real beauty, pure white, plump and tall, with a bright red comb and a proud *panache*. It was love at first sight and I bought the *coq* immediately. The farmer and I put him in a box and loaded him into my vintage Mini Cooper for the quick ride home.

I called him Rico (short for "cocorico") and built a coop for him in the garden myself. Whenever I was out there, he would look at me and plump up his white chest, sing his chant, and stand fierce.

My original lover was trying to impress me and get my attention. I found myself sneaking off to visit with him at all hours and expected a sign of recognition. The *coq* made me feel sexy.

My neighbors and family were not as enchanted by Rico as I was. He began singing at 4:00 A.M. I forgot that this was the glamorous village of Saint-Tropez. Most people were on vacation; they stayed up late at night at the bars and restaurants and wanted to sleep all day. Neighbors started to come to my house to ask, "Do you have a *rooster?*" I had no idea how far Rico's chant carried, and people from across town would give me angry looks.

It was a love-hate situation for them, but from my perspective, it was all love. Even if I stayed out very late, I was charmed to hear my lover's call at sunrise. Oscar was on the hate side. I'd built Rico's coop in the *pétanque* (bocce) court, and Oscar couldn't play, which set off some family controversy.

One night toward the end of summer, Rico escaped. I didn't realize roosters could fly. I realized that, with an excess of confidence and empowered by our relationship, he was able to jump over the fence to join me. But now that he was liberated, he had no intention of returning to the coop. We chased him around the yard, but he was too fast. When night came and Patrick and his family arrived for dinner, we put a strategy together to use white bath towels to try to capture him, but Rico evaded our efforts and, after he'd had enough of running away from us, he flew onto the roof. My friends and I ate outside so we could watch him up there, and we had a fantastic night of teasing him. He looked down at us as we laughed and drank wine by candles and garden lights.

After midnight, my guests left, and Rico wouldn't come down. I had no choice but to leave him up there. I went to bed and was woken by howling at 3:00 A.M. I threw open the blue wood shutters and looked outside. The garden lights were still on so I could see the horror: a fox had captured Rico and held him in its mouth! I ran outside to rescue him.

His wing was bloody and his *panache* was destroyed, white feathers flying into the night. When I gathered his body in my arms, his little head fell limp to the side. I held him close and stroked him, in tears. And then, all of a sudden, by pure miracle, Rico lifted his head. He was still alive! I later learned that roosters are prone to heart attacks. My holding him and rubbing him were like rooster CPR.

I saved his life and we enjoyed the rest of the summer together. I felt miserable about leaving him when we returned to New York, but I found a home for him. I gave him back to the farmer who sold him to me in the first place and promised to take Rico back next year. But it wasn't to be. Over the winter, I got a note from the farmer that Rico had been attacked by a wild dog and passed away. I'm thankful for all the joie de vivre Rico brought me on those summer days.

"Joy comes to us in moments, often ordinary moments. sometimes we miss out on the bursts of joy because we are too busy chasing down extraordinary moments"

Brené Brown

Simple pleasures

The best moments of joie de vivre are unexpected, when you relax and let life unfold. If you are always rushing, the opportunity for

joy can pass you by and disappear. On a lazy weekend, slow down for the joy of playing a game and eating outside.

- **Pastis et Pétanque.** On the Riviera in the summertime, the French play a game called *pétanque*. The rules couldn't be simpler: Throw a little wood ball called a *cochonnet* down a hard surface, and take turns rolling larger *boules* at it. The team with the closest ball to the *cochonnet* wins. Players knock opposing teams' *boules* out, which is frustrating or exciting. Anyone of any age can play; teams might have multiple generations. The adult players cool off with a drink called *le pastis,* a healthy splash of anise (a yellow licorice-flavored aperitif) mixed with water. On a sizzling summer day, a drink of *pastis* is refreshing, light, and gives you a little sparkle. I can't say that it improves the quality of one's *pétanque* technique, but who cares? In Brooklyn, right outside of Bar Tabac, several blocks of Smith Street are closed off on Bastille Day (July 14) for a *pétanque* tournament. The celebration is competitive and the New York teams play by the rules. The French play for victory, too, but they will not compromise on having their *pastis* drinks. No matter how you play it, the game is pure entertainment and everyone wins.

- **Le Picnic.** A picnic is rustic romance, a happy celebration of food and life. The French make it simply elegant with a red-and-white tablecloth to lie on, a full wicker basket with a fresh baguette, cheese, fruit, dried sausage, chocolate, fabric napkins, real plates and glasses, and, of course, a bottle of rosé to cheer the beautiful day. In New York, I enjoyed Sunday picnics in Central Park. Framed by the skyscrapers, we used to sit on the great lawn among the Frisbee players, sunbathers, people doing yoga, and families with kids running around. Oscar used to go off to play basketball, and on summer weekends, we watched the Rollerbladers boogie dancing to a DJ mixing old-school beats. Central Park is the lungs of the city and brings happiness to all New Yorkers.

My favorite restaurant

Sitting outside at a café terrace is always a moment of simple pleasure, whether with friends or alone to observe the world. In Paris, it's always the season, heated in fall and under shades in summer—café terraces are everywhere on every street corner. In Manhattan, terraces are not so easy to find, but I have my favorite bistros where almost everyone speaks French, eats French food, and drinks French wine.

Paris Terraces

Mini Palais. In the heart of the Triangle d'Or, the hidden terrace on the first-floor balcony with the imperial column offers a poetic view of the Pont Alexandre III. It's a secret rendezvous for lunch or a romantic gourmet tea with fresh pastries.

Monsieur Bleu. Located at the Palais de Tokyo at a bend in the Seine, the chic Monsieur Bleu has an unrivaled view of the Eiffel Tower in a lively and intimate setting. The menu is original and surprising. I love the salad with tomatoes and strawberries.

Chez Francis. You can almost grab the Eiffel Tower in your hands from the terrace of this lively, elegant restaurant. Inside, the walls, chairs, glasses, and bar are a deep red, lit with golden light, creating a seductive, dramatic atmosphere.

Café Marly. Located in the arcades of the Richelieu wing of the Louvre, you can see the great pyramid by

I. M. Pei—or not, when the installation of the artist/ magician JR who made it disappear. The sumptuous décor designed by Yves Taralon and Olivier Gagnere transports you to the Louvre's past as a royal residence. Enjoy the foie gras for two.

Loulou. As an alternative to Café Marly, try Loulou, located nearby inside the Musée Les Arts Décoratifs with views of the Louvre and the Tuilleries gardens. It's a wonderful place to have lunch after saying hello to the great lady of Paris, Mona Lisa.

Le Comptoir. An authentic and charming French bistro with simple and tasty traditional recipes.

Carette. A patisserie overlooking the Place du Trocadéro makes some of the best hot chocolate in Paris.

L'Oiseau Blanc. The restaurant sits on the rooftop of the Peninsula Hotel, and, with its glass walls and ceiling (in winter) or open-air seating (in summer), it gives diners an unobstructed 360-degree view of all of Paris's landmarks. The food by Alsatian chef Sydney Redel is great, but the view is the star, especially at night when the City of Light dazzles.

New York Bistros

Félix in Soho for the *lapin à la moutarde* and the *rognons* by chef Pierre Landet from Toulouse, and the summertime ambience and inviting terrace on West Broadway for the Europeans and World Cup football games.

Mamo in Soho, originally coming from Antibes, offers delicious Provençal-Italian recipes with a generous touch of sliced truffle.

Lucien in the East Village. With a traditional flair, the kitchen prepares grilled sardines Saint-Tropez style and the perfect Marseille-style bouillabaisse (fish soup with *rouille* and Gruyère) in a friendly ambience.

Le Coucou's chef Daniel Rose presents "a tribute to classic French techniques and dishes" in a refined and very charming setting. My favorites are the *tout le lapin* ("all of the rabbit") and the lavish *mousse au chocolat*.

Mimi in Greenwich Village. Louis Levy, son of the writer Marc Levy, opened this French restaurant with friends. It has a retro décor. The American chef offers simple but original cuisine with *poulet à la moutarde* and a *baba au rhum* for dessert.

Le Bilboquet on the Upper East Side. Philippe Delgrange greets you for a festive, fun, and delicious French meal that could finish with a laugh and a dance. It's famous for the Cajun chicken and a great side of sautéed mushrooms.

Balthazar in Soho with its traditional *steak frites* and bakery.

And don't forget the French signatures in New York: Le Bernadin, Le Grenouille, Daniel, and Jean-Georges.

things that give me joy

1. Good news.
2. An unexpected message or letter from an old friend.
3. A secret glance from across the room.
4. The seduction game.
5. The sound of birds.
6. A beautiful décolleté.
7. My son walking through the door.
8. A friend whispering something scandalous in my ear.
9. My lover reaching for my hand.
10. Flowers.

joy of gifting

We all know people who are excellent gift buyers. They always seem to know exactly what a person needs and wants for Christmas or a birthday. When I've been able to come up with the perfect gift, the joy it brings to the receiver is equaled by my own. It feels sublime to gift well.

I had one of those moments one November. I was talking to my mother on the phone before I went home to Grenoble for Christmas, and she sounded a little sad. She's usually a joyful person, but something in her voice was flat, lacking sparkle. She said it was because I lived so far away and that she missed me. I tried to think of the perfect Christmas gift for her that would lift her out of her *tristesse*.

On Christmas Eve, I finally thought of what to give her, something that always gave me joy: a songbird. I ran out into Grenoble to find a yellow canary. I had to go to a few pet shops until I found a bright yellow bird and, while walking by an antique boutique in the same neighborhood, I found a white retro birdcage in the window for him. I wrapped a big red velvet bow around my canary's new home.

The whole family was in joy when they saw the canary. We called him Noel. My mother was so touched by the present that she had tears in her eyes. I couldn't have given her a better gift.

The canary has changed my parents' everyday life. Now, when we speak on the phone, I hear Noel singing in the background. The idea wasn't so costly, but it became priceless in my mother's heart and brought an additional touch of joie de vivre to the family.

Laugh

Laughing lowers your blood pressure and fills your heart with happiness and lights up your face. Nothing makes me laugh more than:

Le Gendarme

Laughter is one of the most vital pleasures of life. My parents' generation grew up watching and loving Jerry Lewis movies. My generation grew up with Louis de Funès, France's leading comic actor. He made a series of movies about Le Gendarme, the policeman, who gets into sticky scrapes in different moments and locations—*The Gendarme in New York, The Gendarme Gets Married,* and, my favorite, *Le Gendarme en Saint-Tropez.* What made these movies so much fun was his prickly, rude, cranky, hyperactive affect, his hilarious body language (he was a petite man, only five four and often paired with much taller foils), and his theatrical, crazy facial expressions. He passed a few years ago, but I still watch his movies. Two can't be missed: *The Mad Adventures of Rabbi Jacob* (1973), directed by Gérard Oury, is about a racist French businessman, played by de Funès, who's mistaken for a rabbi while fleeing from Arabs. *The Sucker* (1965), also directed by Gérard Oury, is about a gangster who picks up an unsuspecting rube played by André Bourvil to drive his Cadillac with a trunk full of stolen jewels and drugs throughout Italy.

Gad Elmaleh, the French Jerry Seinfeld

Today, the heir of Louis de Funès is certainly Gad Elmaleh, a French Moroccan comedian who brought American-style standup comedy to Paris. He's often been called the Jerry Seinfeld of France. They look alike, they have the same observational sense of humor, and Elmaleh did the French voiceover for Seinfeld's part in *Bee Movie.* They talk about the difference between French and American comedy in a charming episode of *Comedians in Cars Getting Coffee* while driving around in a Citroën. Elmaleh sells out stadiums in France, and he's recently moved to New York to live in Tribeca and perform at Joe's Pub for a small room of two hundred people. Recently, he was acclaimed at Carnegie Hall in New York with his show *Oh My Gad* which is irresistible.

the singing Madman

There's a reason for the phrase "mood music." Melody infiltrates your mind and changes your attitude. Singing a happy tune turns a long car ride into an adventure, a shower into an imaginary rock concert, a day of chores around the house into a dance party.

A legend in France for singing happy songs is Charles Trenet. The biggest singer of the 1950s, he was known as Le Fou Chantant (the Singing Madman) for his ebullient over-the-top style. Some of his French contemporaries like Maurice Chevalier considered him to be the ultimate French singer, a genius at combining poetry with catchy tunes, all of which he wrote himself. Americans know his song "Beyond the Sea," covered by Bobby Darin and others. He sang about happiness and love even though he didn't always have a joyful life. He was persecuted by the Nazis on suspicion of being Jewish, and spent a month in prison in 1963, essentially for being gay. Regardless of his struggles, his message was pure joie de vivre: happiness is simple and accessible to everyone if you just look for it. His classic song "Y'a D'la Joie" ("There's a Joy") is part of the French cultural legacy. Today, the singer Mika reinterprets the old Charles Trenet song "Je Chante," which has become a hit in France and set toes tapping again.

"There's a Joy" by Charles Trenet

There's a joy, hello hello swallows
There's a joy in the sky above the roof
There's a joy and sunshine in the streets

There's joy everywhere, from there, to the joy
All day my heart beats, capsized and staggers
It is love that comes with whatever
It is love, hello, hello ladies
There's joy everywhere, there's a joy

Paris Canaille

Titi Parisienne

The phrase *titi Parisienne* doesn't have a translation in English because *les titi*—street kids, *les gamin*, *les bohèmes* (without the consumption)—are unique to Paris and unique in their attitude, style, and pursuit of joy. The archetypal example for boys is

294 • Catherine Malandrino

Gavroche from Victor Hugo's *Les Misérables,* the urchin in the beret, white shirt, baggy trousers, suspenders, and ankle boots. For girls, Audrey Tautou in 2001's *Amélie* by Jean-Pierre Jeunet captured the free spirit and quirkiness of the piquante *titi Parisienne* with her cropped bangs, mischievous smile, colorful knits, and high-top sneakers.

The Look: A beret, a *marinière* top, men's trousers or a pleated skirt with tights, a button-down cardigan, ballerina flats, and a red lip.

The Life: Devoted to fun and happiness. They carry themselves with bounce, sparkle, and a brightness that the French call *pimpante.* They don't care about money or success. All they need is a job to pay the bills (like Amélie's waitress gig), canvases for painting, a bike to spin around the city, and weekends for dancing on an *accordéon.*

Where to find them: In the neighborhoods of Montmartre, Bastille, and Canal Saint-Martin, and at *les guinguettes,* outdoor taverns/dance halls along the Seine and the Marne. Pierre-Auguste Renoir painted a series inspired by the joyful atmosphere of eating, drinking, and pirouetting to accordion music with friends at these riverside havens, including *La Guinguette au Pied de la Tour Eiffel* and *Le Déjeuner des Canotiers* (*Luncheon of the Boating Party*). *Guinguettes* are as popular as ever, and well worth a visit. My spring recommendations:

1. **Chez Gegene** in Joinville-le-Pont on the Marne. Classic and so French, down to the checkered tablecloths, terrace tables and red geraniums, frescos of dancers and toque-wearing chefs, carousel lights, mussels in broth with *frites,* and waltzing to accordions (and bagpipes).

2. **Le Chalet des Îles** on an island in Lac Inférieur in the Bois de Boulogne. You have to take a short ferry ride to get to the Swiss chalet with beautiful lake views and a décor that will remind you of country clubs and hunting lodges, but a chic *guinguette* version. On a Sunday, they have a great buffet brunch. Accordion music plays during the daytime, and, on hot summer nights, a DJ spins until 5:00 A.M. at the outside dance floor.

3. **La Guinguette de Neuilly,** on Île de la Jatte on the Seine. The authentic French postcard with red awnings, wicker chairs at café tables, checkered tablecloths, string lights, white lace curtains on the four-paned windows, garden terraces with views of trees and the river, a classic bistro menu with a good *steak frites,* and an outdoor dance floor that beckons.

4. **La Guinguette de la Tour Eiffel,** Quai de Suffren on the Seine. Not the same seaside idyll that Renoir captured in 1880, the *guinguette* in 2017 is quaint during the day, and a nightclub with a DJ after dark. People party, dance, and drink with the light of the Eiffel Tower sparkling above.

'Every child is an artist.
The problem is how to remain
an 'artist once he grows up'
                    Pablo Picasso

Taste the Joy

Foods and drinks that remind me of joyful times from childhood.

- **Caramels.** When the French say "bonbons," they mean a square of caramel that sticks to your teeth like glue. I keep a bowl of bonbons on my desk, just in case I need a petite dose of sticky joie de vivre.
- **Nutella.** My mother would make my sisters and me a *tartine* of Nutella every day when we got home from school. I tried to keep up the tradition with Oscar. Even though he's on his own, I always have some Nutella in the pantry to keep happiness at home.
- *Vache qui rit.* Laughing Cow cheese comes in little triangles with a picture of a red, giggling cow on the wrapper. In France, parents give the wedges to children like string cheese in America. If I happen upon a piece, I laugh (along with the cow).
- *Diabolo menthe.* A mixture of mint syrup and sparkling water was my favorite drink as a child. It's the French version of Sprite. I like to have a bottle of mint syrup at home to treat myself with a *diabolo menthe* when the mood strikes. I feel like a kid again, like in 1977's *Diabolo Menthe* (*Peppermint Soda*), a cult movie for teenagers directed by Diane Kuyrs.

Take it easy

The oldest person to have ever lived was a Frenchwoman named Jeanne Calment. She was born in 1875 and died 122 years later in 1997. She met Vincent van Gogh in Arles, her hometown, when she was

Paris est une fête

thirteen (apparently, she found him ugly and obnoxious). Demographer and gerontologist Jean-Marie Robine, who coauthored *Jeanne Calment: From Van Gogh's Time to Ours: 122 Extraordinary Years,* a book about her life, noted some of the possible reasons for her longevity.

- She drank port wine every night.
- She ate two pounds of chocolate a week.
- She smoked two cigarettes a day until the age of 117.
- She was active throughout her life until she had a fall at 115, walking, biking, playing tennis, fencing, roller-skating, and swimming.

- She cultivated her creativity, playing piano and listening to opera.
- Most importantly, Calment was light about life. Robine described her to *The New York Times* in 1997 as unflappable. "I think she was someone who, constitutionally and biologically speaking, was immune to stress. She once said, 'If you can't do anything about it, don't worry about it,'" he said.

It all adds up to one thing: joie de vivre.

I thought of Calment and her way of surfing through life's situations when one day I came home from a business trip around 11:00 P.M. and was greeted at the door by Oscar's father. He asked me about my flight and then he said, "We have a little problem. Oscar in is jail."

I said, "Oh?"

"He jumped the subway turnstile, and had no ID on him. They put him in handcuffs and arrested him."

It was Oscar's nineteenth birthday, and he was spending the night at the police station.

We sent a copy of his ID, had a conversation with the policeman, and had a glass of wine.

"He's nineteen. It's his first time in jail. Let him deal with it," we said. We toasted our son's birthday.

I told this story to some New York friends, and they couldn't believe how lightly I took the news. They would have stormed the police station with a team of lawyers, apparently.

When there is a little drama in everyday life, I try to surf on it. I take the waves and don't try to control them. Of course, sometimes, life is serious and you have to kick harder to swim to the surface. But not always. You don't need to go deep into intensity and stress over every single thing. Otherwise, life could become miserable. If you are effortless and light, you can see the humor in most sticky situations. After a sip of wine, Oscar's plight struck me as pretty funny.

When he came home at 4:00 A.M., he woke me up and said, "Mommy, I'm out of jail."

I said, "Oh, good. Happy birthday, *chéri.* Tomorrow, we'll speak about your experience." And after all, we did laugh together about it. By the way, Oscar had to go to court and did community service, but he swears he will never jump the turnstile again (until he does).

Jeanne Calment had to surf through much bigger waves than this. Her husband died from food poisoning in his sixties. Her daughter Yvonne died at thirty-six of pneumonia, leaving Calment to raise her grandson Joseph, who also died at thirty-six in a car accident. She surfed through her heartaches and her long life with a lively sense of humor. One of her famous jokes was "I've never had but one wrinkle, and I'm sitting on it."

House of Joy

The Fondation Maeght in Saint-Paul-de-Vence is an invitation to an artistic promenade. One of Europe's greatest art museums, the Fondation buildings are modern avant-garde fantasies with inverted domes as rooftops, turning your imagination upside down from the outside. Inside are impressive masterpieces by Bonnard, Braque, Chagall, Kandinsky, Leger, Miró. Playful surprises abound: a mosaic by Pierre Tal-Coat built into an outside wall, one by Chagall in the bookshop, stained-glass windows designed by Braque and Raoul Ubac in the chapel.

You are welcomed into the garden by Giacometti's gigantic black silhouette sculptures called *L'Homme Qui Marche* or "walking men," and then you meander among whimsical fountains and pools (one by Braque called *Les Poissons,* with mosaic fish at the bottom; another of green men that shoot water out of their eyes), and giant metal cats and owls staring at you. In the Miró Labyrinth, you walk through giant mobiles and dream creature sculptures—an egg, a lizard, a fork. You leave the Fondation with all the colors and perfumes of Provence and an art feast in your memory.

Joy to tears

Some of the highest points of emotion that I've experienced in my career is at the very end of a fashion show. It's the culmination of six months of working twelve-hour days and weekends, stress, and the laser concentration of creating a story from the small detail of embroidery to the big picture of a fashion show, and bringing it to life on the stage. When the last girl walks the runway, and you come out from behind the curtain to present yourself to the audience of press, buyers, and celebrities, the pressure is extreme and you feel fantastic relief and the satisfaction of achievement.

In 2000, I put on the Hallelujah! show at the Apollo Theater in Harlem. Along with the tension of not knowing if anyone would follow me uptown at church time on Sunday morning to see it, I wasn't sure if the models would be able to capture the mood I was going for. I'd cast twenty top girls—including Liya Kebede, Audrey Marnay, and Jacquetta Wheeler—and asked them to dance with abandon and happiness at the finale of the show to celebrate a hallelujah of joy. I didn't know if they'd let down their guard to do it as models are used to presenting an air of detachment on the runway.

When the time came for them to be together and dance, I pulled back the curtain, held my breath, and prayed. The twenty girls went onstage, led by the model Chrystèle Saint-Louis Augustin in a yellow bustier dress, dancing and exuding joy exactly as I'd envisioned it to be. All of the tension and anxiety dissolved in that moment and I walked onstage to join them. The audience was on their feet, smiling, applauding, sharing the ebullience. I felt the emotion building in me. The magic had taken over the theater and it brought tears to my eyes.

Another powerful moment of my career came after my 2006 show called Urban Queen. The look of the collection was inspired by Mary J. Blige's words and lyrics from her *Breakthrough* album. The clothes were Swarovski crystals, mink, embroidery on tulle, applications of leather and Chantilly lace. Each piece was a precious jewel, a labor of love. My team of artisans and I worked day and night for months to create such an elaborate collection.

The stage set had to be just as original and inspiring. Instead of a runway, I wanted to build a huge rotating platform. My vision was for the models to walk the periphery of the stage, and then step onto the platform in the center, strike a pose, and stay there for the rest of the show so that, by the end, all the girls would be

be able to admire the garments from all angles, and take in the
full scope of the collection. To do this, each girl would wear only
one look, which meant we'd have to hire forty models instead of
twenty. If we could pull it off, it would be remarkable.

We rented the Roseland Ballroom on West Fifty-seventh Street.
Production designer Jonathan Reed, who worked on all my shows,
created the rotating platform, which was a tall order. It had to turn
slowly and support forty girls. Roseland had a large enough stage,
and it also had a fabulous sound system—an absolute necessity for
Mary to appear and perform at the finale of the show.

The show came together. The top models we'd hired all looked
parfait on the platform and the clothes were beautifully made. We
were watching from behind the curtain when Mary came out at
the end. The plan was for her to just start singing, but she surprised
me by saying, "I want to present my best friend, you don't know
how much I love her, Catherine Malandrino!" She called me onto
the stage. I wasn't prepared for that. Mary started singing "Hate It
or Love It" and changed the lyrics to the song, working in my name
and my clothes. I wasn't expecting the declaration either.

The buildup of emotion—from creating the collection, the difficulties of the show, the music, Mary's introduction—overwhelmed
me. I glanced back and saw my partner and Mary's ex-husband Ken-
du's faces, with tears in the corners of their eyes. We all knew that
we'd achieved something unique together, and emotions were at
their highest point.

The selected audience of 450 guests felt the magic. Then fashion director of Barneys Simon Doonan congratulated me backstage and told me that Urban Queen was a fabulous collection
and one of the best fashion moments he'd ever experienced.

Typically, the joy after a fashion show lasts only for a short time, ten minutes, long enough to share it with my team. I go right to them to thank them for working so hard, to say "We did it!" and collapse into each other's arms. An hour later, you've already come down from the intense high and are overwhelmed again by conflicting emotions. You've worked so hard and expected so much. If you hear someone say "Congrats, it was great!" you can't help but think, *Really? I almost died, and it was just "great"?* Even if the audience seems to enjoy the show, their reaction can't meet your expectations. You start to worry about the reviews, whether the buyers loved the clothes, and if the orders will come as expected. Your emotions are rapidly changing, veering from one extreme to another, and you don't know what you feel anymore. Somehow, you have no time to recover from the intensity; you are already designing the next collection.

Months of hard work gets you a few minutes of extreme joy, but it's worth every second. Looking back over my twenty years as a designer, I loved all of my collections for the beauty, diversity, and pain that I lived through to create them. I'm so thankful I've been able to enjoy success this way.

When I gave birth to Oscar, I experienced intense pain and tears of joy, too. It's a miracle that our bodies are able to create life. For a mother, the joy of creation is the greatest reward.

" There is no
coincidence
Only
Mendez vous "

jian Cocteau

J'ai *deux amours,* like the song by Josephine Baker says: New York and Paris. For the last twenty years, I've created an imaginary bridge between these two worlds. By crossing it, I weave the cultures together and create a unique tapestry for my life. So far, with a wink, I've pointed out the differences between the French and American ways of life. I think it all comes down to . . .

Big dreams and small pleasures

A major cultural difference between my two countries is a matter of scale.

In France, they are all about *charme, mignon* (cute), and *petit* (tiny)—*petit ami, petit déjeuner, petit café.* Thinking small allows us to enjoy the simple pleasures of life. Sometimes, French people are so precious that they get caught up in the romance and charm of tiny things, and forget about the big picture.

American culture is all about dimension—bigger is better, "go big or go home," gigantic XXL boobs, asses, TVs, and brunch. Americans speak in superlatives. Everything is "great," "awesome," and "incredible." Even if you do nothing special for a friend, they say, "You're the best!" Having big dreams and big ideas *is* fabulous. However, living large might mean failing to appreciate *les petites choses de la vie,* the little things of life.

The best of both worlds is to dream big but also to be able to appreciate the magic of daily life.

American and French patriotism

Red, White, and Blue. French and American flags share the same colors, but the two cultures use them in different ways. Americans are very proud of the flag and will wave the colors all year long. Stars and stripes are in the street, flying under the balcony of buildings, on a pole in the park.

In France, the flag is hardly ever shown except on July 14, Bastille Day, when they celebrate the birth of the republic. The French are very discreet about showing the colors and don't wave it publicly. Their relationship with it is more introverted and intimate. When they see the flag, they think about the values of *liberté, egalité,* and *fraternité,* and what it means to be French.

The eagle and the rooster (*l'aigle et le coq*). Americans have *l'aigle,* the eagle. After the signing of the Declaration of Independence in 1776, the founding fathers set out to create a national seal design. Thomas Jefferson, Ben Franklin, and John Adams debated what animal to use as the national symbol. (According to legend, Ben Franklin lobbied for a turkey.) Eventually, a congressional committee selected a design with an eagle, a symbol of strength dating back to ancient Rome. Julius Caesar used an eagle on his standard. The bald bird fits nicely with the American tough-guy ideal from movies. You can picture Clint Eastwood as an eagle quite easily.

The French have *le coq*, the rooster, a symbol that also dates back to ancient Rome. In Latin, the word for "rooster" sounds the same as "Gaul" (what France used to be called). The Romans called *les Gaulois* (the people of Gaul) roosters, and eventually, the French adapted the symbol for themselves. A rooster crows, walks with a bit of a strut, and has a charming *panache*. I think French actor Jean-Paul Belmondo in his youth used to be a classic French *coq*, always showing off, talking loud and proud, strutting his stuff.

Lady Liberty. The Statue of Liberty, a gift from France to America in 1886, was designed by Frédéric Auguste Bartholdi and built by engineer Gustave Eiffel (of Eiffel Tower fame). It represents a Frenchman's vision of American freedom. Size matters in America, so Lady Liberty is a 151-foot-tall, 225-ton XXL figure of strength, heavily draped in robes that conceal her body, holding a book in one hand to represent the law and a torch for the light of progress in the other, with chains at her feet to symbolize the end of slavery.

She was re-created by Bartholdi for the 1900 World's Fair, the Exposition Universelle in Paris, in a French fun size of nine feet tall. After the fair, it was moved to the Jardin du Luxembourg, and stayed there for a hundred years until, in 2012, it was moved to the entrance of the Musée d'Orsay. A bronze replica of the original stands in the same spot at the Jardin du Luxembourg. A second Statue of Liberty in Paris can be found on Île aux Cygnes, an island in the Seine, near the Grenelle Bridge. It's also *petit* at thirty-seven feet, nine inches, and a svelte fourteen tons. The tablet she's holding is a true tribute to my two countries, bearing two dates—July 4,

1776, and July 14, 1789, when the Bastille was stormed and the French Revolution began.

When Americans market Lady Liberty, they do it on a large scale with big foam crowns and giant posters and statues. When the French market Lady Liberty, the replicas are the size of a key chain. Small doesn't make the symbol of freedom any less profound. Size is just a fundamental difference in how the two cultures see the world.

France is a Woman

Marianne is young and beautiful, and a woman of great style. Otherwise known as the Goddess of Liberty, Marianne represents the postmonarchy France, the spirit of freedom and the republic. Not only is she a conqueror, she's feminine and at ease with her body, often appearing topless or showing ample décolleté. During the Revolution, she was more dynamic, even violent. One of the iconic images of Marianne is the 1830 Eugène Delacroix painting *Liberty Leading the People*. In it, she's wearing a Phrygian bonnet, a French flag in one hand, a musket in the other, with her dress torn and chest exposed as she leads the people into battle. During peace, Marianne has been depicted as less confrontational—without weapons, sometimes covered, sometimes bare chested—but always as a symbol of freedom and strength.

French artists and sculptors continue to play with her image. Marianne is a woman of today, alive and vibrant, keeping up with the times. Official busts of Marianne have been modeled on iconic and popular French women—actress Brigitte Bardot in 1968, singer Mireille Mathieu in 1978, actress Catherine Deneuve in 1985, designer and model Inès de La Fressange in 1989, model Laetitia Casta in 2000, among others. Currently, Marianne is modeled on the stylish actress Sophie Marceau.

In America, the personification of the country is Uncle Sam (initials U.S.), an older man with white hair, a goatee, top hat, flag motif trousers, vest, and tailcoat, who first appeared in political cartoons in the 1800s as a symbol of the government, and gained in recognition in recruitment posters for World War I. His image hasn't changed at all in a hundred years. America could take a cue from France and give the national symbol an update. What would Uncle Sam look like for today's world? I'm thinking of the perfect American man to use as a model. He's cool, talented, a unifier with charisma, who also loves to wear a tall hat—Pharrell Williams!

The poetry of Paris

New York seems to have been designed for business and efficiency. The design is a mathematical grid of straight numbered streets and avenues. People talk about meeting on this block or at that corner. The very oldest buildings in New York were constructed in the late eighteenth century, and very few of them still exist. You can find examples of nineteenth-century townhouses in Greenwich Village and Brooklyn Heights or just look to the iconic Brooklyn Bridge (1883). Most of the city was built in the twentieth century—like the Empire State Building (1930) and the Chrysler

Building (1928)—and the twenty-first, like the just-completed Freedom Tower. Compared to Paris, New York is very new.

Paris seems to have been designed for romance and discovery. It's easy to get lost in its labyrinth of gracefully curving streets, with charming cul-de-sacs, passages, arcing hills, intimate squares, and little parks. You can't see beyond the next curve, which makes the experience of walking the city mysterious. Paris is like a poem, lyrical and imaginative, but sometimes confusing for strangers.

The names of the streets stir the imagination.

- Rue des Blancs-Manteaux (4th arrondissement), or Street of White Coats
- Rue des Mauvais-Garçons (4th arrondissement), or Street of Bad Boys
- Rue du Pont aux Choux (3rd arrondissement), or Street of Cabbage Bridge
- Rue des Filles-du-Calvaire (3rd arrondissement), or Street of the Girls from Calvaire

One street leads to a passage, to a tucked-away square. It's as if getting lost is the whole point, so Paris is revealed to you in unexpected ways. From one street to the next, the city can be dark and intimate, or busy and colorful.

The oldest woman in Paris is Our Lady, Notre Dame. Her construction started in 1163, about seven hundred years before Saint Patrick's Cathedral in New York. The oldest private home in Paris was built in 1407 by Nicolas Flamel, an alchemist who claimed to have made a philosopher's stone and discovered the secret of immortality. In a way, he did. His house still stands on Rue de Montmorency in Le Marais, well preserved with the tavern on the first

Paris is a city for lovers everything in Paris inspire love

floor, as always, with a red sign hanging around an ancient street-light that reads AUBERGE NICOLAS FLAMEL, FOUNDED 1407. In Paris, new isn't necessarily fashionable. The French have a fierce loyalty to tradition and the unique and authentic experience of walking the zigzag streets of Paris that hasn't changed for centuries.

Here are some charming street markets to taste good French products:

MARKETS

- **Le Mouffetard** (5th arrondissement) is a busy open-air market in the Latin Quarter with dozens of stalls, fishmongers selling the best sea urchins and cockles—and Ernest Hemingway's house. He referenced Rue Mouffetard in his Paris novel *A Moveable Feast,* calling it "that wonderful narrow crowded market street." Number 134 is Androuet, a *fromagerie* with a red awning that sells over two hundred kinds of cheese. Take a break and go to Le Mouffetard *brasserie* for a *petit café* and a croissant.

- **Montorgueil** (1st arrondissement). Located next to Saint Eustache Cathedral and Les Halles, it's a permanent market street where you can find the best *baba au rhum* in the world and other world-class pastries at **La Maison Stohrer**.

- **Marché Rue de Buci** (6th arrondissement) is at the heart of St. Germain. Hang out at Le Bar du Marché where waiters serve you a glass of wine in a *gavroche* style. The butcher **Le Foll** is known for his rotisserie chicken and **La Pharmacie Rue de Seine** is the tiniest and cutest of Paris. Stop by **Huguette** for seafood take out or **Da Rosa**, the cult grocery store with a terrace, for the best charcuterie.

- **Marché Raspail** (6th arrondissement) biomarket is renowned for its raw chocolate, trays of fresh wheatgrass, and the best selection of organic veggies. Enjoy glamorous and pricey shopping to the musical notes of the *accordéon.*

PASSAGEWAYS

- Paris has over a hundred covered passageways, like pedestrian streets with restaurants and shops under glass ceilings to let in the natural light. It's like being indoors and outdoors at the same time. My favorite is the architectural gem **Galerie Véro-Dodat** (1st arrondissement), built in the nineteenth century, close to where I lived in Les Halles. I always went there to visit my friend Alexis Lahellec and his art gallery with '50s furniture or to try on the heels at the Christian Louboutin store on the other side of the street. The passageway's black-and-white-checkered marble floor, low ironwork, and glass ceiling create the illusion of depth as you walk through it. In spots, the ceiling is painted with gods and goddesses, a classical flourish that goes with the dark wood arched store windows decorated with copper, mirrors, and golden globe streetlamps.

PARKS

- The **Jardin du Palais Royal** (2nd arrondissement) is iconic for its rows of perfectly manicured box trees and its more than 260 black-and-white-striped columns by Daniel Buren, making it a favorite location for photographers and movie directors. The park has three shopping arcades—the Galerie de Valois, Galerie de Montpensier, and Galerie de Beaujolais—along the peripheries, and at the south end of the park, the neoclassic Royal Palace, former home to kings, current home of the French government. Colette, the writer and bon vivant, lived in an apartment in Passage du Perron until 1954. Her window overlooked the gardens of the

Palais Royal. She wrote *Gigi* at this address, and *Paris de Ma Fenêtre (Paris from My Window)*, about the frightening years of the German occupation. A square in the Comédie-Française nearby was named Place Colette in her honor. My favorite shops there are the *parfumerie* of Serge Lutens and the vintage couture dresses of Didier Ludot. I can't walk the arcade without kissing Chef Guy Martin at Le Grand Véfour. **Jardin du Luxembourg** (6th arrondissement) lies at the feet of the Luxembourg Palace, built in the early seventeenth century by French queen Maria de Medici as an homage to her former home, the Pitti Palace in Florence. The palace itself is quite Italian, but the garden—a sanctuary of calm in the heart of Paris—couldn't be more French. Designed by Jacques Boyceau, who'd been involved in the Tuileries and Versailles gardens, the Jardin du Luxembourg has long arcades, rectangular lawns and flowering plots, fountains with copper horses, ornate fountains, box hedges, an orchard of pear and apple trees, and a puppet theater. Dozens of statues line the arcades throughout the park, including a replica of Lady Liberty. Twenty women—nineteenth-century statues of French queens and saints—stand on pedestals around the central square, the matriarchs of Paris watching as children play with toy boats in the octagonal basin.

PLACES

- **Place des Vosges** (3rd and 4th arrondissements) in Le Marais is the oldest square in the city, built in 1605 by Henry IV. The thirty-six houses along one of the most harmonious squares in Paris have the same design, with façades of red brick and white stone stripes, gray-tiled roofs, and chimneys. Le Marais is a happy area of Paris, known for its mix of Jewish and gay communities and boutiques that stay open on Sundays, unlike many other areas of Paris. **Place Vendôme** (1st arrondissement) is a beautiful neoclassic square in the center of Paris around which you will find the mecca of money and luxury (Cartier, Rolex, Chanel, Chaumet, Louis Vuitton, Van Cleef & Arpels, Boucheron, Dior, Piaget, Baumer, and more) and the most expensive diamonds in the world, the Ministry of Justice, and luxury hotels, including the landmark Hôtel Ritz Paris, where Ernest Hemingway invented the Bloody Mary. It was the home of Coco Chanel for thirty-seven years until her death in 1971. Now, her 1,670-square-foot, two-bedroom pied-à-terre, number 302, is called the Coco Chanel suite, decorated as she left it in Chinese furnishings and baroque finishes. The Imperial Suite, the most expensive, evokes the Palace of Versailles in its opulence and famous residents. It's where Princess Diana and Dodi Fayed ate their last meal on Earth. In the center of the square is the bronze Vendôme Column, erected by Napoleon in 1810 with over four hundred bas-relief plates that depict his victory at the battle of Austerlitz. At night, Place Vendôme glows from antique gaslights, setting the smooth white stone pavement ablaze.

MAISONS CLOSES

- From roughly 1800 to 1946, Paris's brothels, *les maisons closes,* on the Right Bank were completely legal palaces of fantasy, art, décor, and pleasures of the flesh. Think velvet drapery, plush couches, mirrored walls, gold everywhere, chandeliers, absinthe, girls in bustiers and high heels, men with mustaches in suits with cravats, and "living paintings" of nude prostitutes in carnal scenarios. All of the "shuttered houses" are now apartment buildings or stores, but you can get a taste of the decadence by visit-

I marry the romance of Paris and the pulse of NY

ing **Au Bonheur du Jour** (2nd arrondissement), a gallery run by Nicole Canet, a former cabaret dancer, located across the street from the infamous brothel Le Chabanais. You'll find Madame Canet's artwork, postcards, and pictures from the golden era of sin, including original photographs of the exclusive toys of the Prince of Wales, Edward VII, who kept a room for himself at Le Chabanais and indulged in carnal delights in a copper bathtub that was filled with champagne, and a "love seat," a rocking chair for sex.

Well-kept French Secrets

On your visit to Paris, shop where the Parisians go for:

- *Parfums* at Serge Lutens. My favorites: A la Nuit, Fleur d'Oranger, and Amber Sultan
- Leather gloves at Maison Fabre
- Military uniforms, vintage and contemporary, at Doursoux
- Cotton clothes at Petit Bateau
- Modern jewelry at Dinh Van
- One-of-a-kind jewelry pieces at Lydia Courteille
- Books for your fashion library at Librairie Galignani
- The *objets* at Tombées du Camion (which means "fell off a truck")
- The roses at florist Au Nom de la Rose
- Beautiful candles at Cire Trudon

- Wacky furniture at Maison Darré
- Auctions of private home collections at Hôtel Drouot
- Curiosities (antique taxidermy, mounted butterflies) at Deyrolle
- Men's ties at Charvet
- Ballerina flats at Repetto
- Portraits at Studio Harcourt
- Everything else at concept stores Colette and Merci

Day trip into a magical world

A few itineraries for romance and adventure outside of Paris:

The Hall of Mirrors in the Palace of Versailles, aka the Galerie des Glaces. In 2007, the famous hallway was reopened to the public after a renovation of the hanging crystal chandeliers, gold paint, marble walls, ornate molding, and, of course, the 357 mirrors. The seventeen arched windows flood the space with so much light, you can see every opulent, extravagant detail. The Sun King, Louis XIV, began construction of the hall in 1678 and commissioned a series of oil murals—painted on canvas and glued into ceiling vaults—about his many military victories in the 1660s and '70s (the king might have been a little narcissistic). The Galerie was used by the French royal family and court for celebrations, including the 1770 wedding of Louis XVI, fifteen, to Marie Antoinette, fourteen. In 1919, the Treaty of Versailles was signed there, ending World War I.

Three million tourists visit the Hall of Mirrors every year, because it's worth it. Come in the morning, and wear your prettiest dress! I'm grateful for the American friends of Versailles who are dedicated to maintaining an active interest in this UNESCO world heritage treasure with their generosity and worked to preserve its history and beauty for future generations. In 2004, they revitalized the magnificent Trois Fontaines Bosquet garden that was created between 1677 and 1679 by André Le Nôtre, one of the most talented landscape architects of all time.

Don't leave without visiting le Petit Trianon, a smaller (but still huge) palace originally built as the private residence of the courtesan Madame de Pompadour, King Louis XV's chief mistress, and later used by his next mistress Madame du Barry. Louis XVI gave the Petit Trianon to his bride Marie Antoinette as her private residence, a place where she could let her hair down (as it were) and escape from the pressures of court. Marie Antoinette, the trendsetting It Girl of her time, allowed only her inner circle into her retreat, including her best friend (girlfriend?), the Duchesse de Polignac, another trendsetter. Sofia Coppola filmed some delectable scenes at the Petit Trianon in her film *Marie Antoinette* (Kirstin Dunst played the queen, Rose Byrne was the duchess), showing off the Oscar-winning costumes by Milena Canonero and incredible Rocchetti Parrucche–designed extravagent wigs, including one with a birdcage housed inside it, which were the height of fashion in the 1770s.

Hôtellerie du Bas-Bréau in Barbizon, thirty miles from Paris, is a charming two-story Tudor with timber beams, a former hunting lodge on the edge of Fontainebleau Forest. In the fall, the restaurant is famous for game specialties, featuring the wild creatures of the wood—grouse, ducks, partridges, pheasants, deer, boars, and hares—and mushrooms. I remember waking up at dawn, taking a horse ride through the forest on the most beautiful trails, and returning to my cozy room for a generous breakfast, a soak in the Jacuzzi, and a nap. In the afternoon, we'd stroll into Barbizon, the village that inspired the early-nineteenth-century school of painting that favored natural, outdoor light, starting with Corot, Rousseau, and Millet, and taken up a few decades later by impressionists Monet and Renoir. In the evening, it was time to drink a glass of Montrachet and savor the great selection of French cheeses in the warm atmosphere by the fireplace.

Le Grand Hotel Cabourg in Normandy, a seaside resort and casino, the epitome of the Old World luxury of the Belle Epoque, looks like a palace, and the guests are treated like royalty. Between 1907 and 1914, Marcel Proust was a regular, always staying in room 414. He wrote about his ocean-view haven in *In Search of Lost Time,* referring to Cabourg as Balbec. Coco Chanel opened her first shop in nearby Deauville, offering a nautical collection of striped leisure clothes in jersey knit.

Nowadays, it's easy to fall under the spell of the Grand Hotel. While walking on the beach boardwalk or through the lobby with hanging chandeliers, velvet drapes and upholstery, and bold patterned wallpapers. For breakfast, have Proust's famous madeleines, small, shell-shaped butter cakes, with tea. In spring, the hotel hosts the Festival of Romantic Films in the spring, awarding the Swann d'Or to the most quixotic movies, actors, writers, and directors of the year. Maybe you will meet someone like Juliette Binoche, a former festival president, while walking on the boardwalk.

je ne sais quoi

romance elegance

Emotion style bonjour

Oui Belle de jour

C'est la vie Mademoiselle

Rendez-vous Au revoir Merci

French Snobbishness

It's not your imagination. It's real. Compared to American enthusiasm and friendliness, the French might come off as rude and annoying. *C'est normal.* It's only to be expected. It's not that the French are judging other people and finding them lacking. They just have high expectations for everything, and supreme confidence in themselves. In some ways, they act the part of the snobby Frenchman just to meet that high standard.

Pardon the French behavior, but when you visit Paris:

- Don't expect anyone to make an effort to help you or speak English. If you ask for directions, they might act annoyed.
- You will be cut in line. The French hate to stand in line. I've always been amazed in New York by how willing people are to queue up. In France, they say "Screw this" and have elevated cutting to an art form. If someone joins a queue right in front of you, with no apparent reason, don't expect an apology. And if you say something, he'll shrug and say "I don't speak English," in perfect English.
- Crosswalks are optional. No one respects the crosswalk lines or the red lights in Paris. People jaywalk whenever, wherever they want. It's one of the reasons the traffic is always so bad.
- Complaining is a national pastime. The French gripe about everything—the traffic (like New Yorkers), taxes, politics, unemployment. They will form a picket line for anything, and only break for a long lunch.
- Cabs are nonexistent. If you can find one, it's probably going the wrong direction. Don't expect the driver to turn around!

About time

In America, time is money. If you don't use it to make a buck, time is wasted. In Paris, they try to slow things down to relish the *douceur de vivre*, the softness of life.

The French make and take time . . .

- To sit on a terrace having an espresso.
- To make a good wine.
- To age a wheel of cheese.
- To eat well and sit together at the table.
- To play piano.
- To create romance.

Five ways to have the attitude of French Woman

No. 1: Say just enough, but don't reveal too much.

No. 2: Never feel like you have to look perfect.

No. 3: Always feel like you should act perfect.

No 4: Forget overexaggerations like "amazing!," "fabulous!," and "OMG!" Instead, downplay by saying, *"pas mal,"* or "not bad."

No. 5: Arrive fashionably late. Don't be the first to arrive, or the last to leave.

Once in your life in Paris, you must . . .

- Light a cigarette.
- Take an espresso at Café de Flore.
- Get lost in the Jardin du Luxembourg.
- Kiss twice to say *"Bonjour!"*

Sacré Français

- "Cheers!" with champagne.
- Wear silk lingerie and heels.
- Say *"Je t'aime."*

Sacré Français

The French are really funny, believe it or not. We showcase our humor in our expressions.

"Il fait un froid de canard."
Literal translation: It's cold as a duck. It just means that it's very cold outside.
American equivalent: Colder than a witch's tit.

"Avoir des oursins dans la poche."
Literal translation: Having sea urchins in your pocket means you are stingy. With sea urchins in your pocket, you don't want to put your hand in there to get cash.
American translation: You're tightfisted.

"Quand les poules auront les dents."
Literal translation: When hens have teeth. Hens don't have teeth and will never have teeth. So it means "never."
American equivalent: When pigs fly.

"Connu comme le loup blanc."
Literal translation: Known like the white wolf. Most wolves are gray or brown; white wolves are very rare. So a man or

330 • Catherine Malandrino

woman known as a white wolf stands out in a crowd and is very well known.

American equivalent: Sticks out like a sore thumb.

"Le miroir aux alouettes."

Literal translation: The mirror of larks. A decoy, or something that is fake.

American equivalent: A red herring.

"Avoir un cœur d'artichaut."

Literal translation: Having an artichoke heart. It means that your heart opens up very easily—perhaps too easily.

American equivalent: Tenderhearted.

"Tomber dans les pommes."

Literal translation: Fall into the apples. It is what happens when you faint.

American equivalent: Keel over.

"Poser un lapin."

Literal translation: Pose a rabbit. Rabbits are known for running away, so when you pose a rabbit, it might disappear. So, this expression is for when you plan to meet someone, and they aren't there because they've disappeared.

American equivalent: Stand someone up.

"Être le dindon de la farce."

Literal translation: The turkey of the plot. The opposite of being the hero of the plot.

American equivalent: The butt of the joke.

"Chat échaudé craint l'eau froide."
Literal translation: A scalded cat is afraid of cold water. It means that a cat injured by boiling water is not going to go into an ice water bath for relief. It learns to fear all water. So, the expression means that if you've been burned, you learn to back away.
American equivalent: Once bitten, twice shy.

"La politique de l'autruche."
Literal translation: To follow the ostrich policy, you just . . .
American equivalent: . . . Bury your head in the sand.

"Les chats ne font pas des chiens."
Literal translation: Cats don't make dogs. It means that a cat will have kittens and a dog will have puppies, and it's the same for people.
American equivalent: The apple doesn't fall far from the tree.

"Il y a anguille sous roche."
Literal translation: There's an eel in the rock. Not just an observation while enjoying a day at the seashore! It means that there's something suspicious afoot.
American equivalent: Something fishy is going on here.

"Poule mouillée."
Literal translation: A moist chicken=a weak man.
American equivalent: Wimp.

New York - French Connections

For a dose of French flair in the Big Apple, I recommend:

Beauty Products. Antiaging chemicals—resveratrol, viniferine, and polyphenols—are found in grapes and grapevines, and Frenchwoman Mathilde Thomas got the idea to use the wines from her family's vineyards in Bordeaux to create Caudalie Paris antiaging skin care products that are sold all over the world (www.us.caudalie .com). In New York, go to the Caudalie Vinotherapie Spa at the Plaza Hotel for a treatment that uses the products, like a Vinoperfect facial, a Crushed Cabernet scrub, or a Wine Maker's massage.

Books. Albertine bookshop/reading room (www.albertine.com) got its name from the hero of Marcel Proust's *À la Recherche du Temps Perdu*. The library based in the French Consulate was created in 2014 by Antonin Baudry and designed by the architect Jacques Garcia, and it offers thousands of French and English books with their own *coups de coeur* recommendations of the volumes they love most dearly.

Coiffure. French women's haircuts always look undone but are still smooth with subtle color. They don't go for a blow-dry or cut very often. Look at Caroline de Maigret for inspiration about the sexy, effortless messy hairstyle. De Maigret speaks about French style in her recent book *How to Be Parisian Wherever You Are: Love, Style, and Bad Habits*, coauthored with Anne Berest, Audrey Diwan, and Sophie Mas. My advice to achieve the look: don't comb your hair too much, use light makeup, dress well, and always wear heels. For a head of hair like you've just woken up after a night of love, visit Laurent D. at Prive on Fifth Avenue (www.privebylaurentd.com), Yves Durif at the Carlyle on East Seventy-sixth Street (www .yvesdurif.com), and Serge Normant on West Twenty-third Street (www.sergenormant.com).

Eyewear. From sunglasses to reading glasses, you can be overwhelmed by the choices at every price and style. Ask for the personal advice of flamboyant French eyewear designer Selima Salaun, an optician and optometrist in Soho (www.selimaoptique.com). She will look at your bone structure, skin tone, eyebrows, haircut, and style to find exactly the right frames to fit your face and personality.

Florist. For an original bouquet, trust Olivier Guigni of L'Olivier Floral Atelier (www.lolivier.com), who pioneered the leaf-wrap vase and brings unexpected color palettes of flowers to your home compositions.

Gallery. In New York, East Hampton, and St. Barts, Christiane Celle's Clic Galleries (www.clic.com) are curated concept spaces featuring a collection of lifestyle objects, paintings, and photographs from French artists Juliette Charvet, Stephane Dessaint, maripol, and the talented photographer Antoine Verglas. He has established a very strong signature of portraits of women, nudes under the sun, that I love. I own a few images of his and display them in my Saint-Tropez home.

Illustrations. Izak Zenou, French illustrator extraordinaire, has created *Parisienne* chic drawings for Chanel, Celine, Guerlain, Laura Mercier, Neiman Marcus, Vera Wang, and Target (among others), worked with every fashion magazine of consequence, and collaborated on book projects like Billy Joel's *New York State of Mind* and Susan Miller's *Astrology Zone*. He's most famous for his twenty-year collaboration with Henri Bendel. Zenou created the iconic Bendel Girl (many examples at www.izakzenou.com). We worked together for the opening of my first boutique in Soho and I treasure a great portrait he made of me. He also designed the cover of this book.

Interior design. For interiors, put your trust in the taste of French designer Valerie Pasquiou (www.vpinteriors.com), known for her sophisticated yet sleek elegance. She marries brio American references and French artists. Today, she is designing a collection of voluptuous furniture for a French atmosphere with an urban edge called Atelier d'amis (www.atelierdamis.com).

Aline Matsika (www.alinematsika.com), who specializes in yacht interiors, has a chic, graphic design aesthetic.

Lingerie. Maison Close (www.maison-close.com) just opened on Grand Street in Soho, and it touts the philosophy "Staging desire and undress morality." The creative and innovative designs by Monsieur le Francais (aka Nicolas Busnel) evoke Helmut Newton in their eroticism and sensuality. Whether chiffon, satin, or sheer, Maison Close lingerie is made for intimate nights or to wear underneath your clothes—or over them. A minibra or lace-up bodysuit under a men's white shirt is so chic.

Pediatrician. Michel Cohen at Tribeca Pediatrics (www.tribeca-pediatrics.com), and other practices throughout America, has been a French friend of mine for twenty-five years. We met at school and then lost track for a while, reconnecting by chance in New

York when he happened to be my friend Selima's pediatrician, one of the best in the city. Since I had Oscar, Michel hasn't been far from me. His philosophy: take care, but take it easy.

Specialty foods. Ariane Daguin (www.dartagnan.com), chef and author, from the countryside of southwest France, brings us the best foie gras, semiboneless quail, and organic chicken from the finest restaurants and food stores in America at D'Artagnan. She is passionate about quality, and her catering takes you from the farm to the fork.

Merci beaucoup

A special thanks to the French government, the French ambassador to the United Nations François Delattre, and the cultural counselor/permanent representative of French Universities Bénédicte de Montlaur for honoring me with the Chevalier medal and the Ordre des Arts et des Lettres award in the salon of the French Embassy in New York in 2015 for my contributions to the enrichment of the French cultural inheritance.

Catherine's Proust questionnaire

If you were a dress: The "Flag" dress from my 2001 collection

Fashion references: Coco Chanel, Jeanne Lanvin, Madeleine Vionnet

Favorite fashion photographer: Guy Bourdin, Richard Avedon

Favorite texture: Silk

Favorite color: A ray of light and red poppy

Favorite fashion accessory: High heels

Favorite jewel: A pinky ring

The look you prefer for a man: Alain Delon meets Steve McQueen

If you were a novel: *Belle du Seigneur* by Albert Cohen

If you were an artist: Sonia Delaunay meets Picasso

If you were an element: Fire

If you were a piece of furniture: "Summer Rain" chandelier by Christophe Pillet

If you were a movement: Horses galloping

If you were a song: "Walk on the Wild Side" by Lou Reed, remixed with "Chabadabada" by Francis Lai

If you were a song: A bird's song

If you were a dance: Tango

If you were a fairy tale: My life

If you were a lullaby: "Frère Jacques"

If you were a dream: I would fly

If you were a word: Hallelujah!

If you were a city: Paris, New York, and Saint-Tropez

If you were a holiday: Provence

If you were a mirage: Lady Liberty

What is your present state of mind: In love

Your fashion motto: Imagine

Reader's Guide

1. Dreams

Avedon, Richard. *Avedon Photographs: 1947–1977*. Farrar, Straus & Giroux, 1978.

Benaïm, Laurence. *Yves Saint Laurent*. Grasset, 2002.

Bourdin, Guy, and Shelly Verthime. *Guy Bourdin: In Between*. Steidl, 2010.

Charles-Roux, Edmonde. *Le Temps Chanel*. La Martiniere, 2004.

Golbin, Pamela. *Madeleine Vionnet*. Rizzoli, 2009.

Knox, Kristin. *Culture to Catwalk: How World Cultures Influence Fashion*. A&C Black, 2012.

Koda, Harold. *Poiret*. Metropolitan Museum of Art, 2007.

Kyoto Costume Institute. *Fashion: A History from the 18th to the 20th Century*. Taschen, 2015.

Lutens, Serge. *Serge Lutens*. Assouline, 1998.

Mackrell, Alice. *Art and Fashion: The Impact of Art on Fashion and Fashion on Art*. Batsford, 2005.

Newton, June and Helmut. *Helmut Newton: SUMO*. Taschen America, 2009.

Padilha, Roger and Mauricio. *Antonio Lopez: Fashion, Art, Sex, and Disco*. Rizzoli, 2012.

Schiaparelli, Elsa. *Shocking Life: The Autobiography of Elsa Schiaparelli.* Victoria & Albert Museum, 2007.

3. Beauty

Guiliano, Mireille. *French Women Don't Get Fat: The Secret of Eating for Pleasure.* Alfred A. Knopf, 2005.

4. Seduction

David, Tim. *Magic Words: The Science and Secrets Behind Seven Words That Motivate, Engage, and Influence.* Prentice Hall Press, 2014.

De Laclos, Pierre Choderlos. *Les Liaisons Dangereuses.* Durand Neveu, 1782.

Sciolino, Elaine. *La Seduction: How the French Play the Game of Life.* Times Books, 2011.

Süskind, Patrick. *Perfume: The Story of a Murderer.* Vintage, 2001.

5. Amour

Colette, Sidonie-Gabrielle. *Cheri.* Calmann-Lévy, 1920.

———. *Gigi.* 1944.

De Beauvoir, Simone. *The Second Sex.* 1949.

De Sade, Donatien Alphonse Francois. *The 120 Days of Sodom.* 1904.

Desclos, Anne. *The Story of O.* Jean-Jacques Pauvert, 1954.

Despentes, Virginie. *Baise-Moi.* Grove Press, 1999.

Duras, Marguerite. *The Ravishing of Lol Stein.* Gallimard, 1964.

Flaubert, Gustave. *Madame Bovary.* Michel Lévy Frères, 1857.

Gaitskill, Mary. *Bad Behavior.* Poseidon, 1988.

Hardy, Françoise. *L'Amour Fou.* Albin Michel, 2012.

James, Joyce. *Ulysses.* Sylvia Beach, 1922.

Jardin, Alexandre. *Le Zèbre.* Gallimard, 1990.

Lawrence, D. H. *Lady Chatterley's Lover.* Tipografia Giuntina, 1928.

Miller, Henry. *Tropic of Cancer.* Obelisk Press, 1934.

Nabokov, Vladimir. *Lolita.* Olympia Press, 1955.

Nin, Anaïs. *Delta of Venus.* Harcourt Brace Jovanovich, 1977.

Sagan, Françoise. *Bonjour Tristesse.* Rene Julliard, 1954.

Sartre, Jean-Paul. *Being and Nothingness.* Gallimard, 1943.

Soeur Emmanuelle. *Confessions of a Nun.*

Westhoff, Denis. *Sagan et Fils.* Le Livre de Poche, 2013.

6. Inspiration

De Recondo, Leonor. *Pietra Viva.* Sabine Wespieser, 2013.

7. Audacity

Pépin, Charles. *Les Vertus de L'Échec.* Allary, 2016.

Von Furstenberg, Diane. *The Woman I Wanted to Be.* Simon & Schuster, 2014.

9. Joie de Vivre

Allard, Michael, Jean-Marie Robine, and Jeanne Calment. *Jeanne Calment: From Van Gogh's Time to Ours: 122 Extraordinary Years.* Thorndike Press, 1999.

10. Rendezvous

Cohen, Albert. *Belle du Seigneur.* Éditions Gallimard, 1968.

De Maigret, Caroline, Anne Berest, Audrey Diwan, and Sophia Mas. *How to Be Parisian Wherever You Are: Love, Style, and Bad Habits.* Doubleday, 2014.

Hemingway, Ernest. *A Moveable Feast.* Scribner's, 1964.

Proust, Marcel. *In Search of Lost Time.* Grasset and Gallimard, 1913–1927.